Governing Global Finance

Governing Global Finance

The Evolution and Reform of the International Financial Architecture

Anthony Elson

palgrave
macmillan

GOVERNING GLOBAL FINANCE
Copyright © Anthony Elson, 2011.

First published in 2011 by
PALGRAVE MACMILLAN®
in the United States—a division of St. Martin's Press LLC,
175 Fifth Avenue, New York, NY 10010.

Where this book is distributed in the UK, Europe and the rest of the world,
this is by Palgrave Macmillan, a division of Macmillan Publishers Limited,
registered in England, company number 785998, of Houndmills,
Basingstoke, Hampshire RG21 6XS.

Palgrave Macmillan is the global academic imprint of the above companies
and has companies and representatives throughout the world.

Palgrave® and Macmillan® are registered trademarks in the United States,
the United Kingdom, Europe and other countries.

ISBN: 978–0–230–10378–8

Library of Congress Cataloging-in-Publication Data

Elson, Robert Anthony, 1941–
     Governing global finance : the evolution and reform of the international
financial architecture / Anthony Elson.
          p. cm.
     Includes bibliographical references and index.
     ISBN 978–0–230–10378–8
          1. International finance. 2. Banks and banking, International.
     3. Financial crises. 4. Global Financial Crisis, 2008–2009. I. Title.

HG3881.E445 2011
332'.042—dc22   2010031399

A catalogue record of the book is available from the British Library.

Design by Newgen Imaging Systems (P) Ltd., Chennai, India.

First edition: March 2011

10 9 8 7 6 5 4 3 2 1

Transferred to Digital Printing in 2011

To Marjorie

Contents

Figures and Tables

Figures

Tables

CHAPTER 1

Introduction

In September 2008, policy makers in the major financial center countries feared a collapse of the international financial system and an economic crisis unprecedented since the Great Depression of the early 1930s. Indeed, in the space of a couple of months, a problem that had developed in the subprime mortgage market of the US financial system was transformed into a global financial crisis. The size of this financial shock and the speed of its transmission were largely unanticipated by market analysts and policy makers. The economic and financial costs of this crisis in terms of lost output, unemployment, and the decline in personal wealth have been enormous. The crisis has also raised important questions about the stability of the international financial system and the actions that are needed to reinforce the collective governance of that system.

This crisis marked the end of the latest phase in the globalization of finance that has been under way since the late 1950s. As a window into these recent events, this book attempts to explain the main developments in financial globalization that have taken place during the post–World War II period and to examine the institutional and other cooperative arrangements for collective governance that governments have put into place to promote an orderly development of the international financial system.

Financial globalization refers to the increasing size of cross-border financial flows among countries and the growing integration of capital markets across national borders. It is an attribute of the larger phenomenon of economic globalization by which the production of goods and services, trade and finance have transcended national borders in response to advances in communication and transport, on the one hand, and reductions in policy-based barriers to cross-border transactions in goods, services, and financial assets, on the other. Financial globalization has also been driven by innovation in the development of new financial instruments, which have expanded the reach of financial markets or have facilitated the management of risk. The development of so-called structured finance in the form of new securitized instruments and the expansion in the use of credit derivatives were major factors in the latest phase of financial globalization leading up to the current crisis.

Economic and financial globalization have been hailed by many as the process by which the benefits of capitalist development rooted in the industrial revolution of the nineteenth century will be diffused throughout the world in an inexorable process that will bring about global prosperity. The benefits of globalization have clearly been visible and important, but they have been skewed in favor of certain countries and uneven in their distribution of costs and benefits. In addition, as reflected in the antiglobalization protests around the turn of the last century, globalization has exceeded the power of national governments to control its development and to limit collateral damage to other spheres of the global system, such as the environment. The growth of the global financial system has also been prone to certain cycles of boom and bust that have caused substantial harm to developing and emerging market economies in the past and now most recently to the global economy.

The fact that economic and financial markets have become increasingly global in scale, while governmental control and accountability are still predominantly based on the nation-state, represents the fundamental challenge of globalization. Within the national sphere, a proper system of collective governance arrangements in terms of financial regulatory regimes, financial safety nets, common legal and accounting procedures need to be in place to support a healthy development of a domestic financial system. However, there is no global political authority to establish comparable arrangements at the international level. In its place, governments have devised a variety of institutional and cooperative mechanisms, which have come to be known as the international financial architecture (IFA), that are needed globally to promote an orderly process of financial globalization.

The IFA in its current form has followed a clear evolutionary path since the end of World War II and has expanded into a variety of formal and informal arrangements, both public and private. The concept of the IFA first came into use in connection with the debates on international financial reform, which took place in the late 1990s in response to a series of financial crises among emerging market economies that called attention to the need for greater international coordination on financial policy and regulatory issues. After a period of relative calm in international financial markets following the terrorist attacks of 9/11, the idea of IFA reform has surfaced again in policy debates among the Group of 20 (G20) industrial and emerging market countries that have tried to formulate a response to the global financial crisis since November 2008.

This book seeks to explain the factors that gave rise to the near collapse of the international financial system in late 2008 and the reasons why the IFA was unable to prevent the financial crisis that has occurred. In particular, the book attempts to deal with the following questions: What is the IFA, and why is it needed? How has the IFA evolved during the post–World War II era in response to changes in economic and financial globalization? Why was it not working in being able to prevent or anticipate the global financial crisis that erupted in late 2008? And how does the IFA need to be reformed to make it work more effectively in the future?

Main Outline of the Book

The rest of this book attempts to trace the key markers in the evolution of financial globalization during the post–World War II period and in the development of the IFA, with a view to explaining the background and causes for the recent global financial crisis. The book concludes with recommendations for the reform of the IFA as a means of minimizing the risk of future financial crises. The narrative and arguments of the book are laid out in the following chapter sequence.

Chapter 2 provides a brief review of the nature and evolution of financial globalization in recent decades, as reflected in a variety of quantitative measures and regulatory changes. In addition, the chapter explores the particular market failures that can arise in financial globalization and the public goods that the IFA needs to provide to deal with these failures. The chapter concludes with a brief description of the IFA, as it existed before the onset of the recent financial crisis.

Chapter 3 provides an historical context for considering the current age of financial globalization by tracing the evolution of financial globalization since the time of the gold standard (1870–1914), which has been called the first era of financial globalization. The chapter also examines the formal and informal arrangements that underpinned the IFA during the period leading up to World War II. Particular attention is given to the origins of the post–World War II IFA during the Bretton

Woods system (1945–73) and the special roles given to the IMF and World Bank.

Chapter 4 explores the various cooperative efforts that were made to support the Bretton Woods system, including the critical role that capital controls were intended to play under this system. The chapter then examines the factors that played a role in its breakdown, which led to the first reform of the IFA. This reform resulted in the dissolution of a post–World War II consensus on international financial cooperation and began a process of fragmentation in the IFA and a period of more rapid growth in financial globalization.

Chapter 5 examines the second reform of the IFA following a period of rapid expansion in the international financial system and a series of devastating crises among emerging market economies during the 1980s and 1990s. Particular attention was given to the role of the IMF in crisis management and crisis prevention. This reform also attempted to bring together a number of previously uncoordinated activities within the IFA and to establish safeguards for a further expansion of financial globalization. The reform identified issues of global financial stability for the first time and established the twin peaks of the IMF and the Financial Stability Forum (FSF) for financial system oversight.

Chapter 6 focuses on the recent pattern of private financial flows to developing countries and the challenges of financial globalization for low-income countries, in particular. The preconditions and proper sequencing of capital account liberalization are considered. The role of official development finance within the IFA in filling a "missing market" for the financing needs of low-income countries is discussed. The key role of the World Bank in development finance, the problems of aid effectiveness, and official debt restructuring via the Paris Club are also examined in this chapter.

Chapter 7 focuses on the most recent period of financial globalization leading up to the global financial crisis of 2008–9. The chapter examines the macroeconomic, microeconomic, and ideological factors that helped to bring about the crisis. The chapter also identifies the common causes of the recent crisis and the emerging market crises of the 1990s in terms of heavy reliance on foreign capital inflows, monetary and regulatory ease, and unsound banking practices.

Chapter 8 looks at the role of the IFA in carrying out its responsibilities of crisis prevention and crisis management relating to the recent crisis. In the area of crisis prevention, the chapter examines defects in the international adjustment mechanism, the oversight of global financial stability, international financial regulation, and the international lender of last resort mechanism. The absence of an effective international forum to focus political debate on emerging risks in the international financial system and to coordinate policy responses is also highlighted. In the area of crisis management, the chapter focuses on the role that the G20 has played in the international coordination of policy responses, the mobilization of financial resources to deal with the effects of the crisis, and the preparations for a postcrisis world.

Chapter 9 evaluates the third reform of the IFA that is under way as a result of the G20 process that began in November 2008. It identifies the main areas in which changes are being made, as well as those areas in which the reforms are likely to fall short and areas for reform that have not been addressed thus far.

Chapter 10 concludes the study and attempts to draw lessons from the history of reform of the IFA. It also identifies the critical areas for reform action in the future.

An appendix appears at the end of the book, which provides a brief summary description of each of the committees, groups, and institutions that make up the IFA.

Key Themes of the Book

Many themes are present in the narrative of this book, which are useful to summarize at the beginning.

1. Since the mid-twentieth century, the globalization of finance has been an important force in the integration of the global economy. By all measures, it has expanded rapidly, especially since the mid-1970s as actions to liberalize domestic financial markets and dismantle controls on cross-border capital movements took hold in the advanced countries. The suddenness of the eruption of the current global crisis is testimony to the intensity of interdependence of national capital markets among the advanced and emerging market economies that has taken place since the turn of the new century.

2. The IFA has also expanded in response to financial globalization as governments have struggled to put in place a workable arrangement for collective governance of the international financial system that would promote its sound development, while minimizing its propensity to periodic crisis. This process has evolved in an ad hoc and incremental fashion, which has relied increasingly on informal cooperative arrangements (of both a public and private

nature) and adaptive reforms of existing institutions, rather than any attempt at grand redesign, to deal with deficiencies and to fill gaps in the IFA.

3. Throughout the post–World War II era, there has been a tension in the development of global finance between the importance given to financial liberalization to promote market efficiency and the weight given to systems of governance to limit the negative effects of unfettered markets. In the immediate postwar era, the balance of collective decision making was overwhelmingly in favor of the latter, whereas four and a half decades later at the beginning of the 1990s, the pendulum had swung sharply in favor of market efficiency and a belief in the self-regulating power of markets. In the wake of the current financial crisis, a new balance will need to be struck between these two forces.

4. The IFA has evolved mainly in response to the periodic onset of crises in the international financial system, in much the same way that governance arrangements for financial systems at the national level have evolved. Prominent among these crises have been the collapse of the Bretton Woods system in the early 1970s, the international debt crises of the 1980s, and the financial crises of emerging market economies of the 1990s. The global financial crisis of 2008–9 will become another benchmark in this evolving process of reform.

5. The IFA has become increasingly complex and fragmented over time in a way that has hindered its effectiveness, as regards both crisis prevention and crisis management. It is also complicated by a redundancy and overlapping of functions among different institutions and groups. Although the origins of the current crisis can be traced to regulatory failure, flaws in the corporate governance and risk management of large financial institutions, and policy lapses in the United States, the IFA failed to deal with imbalances in the global economy and the risks to global financial stability that were building before the crisis. Weak coordination of actions to deal with impaired banks with large cross-border exposures and the absence of an effective international lender of last resort mechanism fostered contagion once the crisis erupted in the center country (USA).

6. As the pace of financial globalization has intensified over time, the need for a strengthened IFA to govern the international financial system has also increased. Given that political legitimacy only exists at the level of nation-states and the reluctance of

national governments to cede sovereignty to international bodies, the international system faces a continuing challenge of building effective forms of cooperation and coordination in the financial domain. At the same time, countries want to maximize the degree of national control over economic and financial policies and determine the pace at which they achieve integration into the international financial system.

In the light of these themes, the recent global crisis has pointed to the need for a greater harmonization of rules for the regulation of financial institutions with significant cross-border activities and for their resolution in the event of insolvency. At the same time, there needs to be stronger international oversight of national regulatory regimes and a more effective administration of the international adjustment mechanism. These changes can only be achieved, if there is in place an effective governance arrangement for the IFA that involves stronger political oversight and an effective system of national participation and accountability.

Much has been written about the IFA, especially during the second-reform period of the late 1990s when the term first came into general use. Undoubtedly much more will continue to be written in the light of the ongoing crisis. Most of this literature deals with either a particular period of international financial reform or the history of one of the key components of the architecture, such as the International Monetary Fund. In writing this book, I have benefited greatly and drawn many insights from this literature. My purpose in this study has been to provide a relatively concise chronicle of the principal markers in the evolution of the IFA with a view to understanding how it has come to take the shape that it has and how it was able to cope, effectively or not, with the current crisis. This background is essential for any attempt to bring about its future reform.

My interest in this topic has developed over many years since the time I was a graduate student in international economics at Columbia University. It was also nurtured by many years of service on the professional staff of the IMF where I had an opportunity to participate in a wide range of its activities, which constitute a critical part of the IFA, namely its surveillance, financing, advisory, training and evaluation functions, as well as its links with the Paris Club on official debt restructuring operations and poverty alleviation work of the World Bank. This experience also allowed me to witness from an operational perspective some key developments associated with the reform of the IFA such as the Latin American debt crisis of the 1980s, the Asian financial crisis of the late 1990s, and the development of international standards and codes in conjunction with the Financial Stability Forum. During the past several years, I have gained further perspective on the IFA from teaching courses related to this topic at the Duke University School of Public Policy, the Johns Hopkins School of Advanced International Studies, and Yale University and from serving as a consultant to the World Bank and an NGO (New Rules for Global Finance) that has been active in the promotion of governance reform of the IMF.

In the course of writing this book, I wish to acknowledge the excellent research assistance I received from David Bulman, including the preparation of figures and the provision of inputs for the appendix. I am also grateful to Gordon Bodnar, James Boughton, David Bulman, and Domenico Lombardi for providing comments on an earlier version of the book manuscript. None of them of course should be implicated in any of the judgments, conclusions, and recommendations found in the book.

CHAPTER 2

Financial Globalization and the International Financial Architecture

This chapter provides a brief review of the recent evolution of financial globalization and examines the rationale for the international financial architecture (IFA). It also describes the main institutional features of that architecture, as it existed before the current global crisis. The succeeding chapters (chapters 3–5) attempt to explain how it came to take the shape that it has.

The Recent Evolution of Financial Globalization

Financial globalization has been a major feature of international economic relations in the second half of the twentieth century and an important aspect of economic globalization. The suddenness of the onset of the current global financial crisis was a striking, but painful, example of the rapid growth in financial interdependence among the advanced and emerging market economies. This process has largely been a market-driven phenomenon that has affected countries to different degrees, depending on their location and income level.

Financial globalization has many roots and justifications. At its simplest level, the demand for foreign finance will grow with the development of foreign trade, as exporters and importers seek short-term foreign lines of credit to support the production of tradable goods on a revolving, self-liquidating basis. In the absence of barriers to foreign capital inflows, investors in one country will seek equity stakes in profitable companies abroad, in the form of foreign direct investment (FDI), because of domestic market conditions or significant export potential.

A particular form of FDI that is relevant to financial globalization is the acquisition by large banks in the advanced countries of equity stakes in bank operations in emerging market or developing countries, and the opening of branch operations or subsidiaries in foreign countries. FDI flows have been strongest among the advanced countries, especially with the growing activity of multinational corporations, and have been an important force in bringing about a convergence of economic growth rates among these countries. They have also been an important source of growth for many emerging market economies in East Asia (in particular, China) and Latin America.

More generally, the international trade in financial assets and the operations of international capital markets play an essential role in intermediating savings in one part of the global economy to investment in another part, in the same way that financial markets operate across different regions within national borders. They also provide a means for diversifying risk for domestic firms and individuals, for example, in the case of a small economy with high savings and a limited domestic capital market. In addition, the trade in financial assets can provide countries with a mechanism for compensating a shortfall in exports due to some exogenous shock or accommodating an important long-term investment without a severe compression of consumption ("consumption-smoothing").

In a world of interest and exchange rate volatility, active trade in financial assets among countries will engender the demand for derivatives, by means of which investors can hedge against the exchange and interest rate risk inherent in foreign portfolios. Such demand has given rise to a huge growth in interest and exchange rate swaps in international capital markets. In the last decade, the growth in derivative trading was one of the strongest components of international financial transactions, and it became a major source of instability in the global financial system, as explained in chapter 7. Financial innovation (e.g., in the form of new securitized products) has also played an important role in the latest wave of financial globalization since the beginning of the new century.

The globalization of finance that took root and expanded during the last quarter of the twentieth century was the natural accompaniment of the growth in world trade and foreign investment that was supported by the post–World War II international economic and financial arrangements embodied in the so-called Bretton Woods institutions (i.e., the International Monetary Fund [IMF] and World Bank) and the General Agreement on Tariffs and Trade (GATT), which was the predecessor to the current-day

World Trade Organization (WTO). In the early post–World War II era, international trading in financial assets was relatively limited given widespread controls on capital movements and the tight regulation of domestic financial markets. International financial transactions began to take place during the late 1950s in offshore, unregulated markets outside the reach of national supervisory authorities, in particular the euro-currency or euro-dollar markets based primarily in London, which were used by private banks and firms to bypass restrictions on borrowing or lending activity in heavily regulated national markets to finance international operations.[1] With the liberalization of domestic finance and the removal of national controls on international capital flows that began among the advanced countries during the 1970s, the cross-border exchange of financial assets expanded sharply, first among the advanced countries and then beginning in the late 1980s among emerging market countries. This trend was intensified with the revolution in information and communications technology and the development of derivative instruments noted earlier to cover the risk of currency and interest rate volatility.

Economists have used various quantitative measures to gauge the strength of financial globalization. One commonly used indicator is the growth in the stock of foreign assets and foreign liabilities of groups of countries in absolute US dollar terms or in relation to GDP, based on a pioneering database assembled by Phillip Lane and Gian Maria Milesi-Ferretti.[2] These data cover claims or debt in the form of bond placements and bank loans, FDI, equity holdings, and a residual category, including derivatives and official foreign reserves. Throughout the period since 1970, the largest share of these financial instruments was represented by debt, followed by FDI, and equity holdings. In relation to GDP, these stocks roughly doubled in size during the period from 1970 to 1992; since then, however, they have grown by a factor of three times, mostly on account of activity among the advanced countries (see figure 2.1). Compared with previous decades, the period from 2001 to 2007 showed particularly rapid growth in financial globalization. The growth in the use of securitized financial instruments, the development of large complex financial institutions, and the impact of the euro on the elimination of currency risk for intra-European financial transactions each contributed to the latest phase of financial globalization among the advanced countries.

The growth in transactions in financial assets since 1970 has far exceeded the growth in foreign trade. According to data from the Bank for International Settlements on foreign exchange trading, in 1970 the total value of currency trading was roughly equivalent to the value of

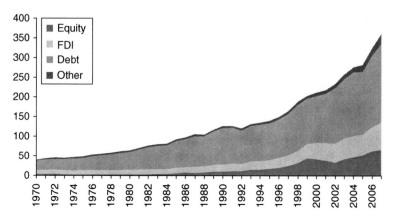

Figure 2.1 Financial globalization (global aggregate assets and liabilities, as percent of GDP)

Source: Updated and extended version of dataset constructed by Lane and Milesi-Ferretti (2007)

global trade. However, by 2007, this ratio had reached 50 to 1, thus signaling an enormous expansion in the trade of financial assets.[3]

As one might expect, the advanced countries accounted for the major share of these stocks, by a factor of roughly 10 to 1 in relation to the emerging market economies of Asia, Latin America, and Eastern Europe, which exceeded the stocks of the rest of the developing world by a similar order of magnitude.[4] Measured in terms of GDP, there was a gradual, steady increase in international financial flows among the advanced and developing countries from 1970 to the mid-1980s, at which point a sharp divergence emerges as the pace of financial globalization among the advanced countries accelerates (figure 2.2). During the first decade of the current century, there has been a further sharp acceleration. This measure of financial globalization across countries is significantly correlated with the level of real GDP per capita and the degree of domestic financial development.[5] In addition, empirical studies have shown that bilateral holdings of foreign assets and liabilities are stronger among countries that share a common language, legal system, and colonial history. Moreover, the willingness of investors to hold external liabilities of a foreign country (and to hold them in the form of equity-like liabilities such as FDI and portfolio equity) is higher for countries with stronger measures of institutional quality and educational attainment.[6]

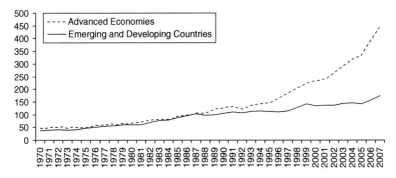

Figure 2.2 Financial globalization for advanced and developing countries (total assets plus liabilities, as percent of GDP)

Source: Updated and extended version of dataset constructed by Lane and Milesi-Ferretti (2007)

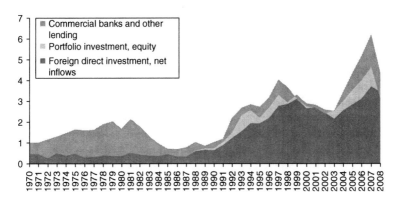

Figure 2.3 Private capital flows to low- and middle-income countries (as percent of GDP)
Source: World Bank, World Development Indicators (WDI)

A rising trend can also be discerned for the emerging market and developing countries, but on a much more muted scale. Within that trend since 1970, there have been three waves in the extension of financial globalization to the developing countries, each larger than the previous one: the first during the second half of the 1970s in response to the oil price hikes engineered by OPEC countries; the second during the first half of the 1990s; and the third during the run-up to the current global financial crisis (figure 2.3). Unlike the previous two surges, the last one involved strong two-way flows of international assets and liabilities of the emerging market economies, which are examined in chapter 7. The boom and bust associated with each of these surges has been the trigger for important changes in the IFA.

Another statistical measure, which economists have used to quantify the extent of financial globalization, is the absolute sum of external current account surpluses and deficits among countries to global GDP. In contrast to the stock measure described in the previous paragraphs, this measure provides a flow dimension to international financial transactions. The current account balance measures the net surplus or deficit of a country's exchange of goods, services, factor income (dividends, interest, and wages) and transfers (e.g., official aid and migrant remittances) with the rest of the world, which give rise to a net accumulation of foreign assets or liabilities. The long-term trend of this measure gives a view of financial globalization roughly similar to the indicator used in the previous paragraphs, with persistence in the size of these imbalances during the 1980s and 1990s and a pronounced widening during the current decade in the run-up to the current crisis (figure 2.4). The phenomenon of growing current account imbalances in the current decade has given rise to much debate about the sustainability of "global imbalances" and their contribution to the onset of the current financial crisis, which is also discussed in chapter 7 of this book. These imbalances were prominently reflected in a large current account deficit of the United States and a large current account surplus of China.[7]

One additional indicator that has been used to gauge the extent of capital market integration across national borders arising from

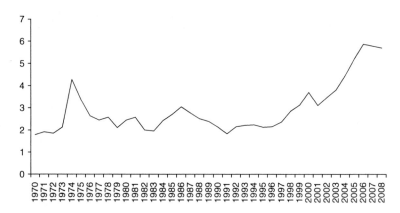

Figure 2.4   Global imbalances (absolute sum of current account imbalances as percent of world GDP)

Source: International Monetary Fund, World Economic Outlook Database (April 2008 and October 2009)

international financial transactions is the difference in interest rates on financial instruments of similar risk and maturity, measured in the same currency (which is encapsulated in the concept of covered interest parity). In a world of perfect capital mobility, such differentials should be minimal or nonexistent as a result of the effect of arbitrage among financial traders. Under the principle of covered interest parity, the emergence of any difference in the price or yield of similar financial assets in different national markets, adjusted for the difference between spot and forward exchange rates, would give rise to sales of one asset and purchases of the other by financial traders (through a process of arbitrage) such that the difference would be eliminated during some finite period of time.

By this test, there has also been a substantial growth in international financial integration among the advanced countries in recent decades and a significant degree of capital market integration. Studies have shown that in the case of the United States and the United Kingdom, for example, interest rate differentials for short-term instruments (e.g., two- to three-month bills), adjusted for the difference between spot and forward exchange rates, were quite variable during the post–World War II period through the end of the 1970s, but since that time they have been reduced significantly and have become negligible. Similar evidence has been presented for comparisons between the United Kingdom and Japan, and between France and Germany.[8]

The measures described earlier all provide de facto evidence of the rise of international financial integration. Other evidence of a de jure nature can also be brought to bear on the measurement of financial globalization. This information relates to the policy decisions of individual governments to relax administrative restrictions on international financial transactions and to remove controls on inward or outward capital movements. Such controls have a role similar to trade or exchange restrictions, which restrict the flow of current account transactions. One of the important achievements of the post–World War II IFA, which is discussed in the next two chapters, was the progressive relaxation of controls on current account transactions (including dividend and debt service payments), which laid the groundwork for a major expansion in international trade during the second half of the twentieth century.

Unlike the case of current account transactions, there has not been any coordinated effort at the international level to bring about a general relaxation of capital controls, except among countries of the OECD and the European Union (EU). The IMF has collected information about the nature and coverage of capital controls by individual countries for many years in its Annual Report on Exchange Arrangements and Exchange Restrictions. These reports provide a simple binary measure for the presence or absence of controls on a variety of different capital transactions, which can be used to trace the evolution of capital account liberalization of one or a number of countries. One limitation of this measure is that it does not provide any indication of the intensity of these controls or the degree to which they have been enforced.

Capital controls are imposed on external financial transactions of individuals and corporations for purposes of influencing the external payments situation of a country or for macroeconomic policy reasons. They can apply to inward or outward movements of capital, and they can be general or selective in their coverage and quantitative or price-based in their application. The imposition of an unremunerated reserve requirement on short-term foreign borrowing by firms or individuals would be one example of a price-based capital control. The requirement to maintain a portion of the local currency proceeds generated by such borrowing in an account in the central bank that does not pay interest increases its effective cost to the borrower as the amount of the loan that can be used is reduced. Other forms of price-based capital controls that have been used in the past involve separate exchange rates for capital, as distinct from current account transactions, and the imposition of taxes on capital inflows.

Capital controls are usually distinguished from other kinds of limits on external transactions of financial institutions, which take the form of prudential requirements. In the latter case, limits may be set on the open foreign position of banks (their net asset or liability exposure), guidelines issued on the matching of foreign assets and liabilities, and reserve requirements set on foreign borrowing, which usually form part of the regulatory framework for banks, along with capital adequacy requirements. A sound regulatory regime for banks has come to be viewed as a prerequisite for capital account liberalization.

According to a recent data set that has been compiled by Professors Menzie Chinn and Hiro Ito, one can see a pattern of capital account liberalization that is sharply distinct for advanced and developing countries and that conforms broadly to the pattern of financial globalization depicted in the charts discussed earlier (figure 2.5).[9] This information, like that for tariff and trade restrictions in the case of international trade, provides evidence for the policy changes at the national level that have supported financial globalization. Capital account liberalization has been most pronounced for the advanced countries, beginning in the mid-1970s. This process was led by the United States, which removed all controls

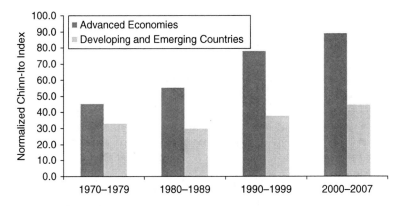

Figure 2.5 Index of financial openness

Source: Chinn-Ito (2006) Financial Openness measure (data extending to 2007, updated February 2009)

on capital flows in 1973, followed by the United Kingdom in 1979 and Japan in 1981. These early actions were instrumental in supporting New York, London, and Tokyo as major international financial centers. By the early 1990s, full capital account liberalization had been achieved for all the industrial countries.[10] This process of liberalization was guided by two regional projects, one inspired by the OECD's Code of Conduct for Capital Movements and the other coordinated under the EU's Directives on the Liberalization of Capital Movements, which became part of community law and practice for EU membership (*acquis communitaire*).[11] The OECD Code was first introduced on a selective basis in 1961, and it was gradually extended in stages to cover all capital account transactions by 1989. The first EU Directive was introduced in 1960 and was extended to cover all capital account transactions in 1988 to support the adoption of the Single European Act, which set a goal for the free movement of goods, services, persons, and capital within the EU by 1992.

In the case of the advanced countries, capital account liberalization was largely an outgrowth of the move toward current account convertibility and trade liberalization that occurred under the Bretton Woods system (1945–73), which is discussed in chapter 3, and the liberalization of domestic financial markets during the 1970s and 1980s. The liberalization of capital controls was also motivated by the realization that such controls became more difficult to enforce in the absence of controls on current transactions, as trade flows could be manipulated to disguise capital account transactions (via "leads and lags" in trade financing and under- and overinvoicing of export and import trade).[12] In addition, with the development of large international banks and multinational corporations with important cross-border activities, domestic pressures for an easing of capital controls grew.

Typically, the process of capital account liberalization in the advanced countries was sequenced in pace with other domestic economic reforms. Once trade liberalization was well under way, controls on long-term capital inflows and trade-related capital flows were dismantled. Controls on long-term capital outflows were removed usually after a sound fiscal position was established (defined as a sustainable fiscal deficit of less than 3 percent of GDP) and controls on domestic interest rates were eliminated. As noted earlier, full capital account liberalization was usually conditioned on having in place an effective bank supervisory and regulatory regime.[13]

With the establishment of the WTO in 1995, certain forms of capital account restrictions for the first time came under the purview of a universal institution subject to international treaty law. Under the General Agreement on Trade in Services (and the Financial Services Agreement of December 1997), countries were required to remove restrictions on capital flows associated with commitments to liberalize trade in services (e.g., financial services), while the General Agreement on Trade-Related Investment Measures (TRIMs) proscribed certain restraints on FDI that restricted international trade (such as local content or trade-balancing requirements). The movement toward liberalization of trade in services followed a successful reduction in barriers to commodity trade negotiated over a period of twenty-seven years through successive multilateral negotiations. The initiative to reduce restrictions on trade in services, particularly in the financial area, is an interesting example of the pressure of large multinational corporations, such as AIG, American Express, and Citigroup, acting on the US government to seek international agreement on the reduction of barriers to their penetration of domestic markets in developing countries.[14]

Among the emerging market and developing economies, capital account liberalization has been a more heterogeneous and uneven experience across regions, with some evidence of reversal in the case of Latin America. By the early 1990s, only around one-fourth of the 155 non-industrial countries reporting to the IMF had established full capital account convertibility.[15] Until the mid-1990s, there was no systematic attempt at the international level to adopt a policy on capital account liberalization outside the advanced countries, and countries were left to their own discretion in this area of international financial policy. East Asia has pursued a more gradual, steady path of liberalization in this regard, similar to that of the advanced countries, albeit with a significant lag. By contrast, Latin America followed a more U-shaped pattern, with an intensification of capital controls during the late 1960s and 1970s consistent with its inward development strategy, followed by a gradual relaxation since the 1980s.[16]

The dramatic shift in official views about freedom for capital movements during the course of the latter half of the twentieth century deserves some attention. At the time of the Bretton Woods Agreement in 1944, with the recent memory of the monetary chaos of the interwar years, controls on capital flows, in particular of a short-term nature, were considered a necessary part of the international monetary order. FDI and long-term portfolio flows were viewed as "productive" or beneficial for economic growth and prosperity, but short-term or "speculative" capital flows were seen as a destabilizing force in the international monetary system. Fifty years later, the prevailing orthodoxy was that capital account liberalization should be actively promoted as an element of the international monetary order. As discussed later in chapter 5, this view was embodied in the proposal in 1997 to include capital account liberalization as one of the objectives and purposes of the IMF. This shift in thinking reflected not only changes in economic paradigms, which had come to view heavy government intervention in the economy as inimical to economic prosperity and welfare, but also the influence of leading economic powers in the international system and private financial interests. In this connection, Gerald Helleiner (1994) has argued that financial globalization was strongly favored by liberal economists in charge of the US Treasury under the Ford and Reagan administrations who advocated a leading role for US-based financial institutions in the international financial system, which led to growing competition with the United Kingdom, Japan, and the EU, as these governments supported global expansion by their domestic financial institutions as well.

The Role of the International Financial Architecture

As noted earlier, the IFA refers to the collective governance arrangements that governments have put in place to safeguard the operations of the international monetary and financial system. By international monetary system is meant the exchange rate and payments arrangements that exist among countries to allow for the international exchange of goods, services, and financial assets and the management of official international reserves, which central banks and traders can use for the settlement of exchange transactions. The international monetary system is analogous to the domestic payments system in a national economy, which allows for the orderly exchange of goods and services through cash and bank account transactions. The international financial system includes the international monetary system, as well as the network of governments, financial institutions, and private investors, which engage in the cross-border exchange of financial instruments in local or global capital markets. These markets are underpinned by an increasingly interconnected infrastructure of central counterparties, central securities depositories and large value payments systems that make possible the clearance and settlement of cross-border transactions in debt and equity securities. The international financial system is far larger in scale than the international monetary system and is dominated by private institutions and investors, which manage most of the transactions in financial assets.

The outbreak of the global financial crisis in late 2008 points to the obvious need for the IFA to minimize the risk of such an event in the future and to mitigate its impact. Crises are an inherent feature of financial markets at both the domestic and international levels. Because financial transactions are intrinsically intertemporal in nature and involve significant risk as to the payment of interest and return of principal in the future, financial systems are prone to crises when confidence is eroded. In domestic finance, this risk has been explained as the result of "asymmetric information" operating on both sides of the balance sheet of a financial institution, which can give rise to failures in financial markets. On the liability side, depositors have less than perfect information about the motives and intentions of bank managers regarding the use of a bank's resources. Bank managers can be prone to "herding" behavior in the upswing of an economic cycle and take on more risk in the search for higher returns. At the first sign of a problem in the bank's operations, in the absence of full disclosure by the bank, depositors may panic and seek to withdraw their deposits, thus imperiling the liquidity or solvency of the bank.

On the asset side of the bank's balance sheet, bank managers have less than perfect information about the motives and intentions of investors seeking access to bank credit. This asymmetry of information can lead to "adverse selection" in that those investors with the most risky ventures or who do not intend to repay the bank will be first in line to seek bank credit, thus giving rise to "moral hazard" on the part of potential borrowers. These market imperfections arising from asymmetric information can lead to credit rationing, higher charges on bank lending rates, more screening, or the absence of credit for new business ventures.

To deal with these market failures in domestic finance, and the financial crises that can be associated with them, governments in most countries have established collective governance arrangements nationally, such as deposit insurance to protect depositors and bank regulatory frameworks and supervision to monitor bank operations, loan administration, and risk management. In addition to regular bank supervision, governments need to have regimes in place to deal with insolvent banks and a "lender of last resort" mechanism or financial safety net (usually in the Central Bank) to provide emergency liquidity to viable banks in the event of widespread panic or crisis.

These same problems of asymmetric information and market failure operate in the international financial system and give rise to the need for some form of government intervention or collective action to minimize the risk of financial crises or deal with its aftereffects. The apparatus that exists at the international level to fill this need is the IFA.

The IFA can also be viewed as a mechanism for the provision of certain global public goods that are essential for the proper functioning of the international monetary and financial systems. Global public goods constitute those services or functions to support the international system that no individual country has the capacity or incentive to provide. At the national level, individual governments provide the public goods needed for the effective functioning of the financial system, but at the international level, such provision requires various forms of intergovernmental cooperative and institutional arrangements.

The essential problem that belies the effectiveness of the IFA is that economic and financial globalization has intensified economic interdependence in the global economy, while governmental structure and accountability arrangements have remained primarily nation-based. The challenge for the IFA is to serve as an effective collective governance arrangement for the international financial system in a world of nation-states and in the absence of a world polity and supranational governmental authority. At the regional level, this divergence in the scope of economic and political arrangements can be resolved through federations and supranational governmental arrangements, of which the best example is the EU. At the global level, however, what has developed is a loose network of institutional and other cooperative arrangements that are imperfect at best and need to be adapted over time.

Over time, the IFA has evolved in response to financial globalization and has been designed by the collective decision making of governments to provide public goods in the following seven areas. The first is the oversight of the international monetary and financial systems with a view to the promotion of global financial system stability. The second is the oversight of the international exchange rate system with a view to the promotion of an effective adjustment mechanism for the orderly resolution of large payments imbalances among countries. The third is a coordinating mechanism for the harmonization of rules for accounting, auditing and the regulating of financial institutions with significant cross-border activities and for the control of money laundering and the financing of terrorism. The fourth is the provision of an international lender of last resort mechanism for international crisis prevention and management. The fifth is an arrangement for the resolution of sovereign debt defaults. The sixth is a mechanism of development finance to promote the transfer of real resources to low-income countries, which participate only marginally in the international financial system. The final area is one of knowledge sharing and the provision of analysis, technical assistance, and training to improve countries' participation in the global economic and financial system.[17]

Initially, at the dawn of the post–World War II era, the IFA was centered in the operations of the Bretton Woods institutions (the IMF and World Bank), as explained in chapter 3 of this book. However, over time, the architecture has become much more diverse and complicated, as new problems arose in the functioning of the global financial system, and new forms of international cooperation were needed to deal with defects and gaps in the system, which any single country was incapable of addressing. One of the problems in this institutional evolution is that, in the design of the postwar IFA, no single institution was given responsibility for oversight of the international financial system and the operations of international capital markets, given the extent of controls on international financial transactions and the predominantly domestic orientation of financial institutions.

In filling this gap in the period up to the current crisis, the IFA had evolved into a mix of public and private institutional arrangements, both formal and informal. It also combined aspects of both "hard" law, as represented by the three universal, treaty-based institutions (the IMF, World Bank, and WTO) and "soft" law, as represented by a variety of cooperative regulatory arrangements coordinated by the Financial Stability Forum (FSF). The growth of these cooperative networks that promote international standards ("soft" law) for the harmonization of national rules in areas such as accounting, auditing, financial regulation, and the basic infrastructure of financial markets has been highlighted by many analysts as a key feature of international relations during the last twenty-five years or so.[18]

The two peaks of the IFA were represented by the IMF, with its oversight responsibilities for the international monetary and financial system and financing mechanism for international liquidity support, and the FSF operating in cooperation with the Bank for International Settlements (BIS), which was intended to coordinate the infrastructural aspects of the system, such as accounting and international financial regulation (figure 2.6).[19] The IMF in some ways has taken on the embryonic form of a global central bank, while the FSF could be viewed as a loose analogy to a global financial regulator. The FSF was intended to promote information sharing and coordination among various individual groups seeking to coordinate activities mainly among the advanced countries, notably in banking regulation (BCBS), securities regulation (IOSCO), insurance supervision (IAIS), and accounting and auditing (IASB). Sovereign debt workouts were managed in a mixed system of ad hoc public (Paris Club) and private arrangements (London Club). In addition, the IMF and World Bank were key players in the fields of development finance and international knowledge sharing. The WTO was the only universal institution with selective jurisdiction in capital account transactions related to trade in services and foreign direct investment in member countries, while regional organizations such as the European Commission and the OECD played an important role in promoting capital account liberalization among their membership. The OECD also supported international collaboration in the field of anti-money laundering and combating the financing of terrorism through the Financial Action Task Force (FATF). The IMF and OECD, along with informal country groups or "clubs," prominently the G10, G7, and G20, all played important, but overlapping roles in promoting international policy coordination among the advanced countries. The G7 countries operated as the de facto steering committee of the IFA in setting the agenda for its management and reform.

As noted earlier, the configuration of the IFA had become excessively fragmented and uncoordinated in the lead-up to the present crisis. There were also serious shortcomings in its governance arrangements that prevented it from operating effectively. The divergence between "hard" law institutions and "soft" law organizations within the IFA also raises questions about its legitimacy and accountability. In addition, there were clear gaps in the scope of financial regulation, defects in the design of bank capital requirements, and weaknesses in the surveillance and oversight of international financial stability that created distorted

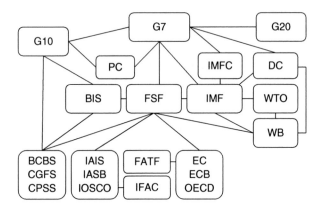

BIS	Bank for International Settlements
BCBS	Basel Committee for Bank Supervision
CGFS	Committee on the Global Financial System
CPSS	Committee on Payment and Settlement Systems
DC	Development Committee
EC	European Commission
ECB	European Central Bank
FATF	Financial Action Task Force
FSF	Financial Stability Forum
G7	Includes Canada, France, Germany, Italy, Japan, United Kingdom, and United States
G10	Includes G7 countries plus Belgium, the Netherlands, Sweden, and Switzerland
G20	Includes G7 countries plus Argentina, Australia, Brazil, China, European Union, India, Indonesia, Mexico, Russia, Saudi Arabia, South Africa, the Republic of Korea, and Turkey
IAIS	International Association of Insurance Supervisors
IASB	International Accounting Standards Board
IFAC	International Federation of Accountants
IMF	International Monetary Fund
IMFC	International Monetary and Financial Committee
IOSCO	International Organization of Securities Commissions
OECD	Organization of Economic Cooperation and Development
PC	Paris Club
WB	World Bank
WTO	World Trade Organization

Figure 2.6   International financial architecture (2007/8)

incentives for risky behavior of financial institutions and the misreporting of balance sheet risk.

It is important to note that the IFA has become a somewhat loose and amorphous structure, which does not exist outside the influence of international politics. Throughout much of the post–World War II era, the evolution of the IFA has been guided and influenced by the advanced countries and the United States, in particular, which have been committed to the development and preservation of a liberal international economic order. The international gold standard of the nineteenth century was underpinned by the strong commitment of the United Kingdom and the power of its central bank and financial sector. In a somewhat similar fashion, the post–World War II IFA has been strongly influenced by the economic policy interests of the United States and the impact of its financial sector. However, since economic policy decisions reflect the influence of domestic political forces, international policy choices of the United States have not always been consistent with the objectives of the IFA. In addition, in an increasingly multipolar world, the power structure within the IFA has become increasingly unrepresentative and a source of weakness in its governance structure, which has undermined its effectiveness.

Summary and Conclusion

In the middle of the last century, capital markets among the advanced countries were highly segmented, and international capital flows were subject to extensive regulation. With the revival of foreign trade and investment activity, this situation began to change during the 1960s as offshore trading in Eurodollar and Eurocurrency markets took hold in an effort by international banks and firms to bypass national controls on capital movements. During the last quarter of the twentieth century, the process of financial globalization emerged in greater force as the advanced countries began to dismantle capital controls within a wider framework of financial liberalization. The growth in financial transactions was particularly strong during the first decade of the current century. During the last two decades, the pace of financial globalization has begun to embrace a wider range of countries, first among the so-called emerging (financial market) economies and some low-income countries. These trends can be discerned in a number of statistical measures and aggregates. The growth in financial globalization has responded to both market forces and policy choices among its major participants.

The IFA represents the collective governance arrangements that governments have instituted to deal with the challenges and problems associated with financial globalization. Before the current global financial crisis, it had evolved into a complex and heterogeneous mix of institutions, clubs and groups, both formal and informal, public and private, which have been created to provide a variety of essential public goods to support the operations of the international monetary and financial systems. The two poles of the architecture were the IMF and FSF, which can be viewed as weakly embryonic forms of a global central bank and single financial regulator within an imagined global polity. The current crisis has shown that this architecture has not functioned effectively and is in need of further reform.

CHAPTER 3

The Evolution of the
Global Financial Order

This chapter provides a brief historical background for the development of financial globalization in the late twentieth and early twenty-first centuries described in the previous chapter. Although financial globalization has taken on many new forms since the 1980s, it is not a new phenomenon. International banking can be traced back to the Middle Ages, but financial globalization on a large scale began to take hold in the period of the international gold standard (1870–1914). This period was followed by a collapse of financial globalization due to the breakdown of the international economic system caused by two world wars and the Great Depression. This chapter traces out the rise, decline, and resurgence of financial globalization in the period since the gold standard and the origins of the present-day IFA in the early post–World War II era.

Throughout this period, official views about the free flow of capital have varied, according to the different weights policy makers have placed on exchange rate stability and domestic policy autonomy. Although support for unfettered flows of capital was characteristic of the gold standard era, government intervention and control of capital flows were viewed as normative for most of the period from 1931 to the mid-1970s. Capital account liberalization and support for financial globalization since the mid-1970s represent a return to an earlier age of globalization, but with very different weights assigned to exchange rate stability and domestic policy autonomy.

The trade-offs facing policy makers regarding exchange rate stability, capital mobility, and domestic policy autonomy are commonly referred to in the economic literature as the Open Economy Trilemma or Impossible Trinity. The first section of this chapter reviews how the Trilemma can be used to demarcate the four periods of the global financial order noted in the previous chapter. This discussion is followed by a brief review of the antecedents for the post–World War II IFA that derive from the experience of the gold standard and the interwar period.

The Open Economy Trilemma

The open economy trilemma or impossible trinity is derived from the basic principles of open economy macroeconomics, which postulate that a country cannot simultaneously maintain exchange rate stability, an open capital account, and monetary policy independence.[1] In a world of highly integrated capital markets, a country can only pursue two of these objectives at the same time. If a country wishes to pursue an independent monetary policy and thus maintain control over the level of domestic interest rates, it may either maintain a fixed exchange rate with capital controls or allow the exchange rate to fluctuate with freedom of capital flows. To illustrate why this is the case, consider the example of a small open economy with a fixed exchange rate regime. If the country wishes to pursue an expansionary monetary policy, action by the central bank to lower short-term interest rates through an increase in bank reserves, in the absence of capital controls, would lead to capital outflows as investors would seek higher-yielding assets abroad. This response on the part of investors would lead to a reduction in the central bank's international reserves and a corresponding reduction in base money and the supply of reserves in the domestic money market. This reduction would neutralize the increase in reserves arising from the initial action of the central bank, thus negating the intended effect of monetary policy. Accordingly, the only way to prevent the neutralizing effect of capital flows in this example of a fixed exchange rate regime would be to impose capital controls.

Although most of the advanced countries today have opted for monetary policy independence with a flexible exchange rate and an open capital account, other countries have made different choices. Hong Kong, for example, maintains a fixed exchange rate under a currency board arrangement with full freedom of capital flows, which is suitable for its role as an international financial center. As a result, domestic interest rates in Hong Kong cannot differ from comparable interest rates in the offshore market, which implies that the Hong Kong Monetary

Authority cannot use monetary policy to adjust interest rates for domestic stabilization purposes.

The impossible trinity can also be used as an organizing principle to understand the policy trade-offs, which the majority of countries have accepted in each of the four periods of monetary order noted earlier: the international gold standard (1870–1913), the interwar period (1919–39), the Bretton Woods system (1945–73), and the post-Bretton Woods system (1973–today). During the gold standard era, countries accepted a binding commitment to maintain fixed exchange rates for their currencies in terms of gold and full freedom for capital movements which, according to the trilemma, necessarily subordinated domestic policy objectives to these constraints. During the interwar period, except for a relatively brief period in the second half of the 1920s when the gold standard was reinstated in somewhat modified form, countries resorted to extensive exchange and capital controls and pursued competitive exchange rate depreciation to achieve domestic stabilization objectives. These choices reversed the commitment of the gold standard and subordinated external policy objectives to the dictates of domestic policy stabilization.

Under the Bretton Woods system, it was agreed that fixed (but adjustable) exchange rates were necessary to support a revival of international trade, along with capital controls to maintain domestic policy autonomy in support of full employment. In this way, capital controls were viewed as essential to support a restoration of the exchange rate stability that had characterized the gold standard, while allowing domestic monetary and fiscal policy to support postwar recovery. With the growing force of international capital flows, the Bretton Woods system was abandoned in the mid-1970s in favor of a mixed system in which the majority of countries have moved toward a regime of flexible exchange rates and capital account liberalization to allow for domestic monetary policy autonomy. Given the wide disparities in the level of economic development among countries today and differences in the extent of their financial integration, any strong generalization about exchange rate regimes and capital account liberalization is difficult to sustain. Nevertheless, one can detect a clear tendency among countries to move in the direction of more flexible exchange rate regimes and more open financial systems.[2]

Thus over a period of approximately 100 years, the international financial system evolved from a regime of full financial globalization and unfettered freedom of capital movements to a completely closed system and then once again to a regime of free capital movements in our own time. This U-shaped pattern of financial globalization has been well documented by economic historians and has given rise to the notion that there have been two periods of economic globalization, namely the period of the international gold standard and the so-called post-Bretton Woods system.[3] According to many of the measures described in the previous chapter, the current age of economic and financial globalization only recovered or exceeded certain dimensions of the previous age toward the end of the twentieth century.

It is also important to recognize that a key difference between the two eras of globalization is that in the first era domestic policy considerations were completely subordinated to the necessity of fixed gold parities. In the current era, given the rise of democratic politics and organized labor groups, such subordination would not be acceptable. According to the impossible trinity, flexible exchange rates have been required to accommodate domestic monetary policy autonomy and freedom for capital movements. An important exception to this pattern has been the experience of the European Union which, during the current era of globalization, decided to limit domestic monetary policy autonomy among its members to achieve exchange rate stability and full freedom of capital flows within (and outside) the union. At the union level, flexibility for the euro has been adopted consistent with the regional monetary policy administered by the European Central Bank and the absence of capital controls.

The next section of this chapter reviews the architectural arrangements for the gold standard and the interwar period and the influence of that experience for the design of the post–World War II IFA.

The International Financial Architecture before World War II

The international gold standard has been called the first era of globalization because of the extensive international flows of goods, capital, and labor that characterized it. Economic historians have shown that by certain measures, financial and labor flows exceeded comparable flows in the international economy at the end of the twentieth century. For example, in measuring financial globalization in terms of the size of current account imbalances, the period of the gold standard exhibited a greater degree of capital market integration than the current global economy at the turn of the last century.[4] Similarly, stocks of foreign direct investment in relation to GDP were higher for many of the developing countries than they were at the dawn of the twenty-first century. In addition, flows of labor migration measured as a stock of native born population in the new world economies far exceeded those in evidence today.[5]

What is also remarkable about the period of the gold standard is that there was no formal institutional arrangement for the IFA at the time. The only legal basis for the regime was rooted in domestic law, which determined the linkage between domestic currency and gold stocks of the government for those countries participating in the gold standard.[6] The regime was critically dependent on the leading economic role of the United Kingdom as the anchor for trade and finance and its dominance in the global economy at the time. After World War II, this role was ceded to the United States. In keeping with the United Kingdom's strict adherence to the gold standard, all countries implicitly agreed to certain "rules of the game" for exchange rate behavior and the international adjustment mechanism, which represented fully credible commitments for the stability of the regime.[7] There was no institutional machinery to enforce these rules or to promote collective action in the event of disturbances to the system. Nevertheless, the gold standard was underpinned by an informal network of central bank cooperation among the advanced countries. Central banks operated in a fairly autonomous manner, largely outside the influence of domestic political forces, in their policy actions to support the system. Subsequent changes in the IFA can be understood as attempts to formalize and extend that cooperative arrangement, as the international financial system has expanded and become more interconnected.

In the technical literature, it is common to measure the effectiveness of international monetary regimes according to three criteria: adjustment, confidence, and liquidity. An effective international monetary system is one that allows for the orderly *adjustment* of international payments imbalances among its members, provides *confidence* to its members of its stability, and generates sufficient *liquidity* to allow for an expansion in global trade and payments. The gold standard can be judged successful on the first two criteria, but not on the third. Since the supply of gold was not subject to international control and was dependent on the accident of private discovery, there were periods of excess supply and excess demand for liquidity during the gold standard, which led to periods of inflation and deflation with harmful economic effects.

The "rules of the game" for adjustment under the gold standard dictated that countries suffering a balance of payments deficit would shrink their domestic money supply as a result of the drain of gold arising from a payments deficit or pursue a policy of credit contraction associated with increases in central bank discount rates. This process would lead over time to a decline in production, employment, and prices until a point where imports had been reduced and export recovery would take place. For surplus countries, the opposite pattern of adjustment would take place, as an inflow of gold or capital inflows would swell the money supply and domestic credit expansion.[8] For most of the advanced countries, which maintained strict adherence to these rules of the game, capital flows played a stabilizing role and facilitated the adjustment process. For countries in the periphery of the system, where payments imbalances were more intractable, sometimes a temporary suspension of gold parities was necessary to facilitate the adjustment mechanism. After some period of time, original gold parities were usually restored, although countries in Southern Europe and South America had inconsistent records in their adherence to this principle. The inalterable commitment of the core countries (e.g., the United Kingdom, France, and Germany) to fixed exchange rates in terms of gold and the adherence to the "restoration principle" for other countries operated as a commitment device that provided stability to the gold standard system and allowed short-term capital flows to play a stabilizing rather than destabilizing role under the system.

Adherence to the gold standard and the commitment to make whatever internal policy adjustments were necessary to maintain a fixed exchange rate to gold, or to restore one that had been temporarily abandoned, also provided the assurances to foreign creditors and investors that made possible a high degree of capital market integration during the period 1880–1913. A country's commitment to the gold standard was considered a "seal of good housekeeping" by participants in the international capital markets in that those capital-importing countries that had a strong record of adherence to the gold standard rules enjoyed lower interest charges on their debt than other countries with a poorer record of adherence.[9]

In terms of the public goods that an IFA is expected to provide, the gold standard can be viewed as successful in terms of providing an effective international adjustment mechanism for the resolution of persistent payments imbalances. In this sense, the system was more successful than the international monetary regimes that followed. The success of the gold standard system was reinforced by an informal cooperative arrangement among the major central banks to support each other's temporary need for gold in times of external pressure on a country's gold supply while policy measures were introduced to stem the loss of gold. At other times, rescue loans might be arranged on an ad hoc basis by private investment firms (e.g., Barings, J.P. Morgan, or Rothschilds), acting in concert with central banks of certain countries.[10] This informal arrangement of rescue loans represented an early, limited form of an international lender of last resort function, which the IFA is also expected to provide.

International capital flows were predominantly private in origin and destination during the gold standard and took the form of interbank loans, bond placements, and direct investment. Flows of bond finance and foreign direct investment were particularly important between developed and developing countries, and in particular between the United Kingdom and territories of new settlements in Latin America and other destinations of European migrants. The development of infrastructure (e.g., railroads, ports) and natural resource extraction was often the attraction for foreign investors, as these activities would generate a stream of revenues with which to service debt finance. Both governments and private companies in the periphery were active borrowers in the international capital markets. The UK economy was highly dependent on export trade and provided a substantial share of its national saving in foreign capital investment to finance that trade. Its financial markets were the most developed in the global economy at the end of the nineteenth century and played a predominant role in the intermediation of global savings and investment. By most accounts, it would seem that international investment conformed to the expectations of neoclassical growth theory in that it flowed to destinations where capital was scarce and marginal returns were highest, thus fulfilling the role of development finance under the informal IFA of the time.[11]

Notwithstanding the effective operation of the gold standard, the international financial system during this period was not immune to shocks and crises associated with boom-bust cycles of lending. Domestic banking crises were common at the time because of the lack of effective supervision and a national safety net of deposit insurance and lender of last resort financing. Currency crises also occurred among the developing countries adhering to the gold standard, although on a much less frequent basis than in the period since 1973 (under the post-Bretton Woods system). According to a study by Michael Bordo and Barry Eichengreen (2002), the incidence of a financial crisis (banking or currency or both) was around twice as large during the period after 1973 than it was during the period of the gold standard because of the lower likelihood of a currency crisis and of a spillover of a banking crisis into a currency crisis (twin crises).

Sovereign debt defaults also occurred because of weak fiscal management in the developing countries and/or periodic shocks associated with a sharp decline in the terms of trade of the debtor country or a recession in a core lending country. Most defaults were concentrated among countries of the European periphery or in Latin America.[12] In the case of sovereign debt defaults, workout procedures were managed on an ad hoc basis by private bondholding groups without formal government intervention. The most famous of these informal, private sector arrangements was the Corporation of Foreign Bondholders (CFB), which acted as a representative group for holders of bonds issued in the London market. Other similar groups existed in many of the other major economies, but none of these had the longevity or seniority of the CFB.[13] Debt workouts were costly for the defaulting country in terms of output contraction and their isolation from the international bond market, but with time and the negotiated restructuring of debt in default, borrowing could resume. The average time of default during the period of the gold standard was around ten years, which is significantly longer than in more recent times. The terms of a debt workout generally took the form of a capitalization of interest arrears, a payments moratorium or extension of debt maturity, and, in some cases, a reduction in the payment of interest and/or principal.[14] In certain situations where creditor committees could not bring about a resolution to a debt crisis, military intervention (or "gunboat diplomacy") might take place as in the case of the US and European creditors vis-à-vis debtors in the Caribbean or South America. The blockade of Venezuela by naval forces from Germany, Great Britain, and Italy during 1902–3 is an extreme example of creditor coordination in the use of trade sanctions to enforce debt repayments.[15]

The gold standard collapsed with the onset of World War I, but in the aftermath of the Treaty of Versailles in 1918, efforts were made to reestablish it, in the form of the gold exchange standard, which were largely successful by 1925. During this period, two important institutional innovations were made which set important precedents for the IFA of the post–World War II era. One was the creation of the League of Nations in 1920 and, in particular, its Financial Committee and Economic and Financial Organization (EFO) which, in certain respects, were precursors of the IMF. The other was the creation of the Bank for International Settlements (BIS) by the European countries in 1930 to manage some of the World War I reparation payments by Germany and to provide a forum for central bank cooperation in Europe.[16] Both of these institutions formalized arrangements for international consultation in the international financial sphere and cooperation among central banks of the leading economic powers of the time, which had not existed previously.

The League's economic and financial operations set important precedents for the development of the postwar IFA.[17] One was its formal consultative machinery to promote international discussion and policy collaboration. In addition to the deliberations of the League's Financial Committee, which included private bankers and officials from national Central Banks and Finance Ministries, the League organized a series of international conferences during the 1920s, which laid the groundwork for the restoration of the gold standard in the modified form of the gold exchange standard. Under the revised standard, certain core countries in Europe and North America reestablished their commitment to the gold standard, while other countries adhered to a mixed system whereby both gold and foreign currency liabilities of the core countries were counted as official international reserves. Although the League did not have any financial resources of its own, the Financial Committee served as a coordinating body for the organization of privately financed stabilization operations with a number of Central and Eastern European countries that allowed them to regain exchange rate stability following World War I. Typically, the League would appoint a Commissioner to each recipient country who would oversee the implementation of economic reforms to facilitate the stabilization objectives agreed between the borrowing country and the Financial Committee. Such operations set a clear precedent for IMF stabilization programs in the post–World War II era, the application of "conditionality" to IMF lending, and the temporary posting of IMF resident representatives to borrowing countries to assist country authorities in the implementation of an adjustment program.

The League's economic activities also created an important precedent for the work of an international secretariat in the surveillance of the global economy. During the 1930s, in particular, the Economic Intelligence Service of the EFO began the systematic collection and compilation of international statistics for member countries and the global economy and produced a number of important analytical studies on the global economy. These activities can be seen as precedent for the work of the IMF in the collection and dissemination of international statistics and the development of its multilateral surveillance function, as manifested in its publication of the World Economic Outlook and Global Financial Stability Reports. Some continuity between the work of the League and the IMF was achieved by virtue of the fact that some of the senior staff assigned to the IMF in its early years had prior experience in the League's economic and financial activities.

The early history of the BIS was much more limited than that of the League's economic and financial activities. As noted earlier, it was not only created with a particular war-related function, but also began to function as a forum for central bank coordination and consultation in the European context that would take on greater significance in the post–World War II IFA.[18] With the establishment of the IMF, the BIS was expected to be closed down because of the antipathy of some of the Allied Powers for its acceptance of debt service payments from Nazi Germany on BIS investments, which were financed in part by gold looted from occupied territories.[19] However, the European central banks, which were its main constituent members, decided to maintain the BIS as a forum for regional central bank cooperation. Beginning in the 1950s, it began to take on more important functions in the IFA with its support for the European Payments Union and its venue for meetings of the G10 central bank governors.

Notwithstanding this embryonic development of institutional arrangements for the IFA during the 1920s and the restoration of the gold standard in 1925, this regime was unable to survive the effects of the Great Depression at the turn of the following decade. At first, rigid adherence to the gold standard provided a mechanism by which its deflationary effects were transmitted from one country to another, starting with the United States in 1929. Then in 1931, following the insolvency of a major commercial bank in Austria (the Credit Anstalt) in May of that year, a wave of panics spread throughout Europe, which threatened the stability of the exchange rate system. That system was already weakened by severe misalignments among some of the major currencies arising from the inappropriateness of prewar parities that were restored after World War I (in particular, for the United Kingdom). In addition, continuing tensions between some of the belligerents in that conflict (in particular, France and Germany) over the issue of war reparations led to a breakdown of central bank cooperation that had underpinned the stability of the gold standard previously.[20] In contrast with the earlier success of the League of Nations' stabilization loans, the BIS helped to arrange a series of rescue operations in 1931 involving its own resources and those of its member central banks for Austria, Hungary, and Germany each of which failed to stabilize currencies exposed to speculative attack.[21] Apart from the inviability of the parities involved, the amounts involved in the loans were relatively small. In addition, in the case of Germany, France was unwilling to support a second rescue operation because of its ongoing disputes with its previous wartime adversary. With the abandonment of the UK gold parity in 1931 and subsequently that of the United States in 1933, a two-tier status of countries, some adhering to the gold standard and others not, began to develop. In retrospect, economic historians have demonstrated that those countries that departed from the gold standard became the first to experience recovery from the Great Depression.[22]

The 1930s were a decade of international monetary disorder. The advanced countries pursued protectionist policies and competitive devaluations in an attempt to protect domestic employment, and all efforts at international consultation and policy coordination failed, notably the World Economic Conference in London of June 1933, which was undermined by the US government decision to abandon its gold parity. The techniques of exchange and capital controls that had been developed during World War I were widely reinstated and intensified that reinforced the deflationary effects of the Depression. In terms of the policy trade-offs of the impossible trinity, countries chose capital controls and a mixed system of exchange rate policy to provide scope for domestic policy maneuver in support of economic stabilization. Sovereign defaults on bonded debt also rose substantially during the economic collapse of the 1930s, which were resolved through the same process of creditor coordination that operated before World War I under the auspices of groups such as the CFB. In the United States, a similar organization, the Foreign Bondholders Protective Council (FBPC), was formed in 1933 with the encouragement of the US government to act on behalf of American bondholders.

The Origins of the Post–World War II International Financial Architecture

The experience of the 1930s and the Great Depression had a profound effect on the design of the post-World War II IFA. The postwar planners in the United States and United Kingdom were mainly concerned with the reconstruction of war-torn economies and the revival of the global trading and international economic system. This experience also demonstrated how the institutional evolution of the IFA has usually been driven by crisis, a theme that will be born out as well in subsequent chapters of this book.

The experience of the 1930s provided three important lessons that guided the design of the post–World War II IFA under the Bretton Woods system. One was that the institutional arrangements to support the international economic system needed to be reinforced and strengthened to foster cooperation and consultation internationally to safeguard the system. Both the Financial Committee of the League of Nations and the BIS represented some initial attempts to formalize patterns of cooperation among central banks and ministries of finance that had only operated on an ad hoc informal basis during the Gold Standard. However, these proved to be insufficient to forestall the damaging effects of the Great Depression, in part because they were not universal institutions and had only weak supranational authority and very limited financial resources.

A second lesson from the 1930s, which guided postwar planners, was that stable and relatively fixed exchange rates were necessary to support the revival and expansion of international trade that had collapsed during the Great Depression. Currency volatility and widespread resort to exchange controls were viewed as having been destructive of the liberal economic order that prevailed during the gold standard and as having reinforced the deflationary tendencies of the Great Depression. Accordingly, the purposes of the IMF were defined in Article I of the Fund Agreement to include the following six objectives:

(i) To promote international monetary cooperation through a permanent institution which provides the machinery for consultation and collaboration on international monetary problems;

(ii) To facilitate the expansion and balanced growth of international trade, and to contribute thereby to the promotion and maintenance of high levels of employment and real income and to the development of the productive resources of all members as primary objectives of economic policy;

(iii) To promote exchange stability, to maintain orderly exchange arrangements among members, and to avoid competitive exchange depreciation;

(iv) To assist in the establishment of a multilateral system of payments in respect of current transactions between members and in the elimination of foreign exchange restrictions that hamper the growth of world trade;

(v) To give confidence to members by making the Fund's resource available to them under adequate safeguards, thus providing them with opportunity to correct maladjustments in their balance of payments without resorting to measures destructive of national or international prosperity;

(vi) In accordance with the above, to shorten the duration and lessen the degree of disequilibrium in the international balances of payments of members.

The important institutional innovation of the Bretton Woods system was the decision to establish, for the first time, an international legal framework and code of conduct for international monetary relations and to invest the IMF with the authority to supervise the international exchange rate system based on fixed, but adjustable exchange rates and freedom for current account transactions. This regime represented a fundamental change from the informal "rules of the game" of the gold standard. In addition to the obligation to eliminate restrictions on current account transactions, members of the Fund were required to seek its approval for any significant departures from established par values (i.e., adjustments of more than 10 percent) under the system. Members also undertook the commitment to liberalize exchange controls on current payments and move toward full current account convertibility under the guidance and support of the IMF. Members undertaking exchange liberalization or making an adjustment to their par values could count on the temporary financial support of the IMF to facilitate these modifications to their exchange arrangements. This feature of the IMF institutionalized the ad hoc informal arrangements involving private investment banks and central banks of the gold standard and interwar years.

The third and final lesson drawn from the international currency experience of the 1930s was that private capital flows, in particular of a short-term nature, had had a destabilizing influence on exchange rate stability, contrary to the experience of the gold standard. The implication of this lesson was that capital controls were viewed as necessary to support a system of stable exchange rates and to allow policy makers scope for the pursuit of full-employment policies in the economic recovery effort following World War II. The result of this collective decision making embodied in the Bretton Woods Agreement was fully consistent with the principles of the impossible trinity. Specifically, Article VI of the Fund Agreement authorized members to impose capital controls for balance of payments management and prohibited the use of IMF financial resources to finance short-term capital outflows. Curiously, these provisions of the Fund Agreement have remained in place even in the face of broad support for capital account liberalization in the last quarter of the twentieth century during the post-Bretton Woods system.[23]

International agreement on the Bretton Woods system represented a critical milestone in the development of international institutions and the IFA, in particular. In response to the breakdown of the international economic system during the 1930s, the international community, under the leadership of the United States and United Kingdom, recognized the need for public goods provision at the international level for the achievement of certain collective goals. Although the concept and the literature on public goods was not developed at the time of the Bretton Woods Agreement, it was clear to the lead negotiators that international cooperation in the monetary and financial area was necessary to prevent individual state behavior that was detrimental to the common economic welfare embodied in a well-functioning international economic system. As noted earlier, international institutions are needed to provide certain services and functions (i.e., public goods) for the benefit of the international financial community that no one individual nation would necessarily have an incentive to provide. Thus in the absence of collective action, such "goods" would be in short supply.

The Bretton Woods institutions (the IMF and World Bank) were designed to provide a number of specific public goods. First, as both universal institutions, they would provide a permanent international forum for consultation and deliberation on international monetary, financial, and development issues. Second, the IMF was intended to exercise oversight of the international exchange rate system and to promote the orderly adjustment of payments imbalances among countries through an effective exchange rate system. Third, the IMF, through its lending operations with member countries, would provide emergency liquidity to countries facing temporary payments difficulties and to facilitate the process of exchange rate adjustment, where warranted in cases of "fundamental disequilibrium."[24] Fourth, the World Bank through its lending operations was intended to identify worthwhile investment projects in developing countries and to provide long-term financing that private finance would not be willing to provide. Fifth, the IMF was intended to become a clearinghouse for the collection of national and international financial statistics and to develop expertise and analytical research on monetary and financial issues (as called for in Article VIII, section 5 of the Fund Agreement) that could be disseminated to the international community through publications, training, and technical assistance. The Bank would come to play a similar role in the field of economic development.

Notwithstanding the clear legal and institutional basis which the Bretton Woods system provided for the international monetary system, there were important gaps in this early form of the post–World War II IFA as regards the coverage of capital transactions that would have to be filled in as the system evolved. Within the Fund's jurisdiction, certain transactions that are usually considered capital transactions in the analysis of a country's external position were included in the definition of current account transactions for purposes of Article VIII of the Fund Agreement, namely "normal short-term banking and credit facilities and payments for moderate amount of amortization of loans or for depreciation of direct investments (Article XIX)." For its part, the World Bank was intended to provide guarantees to promote direct investment flows and would become a principal provider of official development finance. However, the great bulk of private banking transactions and portfolio flows, which were to become the main component of capital flows during and after the Bretton Woods system, were relegated solely to domestic legal regulation and were excluded from the purview of the IFA. This is not surprising given the emphasis on capital controls of the Bretton Woods regime. In this sense, the postwar planners were looking backward in their view of what needed to be fixed in the international monetary system, and they were not intent on a grand design for some future, anticipated state of the global economy. The coordination of national regulatory regimes for financial institutions would become a prominent feature of the IFA during the post-Bretton Woods system.

Another related gap in the Bretton Woods architecture was the absence of any machinery for the resolution of sovereign debt defaults to official or private bank creditors. The Paris Club and London Club approaches to sovereign debt workouts would become a feature of the IFA, as these problems took on more prominence in international finance during the post-Bretton Woods system. Private bondholder coordinating groups, such as the CFB and the FBPC, while still in existence under the Bretton Woods system, had become obsolete with the disappearance of long-term capital markets for international borrowers under the effects of the Great Depression and World War II.[25]

In addition to the public goods' aspect of the Bretton Woods system, the regime embodied an important distinction between one domain of sovereign national control of economic policy and another sphere in which a legitimate degree of external accountability and supranational oversight was warranted in the management of exchange rates. This essential distinction inherent in the Bretton Woods system between an international commitment to a liberal exchange system under the supervision of the IMF and a domain of sovereign control of domestic policy management has often been encapsulated in the notion of "embedded liberalism."[26] This idea gave coherence to a new regime for the international monetary system, for which there was near-universal support, which was essentially different from that of the gold standard. Under the gold standard, the unalterable commitment of the major economies to the gold standard represented the foundation of the regime and ensured an effective international adjustment mechanism to promote international monetary stability. However, the priority given to international adjustment and fixed exchange rates necessarily involved the full subordination of domestic policy to these goals, according to the principles of the impossible trinity. With the expansion of democratic politics and the growing strength of labor unions under welfare states, such a trade-off became unviable and new "rules of the game" needed to be devised, which came to be embodied in the Bretton Woods system. As in the case of the gold standard, a dominant economic power of the time (the United States instead of the United Kingdom) provided an anchor for the new regime, which was essential for its maintenance given the dominance of the US economy in the international economic system.

Another important innovation in the Bretton Woods system was to depart from the principle of unanimity in decision making among equal members in the League of Nations and to establish majority rules according to a weighted voting system which involved the distribution of voting shares across the membership (of both the IMF and the World Bank) mainly according to measures of economic size and power. In recognition of the equality of nations in the IMF, each member was assigned the same number of "basic" votes in the institution, which were augmented by other votes that were scaled to the size of its "quota," or financial shares in the Fund. At the Bretton Woods conference, the share of basic votes represented around 11 percent of total voting power in the Fund, but over time, as quotas were adjusted upward, while the number of basic votes per country remained unchanged, the share of basic votes was reduced to around 2 percent (as of April 2008 when a decision was taken for the first time to increase their number).

This constitutional arrangement of weighted voting power recognized not only the primacy of the allied powers (and the United States and United Kingdom, in particular) in setting up the post–World War II international machinery, but also their important creditor status in supplying the financial resources for the institution through quota subscriptions. At the Bretton Woods conference, the five largest quotas were assigned to the same five, permanent members of the UN Security Council (the United States, United Kingdom, the Soviet Union, China, and France), and as such they were allowed to appoint their own executive director in the Board of the Fund (all the other thirty-nine original members of the Fund formed constituencies that elected seven other members of the executive board). When the Soviet Union decided not to join the IMF, India, which had the next largest quota, became the fifth largest member when the IMF began its operations in 1946. The

United States and the United Kingdom, with the two largest quotas in the Fund, accounted for 36 percent and 16 percent, respectively, of its total initial quota shares.[27]

In keeping with the cooperative nature of the Fund, a member's quota would also determine its access to IMF financing in terms of tranches. A member's access to its gold or reserve tranche, which was equivalent to 25 percent of its quota, would be automatic, but access to higher tranches up to an initial limit of 100 percent of its quota would be subject to conditions that would vary in intensity with the extent of access. Technically, a member would not borrow resources from the Fund in the form of a loan, but would instead "purchase" convertible currencies from other members made available by the Fund in exchange for its own currency, somewhat in the nature of a swap arrangement between central banks but with a longer term maturity than central bank swaps.[28] Beginning in 1952, these purchases would be phased under "stand-by arrangements," as distinct from loan agreements, for example, of the World Bank. Over the years, financial transactions of the Bank and Fund have been given preferred creditor status by governments and other creditors and thus are not subject to rescheduling because of the public good nature of their lending. This status has allowed these institutions to provide credit at rates of interest lower than those charged by other creditors.

The IMF was only one leg of a tripod of institutions that made up the post–World War II IFA. Trade liberalization was to be managed by the International Trade Organization, which eventually came into existence in more limited form as the GATT (the predecessor to the WTO). The international responsibilities of the IMF and GATT were seen as complementary, as the GATT was to promote reductions in barriers to trade (such as quantitative restrictions and tariffs), while the IMF was intended to promote reductions in exchange controls for current account transactions and an open payments system that is essential for enabling an unrestricted exchange of currency to support a liberal trading system. As noted earlier, the work of the GATT (WTO) that is directly relevant to the IFA came into play only in the mid-1990s with the General Agreement on Trade in Services (GATS) which covers, among other things, financial services and the cross-border activities of private financial institutions, and the General Agreement on Trade-Related Investment Measures that covers trade-related aspects of foreign direct investment.

The deliberations on the World Bank (International Bank of Reconstruction and Development) did not take up much time at the

Bretton Woods Conference because of the primary concern with issues of international payments and exchange arrangements.[29] Under the Bretton Woods system, private capital flows were not envisaged to play an important role in the international financial system, except in the area of foreign direct investment. Financial flows were expected to be dominated by flows of official finance, in which the World Bank had a potentially important role to play. These expectations featured prominently in the objectives of the World Bank as stated in Article I of its Articles of Agreement:

> To provide private foreign investment by means of guarantees or participations in loans and other investments made by private investors; and when private capital is not available on reasonable terms, to supplement private investment by providing, on suitable conditions, finance for productive purposes out of its own capital, funds raised by it and its own resources;
>
> To promote the long range balanced growth of international trade and the maintenance of equilibrium in balances of payments by encouraging international investment for the development of the productive resources of members, thereby assisting in raising productivity, the standard of living and conditions of labor in their territories.

Unlike the IMF, whose financial resources came from the contributions of its members, the World Bank was expected to mobilize its funding through the sale of bonds in the major financial centers (initially New York City), drawing on the full faith and guarantee of its major shareholders, which it would use to make loans to member countries. Because of the importance of establishing the credit-worthiness of the Bank in the New York financial markets, it was decided that the president of the Bank should be an American citizen with close ties to the financial community. By an implicit understanding, it was accepted that the head of the IMF would be a European. These decisions set a precedent in the leadership selection of the IMF and World Bank, which have continued to the present day. The importance of satisfying wary financiers of the Bank also led to an early emphasis in the Bank on project finance in its lending operations for large infrastructural requirements (e.g., power generation, transportation, and roads), which typically could offer a high rate of return and steady stream of revenues.

Until the advent of the Marshall Plan, the Bank assumed an important role in the financing of European reconstruction, for which private financial flows were not available. However, the eclipse of the Bank in its reconstruction role and limited recourse of advanced countries to financial assistance from the IMF pointed to a significant limitation of the Bretton Woods institutions as regards their financial resources. The US plan for the IMF and World Bank, which ultimately determined the scope and operating modalities for these institutions, was far less ambitious in its financial dimension than that of the United Kingdom. The British plan designed by John Maynard Keynes envisaged an International Clearing Union with resources of US$28 billion, or more than three times the original size of the IMF (US$8.8 billion). Keynes's plan was also far more ambitious in its design than the IMF, as it would have created an international currency (Bancor) to replace the use of gold in the settlement of payments imbalances and would have established a mechanism to encourage symmetrical adjustment among both persistent deficit and surplus countries.[30] The absence of an effective mechanism to bring about such adjustment would be a problem for the international monetary system up until the present day.

Instead of a bold new system, the Bretton Woods conference settled on a variant of the interwar gold exchange standard, with the US dollar as the main reserve currency given its large gold holdings and dominant position in the global economy. The long run stability of the system, therefore, was critically dependent on sound economic policy management of the United States. This dependency was based on two factors. One was the nature of the exchange rate system, in that par values of IMF members under the Bretton Woods system were defined in relationship to gold or the US dollar, which in turn was defined in terms of a fixed value to gold. The second factor of dependency was that countries relied on the US economy for a provision of liquidity and financing, in much the same manner as the United Kingdom under the gold standard. Such a role was only sustainable if the US economy maintained approximate equilibrium in its overall balance of payments position vis-à-vis the rest of the world. If instead because of expansionary policies, the US balance of payments position was continually in deficit, then its short-term foreign liabilities would increase indefinitely, thus undermining its ability to provide gold in exchange for any claims accumulated by other countries. Ultimately, this weakness in the system undermined all three attributes of the Bretton Woods system: adjustment, confidence, and liquidity.

The dominance of the dollar-based reserve system was solidified by two decisions that were made by the US government in the early post–World War II period. One was the creation of the Marshall Plan in 1948 for the reconstruction of Western Europe that gave rise to the Organization of European Economic Cooperation as its multilateral administrative and coordinating arm, which was converted to the OECD in 1961. The size of the Marshall Plan was far larger than the combined resources of the IMF and World Bank and quickly replaced World Bank reconstruction loans to European countries. During the period 1949–53, around US$12 billion in Marshall Plan aid was disbursed to the European countries, compared with combined disbursements of around US$2 billion from IMF and World Bank loans during the first five years of their existence.[31] The Marshall Plan was probably the most important aid operation of the US government, both in terms of financial commitments in relation to GDP and in terms of results. Beginning in 1950, the Bank began to shift its lending operations toward the developing world.

The other important decision for the Bretton Woods system was the creation of the European Payments Union (EPU), which was established in 1950 to facilitate the establishment of convertibility among the Western European countries. At the Bretton Woods conference, it had been assumed that the European countries would be able to establish current account convertibility relatively quickly, but this expectation turned out to be unrealistic. Instead, the EPU was set up to provide a clearing arrangement, with the US dollar as the main currency of settlement, to facilitate the settlement of imbalances among the European countries whose currencies were still subject to wartime controls and restrictions. It was only in 1959 when full convertibility of the European currencies was established that the Bretton Woods system could fully come into operation. The EPU was also significant for the prominence it gave to the BIS as its financial and clearing agent. In principle, this role could have been assumed by the IMF, but the European authorities preferred to have one of their "own" institutions fulfill this role, such as the BIS which had already developed expertise for its trustee and agency functions in the management of member central bank foreign reserves.[32]

Once the Bretton Woods system came into more prominence at the end of the 1950s, the "dynamic instability" of the Bretton Woods system started to became a major matter of international concern in debates on the viability of the international financial architecture during the 1960s.[33] Notions of reserve adequacy and reserve diversification were the dominant concerns in these debates. Some of these debates were managed within the IMF, consistent with its role as a consultative forum for discussion of international monetary and financial issues. However, many of these debates were also managed outside the forum of the IMF within what came to be known as the G10 group of finance ministers and central bank governors, which organized their meetings under the umbrella of the BIS.

The growth of US dollar liabilities abroad was an important stimulus to the development of the international financial markets, initially in the form of offshore Eurodollar deposits that were traded among major international banks and used to finance international lending operations. The development of these offshore markets outside the organized domestic financial markets of the major countries was purely a reflection of the wide application of capital controls among the major countries, which continued to be viewed as an essential feature of the IFA. However, over time, as the size of these offshore markets continued to grow, capital controls became less effective. The presence of capital controls also led, as noted earlier, to a significant degree of disguised capital flows through under or over-invoicing of trade and the use of "leads and lags" in trade financing.

Ultimately the viability of the Bretton Woods system became untenable with the continued growth in US foreign liabilities, which undermined confidence among the major creditor countries that the United States would be able to meet those commitments through the surrender of gold.

Summary and Conclusion

To understand the current age of financial globalization that began during the 1970s, it is useful to recognize that this period followed one of roughly similar length (1931–73) during which international capital markets were suppressed because of turmoil in the international financial system during most of the interwar period and government intervention and controls during the early post–World War II era. The efforts to create an IFA for the post–World War II period under the Bretton Woods system essentially were intended to restore a liberal international economic order that would promote global prosperity at least on a par with that of the gold standard era of the late nineteenth and early twentieth century. That era established a degree of economic and financial integration among its participants that would not be restored until late in the twentieth century. However, the domestic policy requirements for the gold standard era no longer became viable with the experience of the Great Depression, and new "rules of the game" for the post–World War II IFA needed to be established. These differences in policy requirements can be understood in terms of the impossible trinity, which postulates that a country cannot simultaneously maintain a fixed exchange rate, domestic monetary policy autonomy, and freedom for capital flows. Only two of these conditions can apply at the same time. During the gold standard era, countries chose a fixed exchange rate and freedom for capital flows and surrendered domestic policy autonomy. Under the Bretton Woods Agreement, the collective choice was for fixed exchange rates and domestic policy autonomy, with controls on capital movements.

The IFA of the Bretton Woods system established an institutional structure and formal code of conduct for the international monetary system that only existed informally or in weak embryonic form previously. Instead of the informal "rules of the game" that underpinned exchange rate behavior during the gold standard, the IMF Agreement established formal, legal obligations for its members in the area of exchange rate arrangements and currency practices. It also formalized cooperative financial arrangements among its members, which existed only on an ad hoc, informal basis during the gold standard period and in weak institutional form under the League of Nations and the BIS during the interwar period. The Bretton Woods system also addressed for the first time the problem of development finance in the international financial system with the creation of the World Bank, but did not cover other forms of international capital flows in view of the highly segmented nature of domestic capital markets at the time. This gap in the coverage of the IFA would have to be filled as the international financial system began to take shape and evolve. The postwar IFA was critically dependent on the anchor of the US dollar and the stability of the US economy in somewhat the same way that the gold standard was dependent on the dominant position of the United Kingdom.

CHAPTER 4

The Breakdown of the Bretton Woods System and First Reform of the International Financial Architecture

This chapter focuses first on the efforts that were made to support the Bretton Woods system and the factors that led to its breakdown. This discussion is followed by a review of the multilateral debates that led to the first reform of the IFA. At this stage of its evolution, the primary focus of the IFA continued to be on improvements in the international monetary system. However, the outcome of efforts to improve the system was profoundly influenced by the growing force of capital flows within the international financial system. The result of this reform effort was a more decentralized and fragmented structure of the IFA. The chapter also highlights the important changes that occurred in the activities of the IMF and World Bank, and the emergence of the G7 as a de facto steering committee for the IFA.

The Breakdown of the Bretton Woods System

The Bretton Woods system operated in full force only during the period from 1958, when current account convertibility of the main European currencies was established, until 1971 when the United States unilaterally suspended the redemption of gold for short-term dollar liabilities held by foreign central banks. By 1964, these obligations began to exceed the amount of monetary gold held by the United States. Apart from the problem of "dynamic instability" noted in the previous chapter, the system had two other flaws: one was that countries were reluctant to adjust their currencies in the face of "fundamental disequilibrium," especially in the case of surplus countries, in part because of the fear of disruptive movements of short-term capital flows that would anticipate such adjustments; during the period 1949–1967, there were exceptionally few adjustments in the par values of the major advanced countries, despite the fact that growth rates of aggregate income and productivity differed significantly across the Atlantic. The other problem under the Bretton Woods system was the growing force of capital flows in unregulated, offshore financial markets such as the euro-dollar market, which made capital controls more difficult to enforce with a view to limiting speculative capital movements. The stock of dollar claims in the euro-dollar market rose from US$15 billion in 1960 (compared with a US gold stock equivalent to US$23 billion) to US$83 billion in 1972 (compared with a US gold stock equivalent to US$10.5 billion).[1] Ultimately, the growing force of speculative capital flows made a regime of fixed exchange rates untenable, in line with the principles of the impossible trinity.

In the face of these problems, a number of important, cooperative efforts both within and outside the IMF were organized to support the Bretton Woods regime during this period. One was the establishment of the General Arrangements to Borrow (GAB) by the G10 finance ministers and central bank governors in 1962 to supplement IMF resources, in amounts of up to US$6 billion, for the management of important stabilization loans to industrial countries.[2] The need for this facility pointed once again to the insufficiency of IMF financing for its operations, notwithstanding periodic increases in its quotas. During the 1960s, the GAB was activated on six occasions to support IMF standby arrangements for the United Kingdom (four times) and France (two times). Some of these operations were supported by parallel credits from the Bank for International Settlements (BIS). The creation of the GAB essentially established an international lender of last resort mechanism in the IMF, which it could use to assist countries in resisting currency speculation, as Article VI of the Fund Agreement proscribed the use of the Fund's own financial resources for financing capital outflows.[3]

The G10 also became a leading forum for the discussion of international monetary issues, in particular related to the question of reserve adequacy and the overreliance of the Bretton Woods system on US dollar liabilities to satisfy reserve needs. These discussions led to the proposal to create an international reserve currency in the Fund, Special Drawing Rights or SDRs, which was approved by the IMF in 1969 (in the first amendment of the Fund Agreement) and came into existence in 1970, just before the breakdown of the regime.[4] The G10 central bank governors also established the first of three specialized committees, the Euro-currency Standing Committee (which in 1999 became the Committee on the Global Financial System), for the purpose of collecting statistics and monitoring developments in offshore international banking markets.

From an institutional perspective, the work of the G10 was important in signaling a preference of the major shareholders of the IMF to control decision making on key issues of the IFA outside the IMF, which would take on greater prominence in the post-Bretton Woods era.[5] The G10 also instituted its own peer review mechanism for macroeconomic surveillance during the early 1960s with the creation of Working Party 3 of the OECD Economic Policy Committee. The creation of these two mechanisms would create some tension within the membership of the IMF, which would become more visible during the reform debates of the 1970s.

A second cooperative arrangement that was established during the 1960s to support the Bretton Woods regime was the activation of central bank currency swaps by the key currency countries. In some cases, these swaps were activated in concert with the IMF stabilization loans, noted earlier, and in other cases to relieve pressures on the US dollar. These short-term lines of credit were typically for a period of three months, renewable at the end of the term. Up until the present time, these swap arrangements have never been institutionalized permanently, but have been activated as and when the need arose. During the 1960s, the US Federal Reserve established swap arrangements (or bilateral lines of credit) with fourteen other central banks (mainly European) and the BIS, which grew to a total value of US$11.7 billion by 1972. The BIS also created a network of swap arrangements with central banks in Europe for support of the UK pound (the Sterling Group arrangement), which was coordinated with IMF credits in certain cases.[6]

The third important cooperative arrangement among the advanced countries to support the Bretton Woods regime was the establishment of the "gold pool" in 1961 to stabilize the international price of gold. This action was taken out of concern that private speculation in the international gold market, in the light of rising US foreign liabilities and a shrinkage in its gold assets, could lead to a divergence between the official and the private price of gold that would undermine confidence in the stability of the US dollar as the anchor of the exchange rate system. Accordingly, in 1962, a compact was agreed among the governments of the Belgium, England, France, Germany, Italy, Netherlands, Switzerland, and the United States to intervene in the London gold market to ensure that the private market price for gold would remain at, or close to, the official price of gold of US$35 an ounce. The BIS provided a secretariat for the management of the Gold Pool. This arrangement was successful until March 1968, when France and Germany decided to withdraw their support, and a two-tier gold market, separating the free market from the official market, was introduced.[7]

During this period, the United States also took unilateral action in its capital control regime to contain the growth in its short-term foreign liabilities abroad. One such measure was the imposition of an interest equalization tax in 1963, as mentioned earlier, and the issue of medium-term bonds denominated in foreign currency (so-called Roosa bonds). In addition, the US government issued voluntary guidelines to limit the growth of foreign assets by commercial banks in 1965 and foreign direct investment by multinational corporations in 1968. Each of these measures gave further impulse to the expansion of the euro-dollar market.

Notwithstanding the underlying flaws of the Bretton Woods regime, it should be recognized that the cooperative financial arrangements established among the IMF, GAB, BIS, and the US Federal Reserve provided strong support to the regime and were successful in a number of individual country cases in stabilizing currencies in the face of speculative attack. This experience stands in mark contrast with that of the early 1930s when international monetary cooperation to put in place the functional equivalent of an international lender of last resort mechanism was more limited and ultimately ineffective.

The Bretton Woods system came to an end in August 1971 when the United States closed its gold window and announced the suspension of any sales of official gold to redeem dollar liabilities held by foreign central banks. This action was prompted by the expectation that France and the United Kingdom were preparing to present the US government with a demand that their short-term dollar claims be converted into gold. This breakdown was anticipated years ahead by a number of analysts, prominently Robert Triffin, who identified the fundamental inconsistency of the Bretton Woods system that relied on continued payments imbalances to supply dollar reserves for the international monetary system.[8] The continuation of such deficits over the long term would ultimately lead to doubts among dollar holders about the ability or willingness of the United States to redeem these for gold, at which point a crisis of confidence would occur. These doubts began to grow, in particular during the latter part of the 1960s, as the United States began to incur larger balance of payments deficits related to the government's simultaneous pursuit of the war in Vietnam and its "Great Society" social programs.

The unwillingness of the United States to subordinate domestic policy management to its international commitments under the Bretton Woods system pointed to what would be a continuing problem for the IFA. The Bretton Woods regime was critically dependent on the stability and leadership of the United States, just as the United Kingdom was for the gold standard. During the interwar years, neither of these two powers was able or willing to assert a stabilizing role in the global system.[9] More generally, the breakdown of the Bretton Woods regime highlighted the problem, in a world of nation states in which international economic policy is subject to the accountability of domestic political arrangements, of how to bring about mutually consistent policy choices among the major countries that promote international systemic stability.

In a world of increasing financial globalization, countries must accept the fact that there is a sphere of domestic policy where they are accountable to other countries to maintain about stability of the international financial system through cooperative arrangements such as the IFA. When that accountability does not exist, crises can occur and systemic stability is threatened. The first such crisis was the breakdown of the Bretton Woods system. This lack of accountability would also be a factor in the lead-up to the global financial crisis of 2008–9.

With the closing of the US gold window in August 1971, the gold exchange standard of the Bretton Woods system came to a close. In its place, the international monetary system devolved temporarily into a pure dollar standard, in which major exchange rates continued to be defined in terms of the US dollar, which was the major intervention currency, reserve currency (store of value), and unit of account for international trade transactions. Over the next two years, attempts were made to maintain the par value system through a series of negotiated adjustments in the value of the dollar, but these were unsuccessful in restoring stability to the system because of speculative capital movements. In March 1973, a period of generalized floating among the major advanced countries began.

Notwithstanding the problems of the Bretton Woods regime, it was nonetheless associated with some successful outcomes in the international economic system. One was the substantial expansion in international trade that was promoted by the reduction of current account restrictions and the maintenance of relatively fixed exchange rates under the IMF system. The volume of global export trade expanded by a factor of six during the period 1950–73, or more than twice as fast as the growth in global output. Such an outcome was essential for the postwar recovery process and global prosperity, more generally. Indeed, the growth in global output was significantly higher during the third quarter of the last century than during the last quarter (2.9 percent vs. 1.4 percent). Most Western European countries established full current account convertibility by 1958, and by 1973, thirty-five members of the IMF had adopted the obligations of the IMF's Article VIII status. Other countries continued to avail themselves of the transitional arrangements of Article XIV, under which the maintenance of selective current account restrictions was subject to periodic review and approval by the IMF.

Certainly the stability of the Bretton Woods exchange rate system and the progressive dismantling of exchange controls among the advanced countries provided important support for the expansion of international trade and global economic recovery. During this period, there was also an explosion in the membership in the IMF and World Bank, with the emergence from colonialism of a number of countries in Africa and Asia. By 1973, membership in the Bank and Fund had grown to 121 members, or nearly 3 times the number that initially joined these institutions. Correspondingly, the size of the Executive Boards in these institutions rose from 12 to 20 members.

The Bretton Woods system was also significant for demonstrating the viability and integrity of the IMF and World Bank as international financial institutions and integral parts of the IFA. With the growth in new membership, as just noted, they became nearly universal institutions (with the exception of the countries of the former Soviet Union). The Bank, in particular, made significant contributions to the flow of development finance to the developing world, thus filling a missing market for such finance in the international system. The Bank's role took on greater reach with the creation of the International Finance Corporation in 1956, which provided long-term funding for private investment projects, and the International Development Association (IDA) in 1960, which was the "soft" loan window of the Bank.[10] The Bank also established its credibility in the major financial centers and was accorded an AAA rating for its bonds in 1959.

The Bretton Woods institutions also developed highly professional secretariats based on high standards of professional recruitment and relative insulation from outside political interference. As such, they began to develop strong depositories of knowledge and experience in international monetary and development issues. In the case of the

IMF, its research department made important contributions to international monetary economics, with the development of the monetary approach to the balance of payments beginning in the mid-1950s and the Mundell-Fleming model which became the foundation for modern open economy macroeconomics (and the impossible trinity).[11] The Fund's statistical publications were also critically important for the public dissemination of comparable international data for its members. In 1964, the IMF created the IMF Institute to promote the training of foreign government officials in issues of monetary and financial policy, as well as the Central Banking Service and Fiscal Affairs Department to initiate a program of technical assistance to foreign central banks and finance ministries in developing countries.

In its research activity and advisory services, the IMF had a strong degree of overlap with the work of the BIS. However, while the membership of the Fund continued to grow following its establishment, the BIS remained largely a European institution for central banks (with the US Federal Reserve, the Bank of Canada, and the Bank of Japan its only non-European members).[12] For these central banks, it provided a number of technical services (e.g., managing the investment of foreign reserves) as well as a forum for the regular exchange of views on central bank policy and operational issues. The BIS was also closely involved with the evolution toward monetary union in the European Union (EU) beginning with the efforts at exchange rate coordination in the mid-1970s. Beginning in the late 1980s, it would begin to expand its membership to include central banks from a number of emerging market economies.

The Reform Process

The first reform of the post–World War II IFA was a relatively lengthy process that endured for most of the decade of the 1970s. It began with a series of debates about how the par value system of the Bretton Woods Agreement could be reinstated and improved regarding the international adjustment mechanism, in somewhat analogous fashion to the international debates surrounding the restoration of the gold standard after World War I. A special committee (the Committee of Twenty or C20) was established within the IMF to conduct the debates during the period 1972–74. The members of this committee mirrored the twenty constituencies represented at that time in the Executive Board of the IMF and thus reflected the full membership of the IMF. Notably, this was the last time that policy debates on IFA reform were centralized in a universal forum.

The C20 produced an "Outline of Reform" for the international monetary system in June 1974 that was designed to create a system of adjustable par values with the SDR, the multilateral reserve asset of the IMF, as the principal reserve asset of the system, instead of gold or the US dollar.[13] Ultimately, disagreements among the major shareholders on many of the details of the reform proposals and the disruption caused by the first of two oil price hikes by OPEC countries during the 1970s derailed the reform process. The C20 debates essentially focused on three major topics, in an effort to preserve the rule-bound system of international monetary management initiated with the Bretton Woods Agreement, which still have some relevance today in discussions of international monetary reform.[14] One was the definition of more specific rules of behavior for adjustment policy to ensure the timely elimination of significant imbalances among countries as part of the international adjustment process. This debate revived to some extent earlier discussions at the Bretton Woods Conference, which was triggered by Keynes' proposal for an International Clearing Union (ICU) and the creation of an international reserve currency (the Bancor), noted earlier, that would have imposed a symmetric burden of adjustment for both deficit and surplus countries. Ultimately, the vision for an ICU was not adopted because of the preference of the United States for a more limited IMF. However, the debate about the effectiveness of the international adjustment mechanism has continued to the present time, as reflected in discussions on the resolution of the problem of "global imbalances" in the lead-up to the recent financial crisis.

Regarding the international adjustment mechanism, a key focus of the C20 debate was on the use of "reserve indicators," initially proposed by the United States, as an objective measure of an underlying disequilibrium in a country's external position. Under this proposal, incrementally larger shortfalls or excesses with respect to some baseline reserve level would serve as a trigger for successive pressures for adjustment action to kick in, as administered by the IMF. Various forms of pressure were considered, such as increasing publicity by the Fund of a member's position with respect to the reserve guidelines or the imposition of financial penalties. The proposal for reserve indicators was favored by the United States as a means of bringing about more timely upward adjustment of European exchange rates in the face of inflationary policies pursued by the United States, which had been a factor leading up to the crisis of the Bretton Woods system. In the end, no agreement among the major countries could be reached on this mechanism.

A subsidiary issue taken up by the C20 in its effort to reinstate the par value system was whether the IMF should have a special role in the oversight of members' capital controls, with a view to defining what controls would be appropriate to minimize the speculative, destabilizing capital flows that became a growing threat to the stability of the Bretton Woods system. The advanced countries viewed this proposal as similar to the OECD's Code of Conduct for the Liberalization of Capital Movements, which had been developed during the 1960s.[15] This proposal was an interesting forerunner of the debate on the Fund's role in capital account liberalization in the late 1990s during the second reform of the IFA. Again, without agreement on guidelines for the management of fixed and adjustable par values, the Fund's role in overseeing capital controls was left in abeyance.

The Role of the SDR in the International Monetary System

The other two major issues of importance in the C20 debates related to the role of the SDR in the international monetary system and the settlement of imbalances in the system. As noted earlier, SDRs had been created in the late 1960s as a supplement to currency-based reserves to provide a mechanism for expanding international liquidity for the global trading and payments system independent of the cyclical or balance of payments conditions of a single reserve currency country, such as the United States. Three annual allocations of SDRs for an amount equivalent to US$9 billion were authorized during the period 1970–72. The C20 reform proposals envisaged a system in which par values would be defined in terms of the SDR, rather than gold or the US dollar, and where the SDR could become the principal reserve asset of the international monetary system used in the official settlement of payments imbalances among countries. The European countries, in particular, were interested in a system of "asset settlement" based on gold or the SDR to replace the de facto dollar standard under which there was no limit on the power of the United States to issue dollar liabilities to finance a persistent balance of payments deficit. Under a multilateral reserve system, the United States would be required to redeem dollar liabilities for SDRs or make policy adjustments to correct its payments imbalance. Such an arrangement would have complemented the proposal on adjustment indicators discussed earlier and restored more automaticity to the international adjustment mechanism that was missing during the Bretton Woods regime.

The creation of the SDR was an unusual experiment in the evolution of the IFA and featured prominently in the reform debates of the early 1970s. As in the case of single reserve currencies, such as the US dollar, SDRs fulfill three functions of an international reserve asset in terms of providing a unit of account, a medium of exchange, and store of value. Initially, SDRs were defined as equivalent to the value of one US dollar and its gold content under the Bretton Woods Agreement, in a similar fashion to Bancor under Keynes' proposal for an ICU. However, with the suspension of US gold sales in 1971 and the devaluation of the US dollar relating to gold during 1971–72, the C20 endorsed the idea of shifting the valuation of the SDR to a basket of currencies. Accordingly, the value of the SDR was defined in terms of sixteen currencies representing the countries with the largest share in global trade, which was simplified to five in 1981 (the dollar, pound, franc, mark, and yen).[16] Countries earn interest on their holdings of SDRs as an international asset and pay interest on their allocations, equivalent to the weighted average of short-term government paper of the countries whose currencies are used to define its value.[17] SDRs are allocated to Fund members in proportion to their quotas. Fund members have agreed to accept SDRs in the settlement of exchange obligations among each other, and all the major currency countries have agreed to accept SDRs in exchange for an equivalent amount of their currencies. With the exchange of SDRs, countries earn interest, on a net basis, if their holdings exceed their allocations and pay interest if their holdings fall below allocations.[18] Only official agencies (i.e., member country central banks or ministries of finance depending upon which institution are the agent for transactions with the Fund, as well as the BIS, the World Bank, and thirteen other multilateral banks) have been authorized to acquire and transact in SDRs. The restriction on the private use of SDRs is an important limitation, which would have to be removed if the SDR was to take on a greater role in the international financial system.

In relation to the use of the SDR, the C20 also recommended further consideration of establishing a Substitution Account in the IMF, by means of which countries could exchange their holdings of national reserve currencies in exchange for SDRs. This feature was particularly attractive to the European representatives in view of their concern with the issue of a "dollar overhang" arising from the continued balance of payments deficits of the United States. In the event, during follow-up debates within the IMF on this issue in 1979–80, agreement on setting up a Substitution Account could not be reached. One of the sticking points was the manner in which potential losses for the IMF in managing the Account would be covered. If the US dollar lost value with respect to the SDR which, as noted earlier, is defined in terms of a basket of the major reserve currencies, then the value of the Fund's holdings of dollar assets would become less than the value of its SDR liabilities and a loss in its net worth position would result. If these losses were not to be absorbed by the IMF directly (e.g., through a sale of some of its gold holdings), they would have to be assigned to the United States alone or the advanced countries in relation to the weight of their currencies in the valuation of the SDR. There was no agreement on this issue.[19]

The Role of Developing Countries in the Reform Debate

The developing countries in the IMF, whose number had grown significantly with the process of decolonization, took a particular interest in the debates on the role of the SDR in the international monetary system. They were strong advocates of an SDR "link" with official development finance, as a means of increasing significantly the flow of real resources to the developing world, which was a "public good" previously identified with the World Bank. The idea behind the "link" was that members of the IMF should determine the need for SDRs not only in terms of the role of international reserves in facilitating global payments and trade, but also in terms of a certain target for aid transfers to the developing world. Instead of separate budgetary allocations of aid from each of the advanced countries, governments collectively through the IMF could determine an additional allocation of SDRs specifically designated for the developing countries, or for development finance institutions to use as a capital subscription backing their loans or grants to developing countries. Alternatively, the advanced countries, which receive the lion share of SDRs, could agree to transfer a certain share of these resources to developing countries.

The link proposal found little support among the advanced countries in the C20 debates, which recognized only the monetary role of the SDR in the international monetary system, as distinct from its potential role in development finance. Nevertheless, it has continued to attract attention up until recently.[20] The link proposal, however, was part of a larger debate within the UN system that took center stage during the first half of the 1970s on the New International Economic Order (NIEO).[21] This debate was given impetus by the oil price shock of 1973–74 that also suspended interest in the C20 reform proposal given the lack of agreement between the US and European powers in the Fund on the means of reviving the par value system, especially at a time of great turmoil in the international financial system. The SDR link was the intersection between the two debates. Ultimately, the final shape of the first reform of the IFA would be significantly affected by the debates on the NIEO.

The debates on the NIEO were important in many respects. First, they represented for the first time a focused discussion on the needs of developing countries within the IFA. Developing countries were in the minority and on the sidelines of debates at the Bretton Woods Conference, which was not the case during the reform debates of the early 1970s. Unlike the Bretton Woods Conference, the needs of the developing countries were given explicit attention in the debates of the C20. The "Outline of Reform" specifically addressed the needs of developing countries in a number of places, for example, in the design of certain financing facilities of the Fund (see the following text). It also recognized the transfer of real resources to the developing countries and development finance as one of the key objectives to be served by the international monetary system. The creation of the SDR could be seen as one way in which this objective was being served, independent of the "link" proposal. For developing countries with limited access to international financial markets, SDR allocations at an essentially risk-free rate of interest provide the means by which they can obtain goods and services from the advanced countries for development purposes.

The NIEO debates were also significant because they raised questions about the nature of the international economic system and the distribution of benefits from the emerging era of globalization. The prevailing international economic order, which advocates of the NIEO wanted to reform, was viewed as evolving toward a laissez-faire regime of largely unregulated flows of trade and finance, not unlike the era of the international gold standard, in which principles of market efficiency were the guiding criteria, without regard to distributional issues. The challenge of the NIEO was to raise for the first time considerations of equity in the international system, in addition to efficiency.[22]

The collective power of the oil producing cartel, composed of developing countries, in bringing about a fourfold increase in the international market price of oil gave confidence to the NIEO advocates that other redistributive changes in the international economic system could be achieved through collective action. In addition to other attempts at commodity price stabilization (e.g., bauxite, tin), the NIEO proponents wanted intergovernmental action on a wide front of trade, investment, and development issues. The G77, which was the main lobby group within the UN system for advancing the NIEO, was particularly aggressive in seeking relief on official bilateral debt. Specifically, the NIEO proponents wanted to establish permanent machinery within the IFA to manage debt-servicing problems of developing countries with official creditors, instead of the informal arrangements of the Paris Club, and more generous terms for debt relief than had been offered by official creditors.[23]

The complaint of the G77 during the 1970s was that the principles guiding Paris Club deliberations were not clear and that the terms of negotiations did not consider the development needs of the borrowing countries in terms of providing for a reduction or cancellation of official debt in certain cases, instead of simply a rescheduling of debt service payments.[24] Over time, the Paris Club did codify its negotiating principles and procedures, but it resisted calls for more generous terms of debt restructuring until the late 1980s. During the second half of the 1990s, debt cancellation for a group of severely indebted poor countries became a major issue of concern in the meetings of the G7.

Within the debate on the first reform of the IFA, pressure from the developing countries resulted in a number of changes in IMF financial operations that expanded their access to nonconditional lending. Some of the willingness on the part of the advanced countries to accede to these demands was seen as compensation for the defeat of the SDR link proposal.

A hallmark of IMF financial operations from its inception was the temporary, relatively short-term nature of its loans (or "arrangements" to make "purchases" from the Fund), which were disbursed during a period of typically one year. This restriction was intended to preserve the revolving character of the Fund's financial resources, consistent with its design as an international monetary institution.[25] As noted earlier, each member can borrow IMF resources in relation to its quota, in the form of credit "tranches," with higher amounts of borrowing subject to higher degrees of conditionality in terms of policy commitments and targets for the improvement in its external payments position. Since the IMF does not normally accept collateral in the same manner as private financial institutions, policy conditionality serves the same purpose in providing some assurance for the repayment of its financial resources.[26] Beginning in the early 1950s, the main instrument used by the IMF in its lending operations was called a "stand-by arrangement" under which the IMF would commit a certain amount of financial resources to a member country that would be disbursed typically on a quarterly basis during a period of twelve months, subject to its fulfillment of certain policy conditions and targets specified in a government's "letter of intent."

One of the results of the NIEO debates was to introduce more flexibility in Fund financial arrangements. The experience of IMF lending to developing countries had shown that a disbursement period of one year, together with the expectation of a relatively quick adjustment of external imbalances in these countries, was not always realistic or feasible. On the basis of these considerations, a new facility (the Extended Financing Facility or EFF) was introduced in 1974 to allow for extended arrangements of three years (instead of one-year stand-by arrangements) with a repayment period up to eight years (instead of the normal period of three to five years for stand-by arrangements). In addition, two nonconditional facilities (the Buffer Stock Financing Facility and Compensatory Financing Facility) were expanded to increase access of developing countries to IMF resources without policy conditions, along with the creation of a special Oil Facility to assist oil-importing developing countries in financing the higher cost of oil imports during the 1970s. Unlike the other two facilities, the Oil Facility was financed by direct borrowing of the IMF from the oil exporting countries and operated more flexibly than the GAB. The Buffer Stock Facility was created to finance developing country contributions to buffer stock arrangements linked to the NIEO concerns about commodity price stabilization funds. The Compensatory Financing Facility (CFF) was also established in the mid-1960s to cover the temporary financing requirements associated with primary commodity price shocks. Recourse by developing countries to the Oil Facility and the CFF increased substantially during the 1970s and accounted for nearly 60 percent of total borrowing from the IMF during the period 1972–78 (and approximately 70 percent of borrowing by developing countries).[27]

The Second Amendment of the Fund Agreement

While work was underway within the IMF on modifying the terms of its lending facilities, debate was proceeding among the advanced countries (mainly the United States and France) on an amendment to the Fund Agreement to replace the commitments on the par value system, on which agreement could not be reached within the C20. This reform, which was agreed in the second amendment of the Fund Agreement in 1978 and formalized the legal basis for the current, post-Bretton Woods era, fundamentally departed from the rules-based regime of Bretton Woods, but significantly expanded the responsibility and scope of the Fund's activities. Instead of a centralized rules-based system of fixed exchange rates administered by the IMF, the second amendment of the Fund created a more decentralized system in which countries were free to choose their own exchange arrangements (e.g., fixed or flexible exchange rates), subject to the oversight of the Fund to ensure that they were managing their exchange rate system in a manner that was consistent with external and internal sustainability. Importantly, this reform recognized that the conditions of the global economy did not allow unanimity of view on a single exchange arrangement that would be appropriate for all members of the Fund, and that countries could have a preference for different exchange arrangements depending on their economic conditions, level of development, and so on. However, once they chose a specific form of exchange rate arrangement, they were expected to communicate this decision to the IMF and fully cooperate with it in ensuring that it was implementing its exchange rate regime in a manner consistent with a stable international monetary system.

One of the key elements of the second amendment of the Fund Agreement was the revision of Article IV dealing with "obligations regarding exchange arrangements." Among other things, the revised language of Article IV recognized the growing importance of capital flows in the international financial system by noting that "the essential purpose of the international monetary system is to provide a framework that facilitates the exchange of goods, services and capital among countries, and that sustains sound economic growth." The reference to "sound economic growth" was intended to signal the importance of development issues for the majority of Fund members.[28] In addition, Article IV established for the first time explicit responsibility for the Fund to "oversee the international monetary system to ensure its effective operation" (which underpins the Fund's multilateral surveillance responsibilities) and to "exercise firm surveillance over the exchange rate policies of members" in meeting their obligations under Article IV (which underpins the Fund's bilateral surveillance responsibilities). These obligations in turn were stated as follows:

"Each member shall:

(i) endeavor to direct its economic and financial policies toward the objective of fostering orderly economic growth with reasonable price stability, with due regard to its circumstances;

(ii) seek to promote stability by fostering orderly underlying economic and financial conditions and a monetary system that does not tend to produce erratic disruptions;

(iii) avoid manipulating exchange rates or the international monetary system in order to prevent effective balance of payments adjustment or to gain an unfair advantage over other members;

(iv) follow exchange policies compatible with the undertakings under this section."

The revision of Article IV changed the role of the Fund from one of monitoring member countries' current account restrictions and progress toward current account convertibility to one of monitoring their exchange rate and macroeconomic policy framework and prospects, more generally. Annual consultations with the Fund, which had been mandatory for member countries adhering to the transitional arrangements of Article XIV, and voluntary for those that had accepted Article VIII status in the Fund, would now be mandatory for all members. The struggle over the terms of the revised Article IV showed that the Fund membership was still attached, in principle, to some form of collective governance arrangement in policy coordination that recognized a zone of policy in which governments were accountable to the international community. The difference with the Bretton Woods system is that zone of policy would now encompass more than the appropriateness of its exchange rate or par value and would include the scope of its external and macroeconomic policy management as well.

There was a clear recognition in the revised framework of Article IV that considerations of external stability could not be divorced from considerations of domestic stability and growth within the Fund's new surveillance mandate. How well this surveillance would be conducted would be a factor leading up to the recent crisis. Many analysts have characterized this regime as a "non-system," since there were no explicit rules as there had been under the Bretton Woods system on how countries would manage their exchange rate regimes. As a result, the IMF has had a continuing challenge in its surveillance exercises in defining acceptable guidelines on exchange rate behavior that has continued up until the current day.

To guide members in the conduct of exchange rate policies, new guidelines on surveillance were developed by the Fund's Executive Board in 1977, which essentially remained in tact until their revision in 2007. From the point of view of the evolution of the Fund's interest in capital account issues, it is important to note that the guidelines provided a number of indicators which the Fund would use in determining if members were complying with the obligations of Article IV noted earlier, which included, among other things, "a change, for balance of payment purposes, of restrictions on, or incentives for, current transactions and capital flows" and "the pursuit, for balance of payments purposes, of monetary and other domestic policies that abnormally encourage/discourage capital flows."[29]

In a symbolic reference to the C20 debates, the revised Fund Agreement also provided for the restoration of the par value system based on the SDR as the central reserve asset, if 85 percent of the Fund membership voted in favor. The use of this supermajority requirement in Fund decision making (which also applied to decisions to increase quotas and to amend the Fund Agreement) in effect gave a veto power to the United States, given that its quota (the largest in the IMF) exceeded that threshold, as well as to the other members of the G10, if they acted in concert. The amended Articles of Agreement also envisaged the possibility of calling into being an IMF Council to provide more direct political direction and oversight of IMF activities than is possible for the Board of Governors. The possible role of the Council in the IFA has featured prominently in current reform debates. Instead of a council, however, the Board of Governors decided to establish an "Interim Committee" as an advisory body for the IMF, which subsequently in 1999 became the International Monetary and Financial Committee. In somewhat parallel fashion, a Committee on the Transfer of Real Resources to Developing Countries (or Development Committee) was established at the same time (in 1974) as the Interim Committee to advise both the World Bank and the IMF on their activities vis-à-vis the developing countries. The establishment of this committee can be attributed to the influence of the NIEO debates on the Bretton Woods institutions.

Changing the Nature of IMF and World Bank Operations

Apart from the new surveillance function of the Fund, the first reform of the IFA marked an important change in its financial operations that modified the character of the IMF from purely an international monetary institution to one with development objectives as well. Under the influence of the NIEO debates, a division of views between advanced countries (the "north") and developing countries (the "south") took on more prominence in the work of the IMF and reform of the IFA. This north-south split was reflected in the emergence of different clubs of creditor and debtor countries in the IMF. The emergence of the G10, as noted earlier, was the first manifestation of this differentiation of membership within the Fund, which was countered by the creation of the G24 in 1971 (as a subgroup of the G77) to represent the interests of the developing countries in the C20 debates. The subsequent formation of the G7 industrial country group, as described below, would represent a further step in the polarization of creditor and debtor groups within the IMF. One way in which this split has become clear is that, after 1978, the major industrial countries of the G10 and G7 chose not to engage in any borrowing operation with the Fund. Before that date, both advanced and developing countries alike had undertaken borrowing operations with the Fund, consistent with its role as the international equivalent of a credit union; while most of the borrowers from the Fund were developing countries, the advanced countries (including the United States) accounted for around 60 percent of the total amount of Fund resources approved under stand-by arrangements during the period 1952–78.[30] The lack of interest in Fund financing on the part of the major European countries can be explained in part by the shift in their focus to regional monetary cooperation and the development of regional stabilization mechanisms during the 1970s, which operated at the level of both the European Community central banks and the council of ministers.[31] This change in the borrowing status of the advanced countries would coincide with a growing attention to the needs of developing countries in IMF operations and a redirection of policy coordination among the advanced countries to groups outside the IMF.

One example of the changing character of IMF operations was the decision in 1976 to initiate a partial sale of the IMF's gold reserves to finance so-called Trust Fund operations, which were long-term, concessional lending to cover the balance of payments needs of developing countries during 1977–81. Trust Fund loans carried an interest charge of ½ percent, with repayment during a period of 5 ½ to 10 years after each disbursement; low (first credit tranche) conditionality applied.[32] This departure from normal Fund practice began in 1975 with the creation of a special Subsidy Account, financed by contributions of member countries outside the normal operations of the IMF, to offset some of the borrowing cost associated with its Oil Facility for low-income members. The Trust Fund operations were the forerunner of what became a permanent feature of subsidized IMF lending to low-income countries under the Structural Adjustment Facility (SAF/ESAF) during the period 1986–98, and then under the Poverty Reduction and Growth

Facility (PRGF) since 1999, which have been closely coordinated with World Bank IDA lending.

While the IMF began during the late 1970s to take on certain development financing operations and focus its lending operations mainly on developing and emerging market countries, the World Bank was changing its lending operations from one with a strong emphasis on capital-intensive infrastructural projects to one with a country policy focus, somewhat similar to that of the IMF. As a result, some duplication and overlap in the lending operations of the two institutions began to emerge, which have remained to the present time and created continuing concerns about the nature of Bank-Fund collaboration in lending operations to developing and emerging market countries.

The decade of the 1970s was also a watershed in the fragmentation and decentralization of the IFA. While more decision making on the global governance of the international financial system began to move outside of the IMF with the growing influence of the G7 and G10, the G10 also began to give more prominence to international financial issues in its deliberations within the BIS. In this connection, as noted earlier, the G10 central bank governors began in the 1970s to establish at the BIS certain standing committees of central bank officials to examine issues related to the expanding flows of international finance, the coordination of bank supervision, and the monitoring of payments, clearing and settlement systems, which operated with little or no involvement of the IMF.[33] These committees would take on more importance within the IFA in the aftermath of the international debt crises of developing countries in the early 1980s, which was directly related to the recycling of petrodollars by large international banks in the wake of the two oil price shocks of the 1970s. This borrowing by oil-importing developing countries marked the first major expansion of the international financial system to encompass the developing and emerging market economies and would lead to the second reform of the IFA, which is examined in the next chapter of this book.

Another sign of a diminished role for the Fund vis-à-vis the advanced countries was the decision of European countries to work toward a regional system of stable exchange rates, which ultimately led to the creation of the euro. For this project of economic and financial integration to be effective, the European countries developed a strong process of peer review of each government's economic and financial policy operating through the European Council of Finance Ministers (ECOFIN) and other fora, such as the Committee of Governors of member states of the EEC, which held its meetings at the BIS. Other peer review arrangements also took on importance for the advanced countries with the regular meetings of Working Party 3 of the Economic Policy Committee of the OECD, as noted earlier. Within the project of European integration, the Fund would play no role other than that related to its annual consultation procedure under the new terms of Article IV. In the deliberations of Working Party 3, the IMF had only an observer status. While each of these peer review mechanisms has their justification in the promotion of policy coordination among the advanced countries, they ultimately weakened the authority of the IMF in its surveillance function. Under this more decentralized system of regional surveillance arrangements for the advanced countries, the IMF would play a less active role vis-à-vis the major industrial countries than it did under the Bretton Woods system and its surveillance role would come to be seen as less than even-handed across the membership.

Both the BIS and the EU also developed limited financing facilities for balance of payments support among the European central banks, thus duplicating, if not undermining, the central role which the IMF had played in this area during the Bretton Woods regime. Within the European Community, the Community Loan Mechanism was established in 1975 to assist member countries in the financing of oil imports, drawing on loans extended by large international banks operating in the euro-currency markets. In the case of the OECD, the United States advocated the creation of a parallel Financial Support Fund of US$25 billion exclusively for OECD members, which exceeded the financial resources available to the advanced countries from the IMF at the time. However, without strong support from the European countries and a decline of interest on the part of the US government, this proposal did not materialize.[34]

Creation of the G7 as the Steering Committee for the Global Economy

The development of the G7 forum of finance ministers and central bank governors was perhaps the most important institutional change in the IFA in terms of its influence over global financial governance up until the current crisis. The G7 forum began as the G5 (the United States, United Kingdom, France, Germany, and Japan) in the mid-1970s to manage the debate of the first reform of the IFA, and in particular, the language of Article IV of the revised Fund Agreement noted earlier, and to discuss economic policy cooperation among the group. The formation of the G5 at the finance ministry level was an initiative of the

United States, and it was seen as an effective counterweight to the G10, in which the European representatives were dominant.[35] Over the next decade, it evolved into the G7 (the G5 plus Canada and Italy), with the participation of both finance ministers and central bank governors, which would become in effect a de facto, self-appointed steering committee for the IFA, operating in parallel with the G7 heads of government (and G8 with the admission of Russia in 1997).[36] It has operated without any formal secretariat, relying instead on the network of informal contacts among subcabinet level treasury staff and senior central bank officials in the major capitals. Most major decisions within the IMF would be agreed in advance by this group, which in effect replaced the G10 as the locus of decision making regarding the IFA. The G7 would come to see institutions such as the IMF and World Bank as key instruments of the IFA for managing problems affecting developing, emerging market and transition countries in the global economy.

The main rationale for this forum is that it has allowed for an effective exchange of views on international economic issues and a peer review process for macroeconomic policy cooperation among key representatives of the major financial powers with strong common interests in the international financial system, in a relatively closed setting that facilitated dialogue and debate. Its major defect, however, is that over time the forum has become increasingly unrepresentative of economic and financial power in the international system and has accentuated the sense of power division within the IMF and IFA, more generally. In addition, its policy coordinating function has not been well integrated with that of the Fund.

During the 1970s and 1980s, the G7 forum focused mainly on issues of macroeconomic policy coordination, on a somewhat episodic basis. Then during the 1990s, the second reform of the IFA became a central focus of its deliberations in the wake of a wave of financial crises in the emerging market economies. Beginning in that decade and continuing in the next, the group also placed heavy emphasis on issues of trade and aid, as well as official debt relief for highly indebted poor countries.

In the period after the second amendment of the Fund Agreement, both the IMF and G7 were experimenting with newly established surveillance mechanisms to support a relatively new system of flexible exchange rates, one formally established under the requirements of Article IV and the other informally established among the G7 finance ministers and central bank governors. In the latter exercises, the IMF came to play a limited role at best. One of the primary objectives in the area of policy coordination which the G7 focused on was exchange rate stability, principally among the US dollar, the Japanese yen, and the German mark. During the post-Bretton Woods era, exchange rate variation among these currencies has proved to be far more volatile than experts and policy makers anticipated when the period of flexibility among the major currencies began in the early 1970s. Swings of 10 percent or more in the real value of currencies on a bilateral basis within a period of a few months have not been uncommon, while misalignments of exchange rates from underlying macroeconomic fundamentals could persist for significant periods of time. Such volatility and misalignment have been hard to explain in terms of changes in underlying economic fundamentals such as differences in business cycles, productivity growth, and current account positions. Exchange rate misalignments among the major currencies are a problem for the international monetary system in that they can distort investment decisions and profoundly affect trading relations among the key currency countries, as well as the competitiveness of other currencies that are pegged to one of the key currencies.

During the last quarter of the twentieth century, the G7 process gradually evolved from one of seeking accommodation of monetary and fiscal policy stances among the participants in its early years to one of loose targeting of exchange rates with episodes of coordinated exchange rate intervention in the 1980s and to a stance of noninterference and loose consultation on macroeconomic policies in the 1990s.[37] The evolution of this policy process from one of policy activism to one of simply information-sharing paralleled a marked change in thinking about economic policy. The 1970s marked the beginning of a counterrevolution against Keynesianism and fiscal and monetary activism in support of full employment and a gradual shift in the direction of fiscal rules and central bank independence in pursuit of medium-term inflation and growth objectives.[38] The sharp expansion in cross-border financial flows also created skepticism about the impact of sterilized intervention on exchange rate movements.

During the 1980s, some efforts were made by the G7 to include the technical input of the IMF. Beginning in 1982, the managing director of the IMF was invited, in his personal capacity, to attend the first part of the semiannual ministerial meetings, at which he was asked to present the views of the IMF on the global economic outlook and the policy requirements to achieve sustainable growth with low inflation in the major industrial countries. Then, in the second part of the meeting, when active policy debate among the ministers would occur, the managing director was invited to leave.[39] Subsequent meetings at the deputies' level involved a senior Fund staff representative in part of the discussions and reliance on the IMF for the provision of a mutually consistent set of projections and indicators for the G7 countries. However, in the key meetings of the G7 ministers, in September 1985 (at the Plaza Hotel) and in April 1987 (at the Louvre), where agreements on coordinated exchange rate intervention were reached, the IMF was neither represented, nor was it involved in the technical preparations. This limited engagement of the Fund generally reflected some mistrust of the IMF among G7 participants.[40]

Most evaluations of the G7 policy process have not been very favorable, as exchange rate volatility among the major currencies has continued to be a problem in the international monetary system and periods of sustained misalignment of major currencies have created problems of resource allocation and trade competitiveness. In one early quantitative assessment of the effectiveness of macroeconomic policy commitments associated with G7 Summit declarations during the period 1975–89 (which reflected earlier agreements at the ministerial level), the extent of policy fulfillment was found to be rather low.[41] In part for this reason and to improve the process of multilateral surveillance, most observers have called for a more structured process with a prominent role for the IMF in guiding the technical underpinnings of the policy exchange and in evaluating county performance in achieving certain agreed objectives.[42] In this connection, the initiative taken by the G20 in September 2009 to have the IMF play a more direct and formal role in its multilateral "mutual assessment" process is an important and positive change (see chapter 8).

Summary and Conclusion

This chapter has reviewed the extensive efforts made to sustain the Bretton Woods regime, the main structure of the IFA established after World War II, and the outcome of discussions that led to its first reform after the breakdown of that regime. The common element of this experience during the 1960s and 1970s was the search for a more stable order for the international monetary system. The Bretton Woods era was a period of relatively robust growth in global trade and output, but it was subject to some important underlying weaknesses that ultimately led to its breakdown. One was the rigidity of exchange rates, mainly among the advanced countries. Governments resisted exchange rate adjustment, and instead relied on domestic policy adjustments to maintain parities that became subject to periodic attack because of the growing weakness of capital controls.

The decade of the 1960s was a period of active coordination among central banks of the industrial countries, the IMF and BIS in the mobilization of rescue operations to ward off speculative attacks. Additional funding for the IMF was also mounted by the advanced countries via the GAB, for it to play a significant role in these operations. This multilateral effort to establish an international lender of last resort mechanism was far more robust and successful than during the gold standard or interwar periods.

The other flaw of the Bretton Woods regime was its excessive reliance on the United States, as the leading reserve currency of the system, to satisfy the incremental demand for international liquidity that accompanied the growth in global trade and production during this period. The issue of maintaining an adequate level of international reserves was not addressed specifically during the design of the IFA at Bretton Woods. The United States played a unique role as a central bank for the global monetary system by lending long-term (e.g., through foreign direct investment) against the issue of its short-term foreign liabilities. This arrangement was satisfactory only in so far as other countries had confidence in the ability of the United States to redeem those liabilities for gold, as called for under the Bretton Woods Agreement. International confidence began to erode during the 1960s as those liabilities expanded and US gold supplies began to shrink, as a result of expansionary domestic policies of the US government. This dynamic instability of the gold dollar system was well anticipated before its demise during the period 1971–73 and led to the creation of the SDR as a supplement to single currency reserves and gold in 1969 and a first allocation in 1970. However, the arrival of the SDR was an issue of "too little, too late."

The breakdown of the Bretton Woods system at first led to an intensive effort managed by the IMF Committee of 20 to work out the details of an improved version of the par value, fixed exchange rate system with clearer rules for adjustment of balance of payments imbalances, more symmetry in the adjustment of surplus and deficit countries, and a central role for the SDR. However, disagreement among the major industrial countries on a number of aspects of the revised system and turmoil in the international economy brought about by a massive oil price shock in 1973 led to the deferral of debate on reconstructing a system of adjustable fixed exchange rates and a move to generalized floating among the advanced countries. Some of the main issues in that debate, such as the role of indicators in triggering balance of payments adjustment, the role of the SDR as a multilateral reserve currency, and a

Substitution Account for US dollars continue to be relevant for ongoing debate on the reform of the IFA.

The recognition of more flexible exchange rate regimes was ratified in the negotiations of a revised Article IV of the Fund Agreement that was approved with the Second Amendment of the Agreement in 1978. This reform established a more decentralized system of exchange arrangements in which each country was allowed to adopt an exchange rate regime of its choice, subject to the requirement that it would cooperate with the Fund in ensuring that its regime was consistent with a sustainable external position and stability of the international monetary system as a whole. These changes resulted in an important shift in the surveillance responsibilities of the IMF, with a new emphasis on its oversight of the international monetary system and its evaluation of each member's macroeconomic policy and prospects affecting its exchange rate position.

The first reform of the IFA also coincided with important changes in the nature of IMF and World Bank lending operations and some fragmentation in its governance arrangements. With the growing importance of developing countries in its membership, the IMF began in the late 1970s to make concessional loans to low-income countries for balance of payments needs, with funding separate from its normal quota-based resources. The World Bank, for its part, began the practice of policy-based lending, as distinct from its traditional focus on project-based lending. These changes would bring the IMF and World Bank much closer together over time in their lending operations and introduced a new developmental focus in the financial operations of the IMF.

In the area of governance, the first reform of the IFA established two new oversight committees for the Bank and Fund at the ministerial level, one the Development Committee to deal with concerns regarding the transfer of real resources to developing countries and the other, the so-called Interim Committee (which became the International Monetary and Financial Committee) to provide advice and guidance on the Fund's activities. Notwithstanding these new institutional arrangements, effective decision making for the work of the IMF and World Bank would reside with the G7 ministerial group, which began to take shape at around the same time. To counter the influence of groups such as the G10 and G7, the developing countries have created their own coordinating group (the G24) to advance their interests on matters related to IMF and World Bank policies. These arrangements have led to some degree of polarization in the memberships of the Bank and Fund between creditors and debtors, which have been accentuated by the fact that after

1978, the advanced countries for the most part have refrained from using IMF financial resources. This change may be explained in part by the decision of the European countries to focus more intensively on their own regional project toward monetary unification with its unique exchange stabilization mechanisms. Some degree of polarization has also been promoted by the reliance of the advanced countries on their own peer review mechanisms in the OECD and the EU, which have operated largely independently of the IMF surveillance work.

With the first reform of the IFA, a more fragmented arrangement of institutional responsibility would emerge that persisted up until the time of the recent global crisis. The IMF's new responsibilities for systemic oversight would overlap or compete with financial system oversight carried out by the G10 governors working with the BIS. Country surveillance activity of the IMF would compete with similar activities conducted by the G7, OECD, and the EU. Financing arrangements would be decentralized among the BIS, the G10 central banks, the European Community, and the IMF. The G7 would become an important coordinating mechanism for some, but not all elements of the architecture.

CHAPTER 5

Emerging Market Financial Crises and the Second Reform of the International Financial Architecture

The second reform of the IFA followed an unprecedented expansion in financial globalization from the mid-1970s until the mid-1990s that encompassed both advanced and emerging market economies. This period of financial globalization was encouraged by the onset of floating exchange rates among the major advanced countries, the removal of capital controls in these countries, and the liberalization of their domestic financial markets. The growth in international financial flows involved at first large banks in the major financial center countries of Europe, Japan, and North America during the 1970s and 1980s and then spread to private portfolio capital (bonds and equity) and foreign direct investment in the 1990s (see figure 2.3). These two periods of sharp upswings in the flow of foreign capital, followed by major reversals, were later repeated in the run-up and aftermath of the current financial crisis. The volatility of these flows has been a continuing problem for the stability of the international financial system.

The growing exposure of developing countries to financial globalization by means of recourse to international banking credits led ultimately to the sovereign debt crises of the early 1980s, which threatened the solvency of the large financial center banking institutions. This crisis in turn led to the first international effort at harmonizing international financial regulations through the so-called Basel Accord of 1988 on capital adequacy standards, which was initially intended for banks in the advanced countries. The second wave of financial globalization involving bank and non-bank flows of finance during the 1990s led ultimately to a series of financial crises in the key emerging market economies. The resolution of these crises led to the second reform of the IFA, which changed its focus to address issues of both crisis prevention and crisis management within the international financial system. The debt crises of the 1980s and the financial crises of the 1990s can be linked in one important way, as the means of resolving the first round of crises led to a second wave of capital inflows that contributed to the second round of crises in the following decade.

The International Debt Crisis of the 1980s

With the oil price shocks of the 1970s, attention at the international level focused on the "re-cycling" of surplus funds generated by the oil producers to oil importing countries, particularly in Africa, Asia, and Latin America. The IMF became involved in this effort with the creation of a special Oil Facility during 1974–75, which allowed nonconditional access to Fund resources by oil importing countries. But most of the recycling of "petrodollars" was handled directly by major international banks in the advanced countries, with the encouragement of their central banks. International banks operating in the offshore Eurodollar market were particularly effective at intermediating deposits received from the oil exporters into medium-term credits or syndicated loans for oil importing countries to accommodate a problem of global imbalances caused by two oil price shocks in the 1970s.

Lending by the IMF under two of its Oil Facilities amounted to the equivalent of US$8 billion, whereas international bank credits to developing countries during 1974–81 amounted to approximately US$200 billion.[1] The expectations at the time were that high oil prices could not be sustained for a long time and that sovereign governments were good credit risks, which meant that international bank credits to developing countries would have a good probability of repayment. Accordingly, general-purpose borrowing (i.e., public sector borrowing for general budgetary purposes without any link to specific investment projects) by the oil importing countries increased sharply.

The creditworthiness of borrowers varied significantly across the developing world. It was relatively high among Asian borrowers because of their generally conservative fiscal management and export-oriented development, but far more mixed in the case of Africa and Latin America. In the latter case, governments in Latin America had traditionally pursued an inward development strategy that downplayed export promotion and was heavily dependent on imports, notwithstanding attempts to foster domestic industries that would produce substitutes for foreign imported goods. With relatively easy access to private international finance, these governments pursued expansionary domestic policies, which significantly increased external current account deficits and public debt burdens in the region. In the wake of the oil price shocks of 1973 and 1978, large international banks were eager to find lending outlets for the huge deposits that they received from the oil producing countries. In the case of sovereign borrowers, lending standards were relaxed and governments in search of financing for budgetary purposes found easy access to foreign credit. Both "push" and "pull" factors were at play in the build-up to the debt crisis of the 1980s.

When a policy of monetary tightening in the United States was initiated in 1980 to deal with a problem of entrenched inflation, interest rates in international money markets, to which the interest rates on bank recycling loans were tied, rose sharply.[2] As a result, the debt service burden on these countries increased substantially, and in 1982 Mexico became the first sovereign borrower to default on its international bank credits. During the 1982–84 period, thirty-two governments across the developing world encountered difficulties in making debt service payments on their international bank credits and entered into rescheduling agreements with commercial banks.[3] What made this crisis a threat to the global financial system was the fact that the exposure of the 9 largest US commercial banks to these countries was equivalent to nearly 200 percent of their capital.[4] Thus the solvency of major banks in the United States, as well as in Japan and the United Kingdom, were at risk.

The debt crisis of the early 1980s triggered the most active period of sovereign debt workouts by the major international banks during the post–World War II period, in close coordination with the IMF. The Fund played a key role in defining with country authorities the macroeconomic and balance of payments framework within which debt refinancing would need to take place. It also took the bold step of insisting in many cases on "new money" loans from the banks along with a rescheduling of debt service payments as a condition for its financial support. This form of "concerted lending," orchestrated by the Fund, was sanctioned by the G7 authorities as a form of regulatory forbearance that allowed the banks to avoid the penalty of making provisions on loans that were in arrears, which could lead to a reduction in their capital position. The Fund's lead role in the management of the debt crisis was recognized by the fact that in major cases, such as Mexico, central banks of some of the advanced countries, together with the BIS, provided "bridge" financing of a short-term nature to cover the time needed to put an IMF financial arrangement in place.[5]

The process of debt rescheduling and refinancing was managed by the banks in an informal, ad hoc framework, known as the London Club. Under this framework, a steering committee of bank representatives and country officials under the leadership of a major commercial bank (e.g., Bank of America or Citibank) would be formed to negotiate the terms of an agreement. IMF staff representatives familiar with the country were almost always involved to provide the committee with an assessment of the country's economic situation and prospects, along with the contours of the adjustment program that the IMF was prepared to support.[6] Once an agreement between the banks and the country officials was reached, the committee would be disbanded.

The international debt crisis triggered a period of difficult economic adjustment for the highly indebted developing economies. Throughout the decade of the 1980s, these countries were encouraged by the IMF and World Bank to undertake "structural adjustment" programs in exchange for their financial support to deal with underlying imbalances in their economies by liberalizing financial and product markets, limiting the scope of public sector activities, and reducing tariff protection and currency overvaluation as a means of restoring external creditworthiness. The principles underlying this approach came to be embodied in the notion of the "Washington Consensus."[7] In retrospect, the assumptions regarding the prospects for a resumption of growth that underpinned adjustment lending and refinancing for the indebted countries were overoptimistic.[8] In Latin America, the 1980s has come to be known as the "lost decade," as average growth in real per capita income for this period was negative for the region.

By the late 1980s, it was becoming clear that this approach to the debt problem was not working to the benefit of the debtor countries, which continued to face severe debt service problems while increasing their debt burden. In addition, the banks resisted further reliance on the practice of debt rescheduling accompanied by new lending and began to make provisions for the eventual mark down of their loans to developing countries. In these circumstances, the US Treasury under the leadership of Secretary Nicholas Brady came to the view that the solution to the debt crisis required debt reduction on the part of the borrowing countries and not simply the provision of new finance tied to structural adjustment programs. With the strong support of the US government, the IMF began the practice in 1989 of negotiating financial programs with bank-indebted countries that made explicit provision for debt reduction through the exchange of new bonds for a discounted value of the bank debt. Some of the proceeds from IMF loans were used for the purpose of buying zero-coupon US treasury bonds to guarantee the principal and interest due on the new (so-called Brady) bonds issued by these countries, which would "enhance" their appeal to commercial banks and potentially other investors because they were issued in bearer form.[9] Through a further round of London Club negotiations, seventeen emerging market countries (including ten in Latin America) were able to reduce their commercial bank indebtedness amounting to US$211 billion by an aggregate amount of around US$85 billion during the 1990–97 period.[10] This experience ushered in a new phase of international bond placements by emerging market economies, as large international banks for the most part withdrew from direct medium-term lending to governments outside the advanced countries. The bonds, which the banks accepted from debtor countries for the cancellation of their bank debt, could be sold to private investors because of the attraction of the "enhancements" they carried. Thus began the development of a new international market for sovereign bond debt, which would play a role in the financial crises of the late 1990s.

The resolution of the debt crisis of the 1980s was handled in an experimental and ad hoc fashion under the existing IFA. It was first seen as a liquidity crisis for the borrowing countries instead of a solvency crisis, and the initial approach was one of bringing pressure on private bank lenders, through the IMF and directly by the G7 governments, to extend "new money" loans and a rescheduling of existing credits as a quid pro quo for official lending from the IMF in support of structural adjustment programs. When it was recognized that this approach of "growing out of debt" would not restore the creditworthiness of the borrowing countries, it was action by the US Treasury, rather than an initiative of the IMF or World Bank, that led to a program of debt reduction. The IMF was the principal implementing agent of this new strategy and offered financial arrangements to support countries in their negotiation of debt exchange operations that allowed them to reduce their debt burden.[11] In view of the length of time (more than a decade) required to complete these sovereign debt workouts and the cost in terms of foregone output for the countries involved, one can ask whether a more efficient mechanism was needed in the IFA to handle problems of sovereign debt workouts. This question would again be raised at the end of the 1990s after a second wave of defaults on emerging market bond debt.

The international debt crisis also set in motion the first attempt at coordinating international financial regulation, which has become an increasingly important focus of the IFA. The Basel Committee on Bank Supervision was established in 1974, as noted earlier, in the wake of two significant bank failures in Europe and the United States with important international ramifications in the early 1970s. In response, the committee established a Concordat in December 1975 that laid down certain basic principles of cooperation between host and parent authorities dealing with the supervision of a large international bank. However, the threat to the solvency of a number of large international banks in Europe, Japan, and North America arising from the debt crisis of the 1980s led to a much more focused effort at international regulatory harmonization that recognized the dual concerns of supervisory authorities about protecting bank soundness and preserving a level playing field for banks in an era of growing international banking activity. The result of this effort was the 1988 Basel Accord on capital adequacy standards.

Unlike the Concordat, which simply established principles for cooperation among financial regulators in the advanced countries, the 1988 Accord established a minimum capital requirement for banks of 8 percent in relation to their loans and investments with different risk weights assigned to broad categories of those assets.[12] It also defined a two-tiered structure of capital, with each tier having equal weight in the computation of the capital requirement. Although intended initially as a standard for the G10 countries, it has gradually been adopted by more than 100 countries, which have viewed its adoption as a "seal of good housekeeping" in the regulatory field. In 2004, the Basel Committee agreed on a revision of the 1988 Capital Accord after many years of debate, which defined a new approach to bank regulation, as discussed in chapter 8.

Emerging Market Financial Crises of the 1990s

The emerging market financial crises of the 1990s followed a major expansion of private portfolio flows to these countries in the years after the resolution of the international debt crisis and a shift in international bank credits from a medium-term to short-term duration. This latter shift was induced, in part, by the new capital accord described earlier, which assigned a relatively low risk weight to short-term interbank lines of credit, in relation to other types of bank lending, for the purpose of computing a bank's capital requirements. Although the crises of the 1980s reflected mainly a problem of excessive public sector borrowing from international banks, the crises of the 1990s represented mainly a problem of excessive borrowing by banks, corporations, and governments from foreign portfolio investors and banks. Foreign investors were attracted by efforts at financial liberalization in the major emerging market economies and a record of high economic growth, particularly among countries in the East Asian region. This new wave of financial globalization gave rise to two problems for these countries. One was the management of macroeconomic policy in the face of large private capital inflows. The other was the proper pace of capital account liberalization to facilitate their integration into the international financial system.

Economic policy management was complicated significantly by sustained private capital inflows or a surge in such flows. If recipient country authorities intervened in their currency markets to absorb the surplus of foreign exchange associated with capital inflows, this action would lead to a large expansion in domestic liquidity with potentially inflationary consequences. However, a tightening of monetary policy, for example, through open market sales of central bank or government paper, would lead to upward pressure on domestic interest rates. An increase in domestic interest rates, in turn, would attract further inflows of foreign capital, thus perpetuating the cycle, while dampening domestic investment. Alternatively, if the central bank limited its exchange market intervention, sustained capital inflows would lead to upward pressure on the exchange rate. Significant currency appreciation, in turn, would have a dampening effect on exports, while encouraging import expansion. These external effects would also have potentially negative consequences for growth, in particular for countries that were pursuing an export-led development strategy. These considerations left emerging market countries with the dilemma of trying to use fiscal policy as a countercyclical tool to offset the expansionary effects of capital inflows or using some mix of monetary tightening, capital controls and limited exchange market intervention. While in principle fiscal policy can be used in this way, from a practical perspective it is difficult to implement given the weakness of fiscal institutions in many developing countries and the lack of flexibility in public expenditure management.[13]

Issues of capital account liberalization had not been a central focus of the Fund's operational work and only drew attention in some of its analytical work in the 1990s as the institution tried to consider developments in this policy area among the advanced countries. As noted earlier, both the OECD and the EU developed codes for capital account liberalization among their membership, which became requirements for emerging market countries seeking admission to these clubs. An early study of the IMF staff in 1993 reviewing the experience of the advanced countries concluded that capital controls were not effective as a long-term defense against speculative capital flows, and that sound domestic policy management, a flexible exchange rate policy, and effective financial sector regulation were essential for dampening the destabilizing effect of short-term capital flows.[14] The IMF's Executive Board gave relatively little attention to issues of capital account liberalization before the 1990s, apart from discouraging reliance on capital inflows as a means of sustaining an inappropriate exchange rate.[15] In the absence of specific guidelines from the board, the staff was generally supportive of capital account liberalization in its policy dialogue if country authorities were interested in pursuing it, which was consistent with the institution's encouragement of financial liberalization, more generally.[16] However, mistakes were clearly made by some of the countries of East Asia, such as Thailand and Korea, which were at the center of the regional financial crisis, in that the governments liberalized prematurely short-term capital inflows in an economic environment in which banking and prudential regulation was relatively weak and a de facto fixed exchange rate was maintained.

Table 5.1   Major emerging market financial crises (1994–2002)

Country	Year	Type of Crisis	Fiscal Cost[a]	Output Loss[b]
			(as % of GDP)	
Argentina	1995	Single (B)	2.0	7.1
Argentina	2001	Triple (B+C+D)	9.6	42.7
Brazil	1994	Single (B)	13.2	–
Colombia	1998	Single (B)	6.3	33.5
Ecuador	1998	Triple (B+C+D)	21.7	6.5
Indonesia	1998	Triple (B+C+D)	56.8	30.1
Jamaica	1996	Single (B)	43.9	30.1
Korea	1997	Twin (B+C)	31.2	50.1
Malaysia	1997	Twin (B+C)	16.4	50.0
Mexico	1994	Twin (B+C)	19.3	4.2
Russia	1998	Triple (B+C+D)	6.0	–
Thailand	1997	Twin (B+C)	43.8	97.7
Turkey	2000	Twin (B+C)	32.0	5.4
Uruguay	2002	Triple (B+C+D)	20.0	28.8
Venezuela	1994	Twin (B+C)	15.0	9.6

B= Banking Crisis   C= Currency Crisis   D= Sovereign Debt Crisis

[a] Net of recoveries
[b] Measured as deviations from trend GDP
Source: Laeven and Valencia (2008)

The emerging market financial crises that began in the 1990s affected primarily fourteen countries, mainly in East Asia and Latin America, during the period 1994–2002 (table 5.1). Since these crises have been discussed extensively in other studies, they will only be referenced here in selected cases to highlight the issues of crisis management and crisis prevention that were central to the second reform of the IFA.[17] These financial crises exhibited certain familiar causal factors as financial crises of the past, but introduced new mechanisms by which they were triggered and propagated from one economy to another via the effect of contagion. In the past, financial crises typically affected either the banking system of a country or its exchange rate peg. In the 1990s, however, crises typically involved simultaneously the banking sector and the exchange rate system (so-called twin crises); and in some cases (e.g., Argentina 2001–2), they were "triple" crises involving a sovereign debt crisis, as well.[18] The economic costs of these crises were enormous, as reflected in their negative effect on economic activity and the increase in public debt associated with their resolution.

In the past, a banking crisis would often follow a period of financial liberalization whereby direct government controls on credit or interest rates were removed, and banks were allowed to operate according to market incentives subject, in principle, to appropriate internal risk management and external prudential oversight by independent bank regulators. Where crises occurred, neither of these constraints were effective, and banks became instruments of speculation and "bubble" phenomena in which credits were extended to increasingly risky borrowers or loans for high-risk ventures were undertaken. Some triggering event, such as a rise in loan defaults, a downturn in property prices (in the case of a building boom), or a tightening of monetary policy would lead to depositors' concerns about the safety of their money, and a panic would set in.

In the case of an exchange rate crisis, typically a country would be running an external current account deficit linked to excessive domestic credit expansion to finance an unsustainable fiscal imbalance, which would put downward pressure on the foreign reserve position of the central bank or lead to an increase in public debt. At some point, domestic residents and foreign investors would realize that the foreign reserves of the central bank were likely to be exhausted or foreign creditors would reduce their lending to the government, at which point panic would set in and a run on the currency would commence.[19]

The financial crises, which affected Mexico in 1994 and Thailand, Indonesia, and Korea in 1997–98, all shared common origins with typical crises of the past, but introduced a new vulnerability in terms of reliance on foreign borrowing often of a short-term nature. Each of the countries was pursuing a fixed exchange rate regime for all practical purposes, even if their currencies, in principle, were allowed to fluctuate. This policy stance created an environment of moral hazard for domestic borrowers in that they came to expect that fixed rate regimes would be maintained indefinitely in the future, so that there was little or no exchange risk involved in servicing their debt. Another common element of these countries is that they had all undertaken programs of capital account liberalization to attract foreign investors, but without proper safeguards in terms of a sound banking system and a robust regulatory regime. These countries' reliance on borrowing in foreign currency has come to be known in the academic literature as the problem of "original sin" that simply recognized the fact that the financial systems of these countries were relatively undeveloped and that foreign investors were not prepared to purchase assets or claims of these countries denominated in local currency.[20]

An additional commonality among these countries was that they were experiencing periods of rapid expansion and growth, some of which reflected increasingly risky investment (e.g., in real estate) financed by foreign borrowing from abroad. Typically, the external current account was in deficit, not because of a serious fiscal imbalance, as was often the case in financial crises of the past, but rather because of excessive growth of private consumption and investment. Before that time, a common view was that such external deficits were not a cause for concern, as private investment was assumed to be based on sound project analysis that demonstrated good prospects for debt repayment.

Reliance on foreign borrowing in these cases was particularly risky as it was often of a short-term nature, which was facilitated by relatively low interest rates abroad. Access by Asian borrowers to funds in Japan was particularly attractive because of low interest rates prevailing there during a period of weak growth and came to be known as the "carry trade." In the case of Thailand, such borrowing was encouraged by the government's creation of the Bangkok Interbank Borrowing Facility. In Korea, foreign borrowing took the form of short-term loans by Korean banks from banks in the advanced countries that, as noted earlier, were encouraged by the 1988 Basel Accord that assigned a relatively low risk weight to interbank lines of credit.

The extensive reliance on short-term foreign borrowing that was characteristic of the countries that suffered financial crises in the 1990s created a significant vulnerability in their national and sectoral balance sheets. This problem can be understood as one of "double mismatches" between assets and liabilities. The first mismatch arises from the fact that short-term liabilities were being used by private businesses and banks to fund long-term assets or investments in speculative or risky activity. In the case of banks, the transformation of short-term resources into longer-term assets is normal activity, but if the short-term funding is denominated in foreign currency and the longer-term investment of those resources is denominated in local currency, this process of inter-mediation gives rise to a second, currency mismatch in addition to a maturity mismatch. With these "double mismatches," the balance sheet risk of the bank or private business is increased significantly. This risk was present in one way or another in all the crises of the 1990s.

Since the vulnerability was related to the capital (or financial) account of the balance of payments of these countries, these crises came to be known as "capital account" crises. The trigger for the crisis can be associated with the same problem of "asymmetric information" between the suppliers and users of funds in domestic bank panics, discussed in chapter 2. In the financial crisis cases, the suppliers of funds, or foreign investors and banks, were exhibiting clear signs of "herding" behavior in the absence of good or full information about developments taking place in the countries they were investing in. On the other side of the balance sheet, the users of funds, and the governments of the countries involved, were not publishing accurate and timely information about economic developments and prospects. In this environment, any sud-den, adverse news or event could trigger a change in expectations of foreign investors and a cessation or withdrawal of foreign funding. This phenomenon of "sudden stops" would then trigger a collapse of imports and domestic spending that, in turn, would require a change in the real exchange rate to bring about a reduction in the current account deficit consistent with lower external financing.[21] Currency deprecia-tion would have a devastating effect on the balance sheets of the private sector, as suddenly their funding was withdrawn, and the local currency value of their liabilities would be considerably higher than that of the assets they were backing, thus giving rise to the threat or event of insol-vency. This rapid sequence of events, involving often a simultaneous outbreak of currency and banking crises (or "twin" crises), would have devastating effects on output and employment.

Once a crisis erupted in Thailand in April 1997, its effects were trans-mitted to other countries in the region through a process of contagion. In some cases, the contagion of "sudden stops" was caused by widespread panic of investors operating in the absence of reliable information, or by the sudden realization that other countries in the region might be in a similar situation as Thailand (so-called wake-up call effect). In other cases, negative economic effects could be transmitted to neighboring countries via important trade or financial linkages that existed in the East Asian region. Many countries were attacked by "sudden stops" in the wake of the crisis in Thailand, but these attacks were milder and less consequential in those countries that had strong reserve positions, such as Singapore and Taiwan. This fact would become an important lesson for emerging market countries once the crises were resolved.

The contagion effects of the Asian financial crises were not restricted to that region alone. In 1998, capital withdrawals and increases in risk premia on emerging market debt affected countries in Latin America and Eastern Europe, as well. In addition, Russia's default on its sovereign debt in 1998 sent shockwaves to the advanced countries, as reflected in the failure of a large US-based hedge fund, Long Term Capital Management (LTCM), which was a highly leveraged investor in Russian debt, among other investments. The activity of this fund was an early example of speculative activity that would be a central factor in the global financial crisis of 2008–9.

Most countries responded to the crises with a combination of exchange rate flexibility and monetary and fiscal policy adjustments, along with a variety of structural reforms to deal with institutional and regulatory weaknesses that allowed serious imbalances to arise. These programs were all guided by the IMF and have given rise to substantial debate and controversy, which will be discussed in the next section of this chapter. Most countries did not have recourse to capital controls in the context of the crisis, except Malaysia, whose experience has also been the focus of much controversy.

The financial crises of the 1990s gave rise to major debates about the effectiveness of the IFA in crisis management and crisis prevention, which played out during the second half of the 1990s, as the crises were unfolding. As in the case of the first reform, the second reform of the IFA was clearly crisis-driven and reflected a process of experimentation and adaptation of IMF procedures and operations, building on its experience in the debt crises of the 1980s. On the side of crisis prevention, one of the significant innovations was the creation of the Financial Stability Forum (FSF) to coordinate the work of international regulatory bodies within the IFA and the program of international standards and codes.

The second reform of the IFA was focused mainly on the impact of financial globalization on emerging market economies and what could be done to safeguard their integration into the global financial system. The crises of the 1980s and 1990s had shown that global financial flows were subject to boom and bust cycles, which could have devastating economic effects on these countries. The reform dealt with the questions of what could be done to tame these cycles and what protections needed to be in place at the international level to minimize the risk of crisis and to manage crisis response. The adequacy of international financial regulation was also subject to significant debate, not only as regards the role of capital adequacy standards, but also in respect of the institutional arrangements at the international level to enhance international cooperation and coordination among national regulators. The notion of global financial stability and the macro-prudential risk assessment of financial sector stability at the national and global level were brought into the scope of the IFA for the first time. The recent global financial crisis has shown, however, that these efforts were insufficient.

The second reform of the IFA, unlike the first reform effort, was almost entirely a top-down effort guided by the G7 countries in a series of summits that took place during the second half of the 1990s.[22] At the ministerial level, in September 1999, the G7 called into being the G20, which included twelve systemically important emerging market economies (along with the EU) as an additional forum in which to discuss some of the proposed reforms to the IFA.[23] The IMF was used to ratify in effect some of the decisions taken by the advanced countries. The "club approach" to decision making made it easier for reforms of the IFA to be considered and agreed, but it created the impression that the second reform was largely intended for the rest of the Fund membership, rather than for the system as a whole. This approach to some extent explains why the reform effort was inadequate to deal with the onset of the current crisis.

Crisis Management and the International Financial Architecture

Reform efforts in the area of crisis management focused essentially on three issues: the nature and scope of conditionality in IMF lending programs for the crisis countries, access limits under IMF facilities and its role as an "international lender of last resort," and the Fund's role in sovereign debt restructuring. As in the case of the 1980 debt crisis, the IMF was clearly the lead agency in the response of the international community. The World Bank, for its part, provided lending on a much smaller scale than the Fund (as part of so-called secondary lines of defense) and focused its technical assistance on certain key aspects of the recovery

Table 5.2   Financial rescue packages for selected financial cases (1995–2003)

Country	Year	Total Commitment	IMF Resources			Other Resources[a]	
		US$ BN	US$ BN	% of Quota	% of GDP	US$ BN	% of GDP
Mexico	1995	38.0	18.0	688	4.4	20.0	5.4
Thailand	1997	13.9	3.9	505	2.2	10.0	5.5
Indonesia	1997	26.3	11.3	555	5.0	15.0	6.6
Korea	1998	40.8	20.8	1938	4.0	20.0	3.8
Brazil	1998	32.9	18.4	600	2.3	14.5	1.8
Russia	1998	15.1	15.1	186	3.5	–	–
Argentina	2000/01	23.1	22.1	800	7.8	1.0	0.4
Brazil	2001/02	35.1	35.1	900	6.9	–	–
Uruguay	2000/01	4.2	2.7	694	14.5	1.5	8.0
Turkey	1999/02	33.8	33.8	2548	17.0	–	–

[a] Other resources from World Bank, other development banks, and bilateral sources
Source: Roubini and Setser (2004)

programs, for example, in the area of bank restructuring and corporate insolvency. Other institutions, such as the BIS, would also play a supporting role in providing "bridge" finance in certain cases to cover the time while an IMF financial arrangement was being put in place. Table 5.2 shows the amount of financing that was made available by the IMF and other lenders in the financial crisis cases.

The Nature and Scope of IMF Conditionality

The conditionality of IMF lending has been the subject of controversy and debate throughout its history. As noted earlier, its basic rationale has been as a safeguard for the temporary use of Fund resources, which are intended to be made available on a revolving basis to its membership. In addition, as noted earlier, since the Fund does not generally accept collateral for its loans, conditionality is intended to provide a substitute for such a guarantee by giving some assurance that policies and adjustments will be put in place to enable the borrower to repay the Fund on a timely basis. In practice, one of the problems that arise in the negotiation of Fund lending programs is the mix of financing and policy adjustment (conditionality) that is employed in reaching a solution to the borrower's external payments problems and the timeframe within which that improvement takes place. In particular, since the time of the first reform of the IFA, there has been a tension within the IMF between the advanced, creditor countries that have favored less financing and more adjustment in Fund lending programs and developing or borrower countries that have favored relatively more financing. Thus, the scope and content of conditionality, as well as the size of the Fund's resources (specifically the overall size of its quotas) have been reviewed and debated within the organization on a continuing basis.[24]

In the financial crises cases of the 1990s, there was also active debate about the conceptual framework of the Fund's financial rescue programs, as well as the scope and content of the specific conditions (or so-called performance criteria) tied to that assistance. Conditionality can take a variety of forms in IMF financial arrangements. Some performance criteria may be expressed as "prior actions" to be completed before the approval and initial disbursement of an IMF financial arrangement. These usually relate to the adoption or implementation of some important policy change, which is judged to be important for the success of the program. Others are quantitative in nature, typically specified on a quarterly basis, which set numerical targets, for example, for the conduct of monetary or fiscal policy consistent with the overall macroeconomic objectives of the adjustment program. Still others may be qualitative in nature and specified as "structural" conditions for the commencement or completion of some institutional or economic reform, or for the completion of a mid-term review by the Fund of the progress achieved under the program. Disbursements under Fund arrangements are typically phased over time, subject to the satisfactory fulfillment of both the quantitative and qualitative performance criteria specified in the arrangement. While these conditions obviously constrain the borrower's access to Fund resources, they also provide interim guidance on the adequacy of the program and the opportunity, in the case of program reviews or noncompliance with program targets, for mid-course corrections, if needed. The policy program to be implemented by a government receiving Fund assistance and the specification of conditionality for a Fund financial arrangement are spelled out in what is called a "letter of intent" that is negotiated between the IMF staff and the government authorities, typically those in charge of the central bank and ministry of finance.[25]

Over time, there has been a tendency for the number of conditions in Fund arrangements to increase. The scope and quantity of structural conditions in the Asian crisis cases was an issue of significant criticism by the governments concerned and outside observers. The main issues raised were whether the scope and quantity of conditions involved were essential for the immediate stabilization of these economies and whether they undermined the confidence of outside creditors in the ability of the government to cope with the demands of the crisis. This criticism was raised, in particular, in the case of Indonesia, for which 140 structural conditions were included in one of the Fund's arrangements.[26] Other complaints have been raised that the US government applied special pressure to ensure that certain conditions related to the liberalization of capital flows and financial services were introduced as conditions for IMF loans. In the case of Korea, the removal of restrictions on foreign firms' participation in the local financial services industry was included as a structural condition in the Fund's financial arrangement, but this measure had been on the government's reform agenda prior to the crisis.[27]

By and large, the criticism of excessive structural conditionality has been accepted within the Fund, and in the period after the crisis, efforts were made by Fund management to streamline the conditionality of IMF programs and define more carefully the relevance of conditions for the macroeconomic objectives of the program. As part of this effort, a clearer division of labor was sought with the World Bank, whereby reforms of a structural nature (e.g., in trade policy, public sector management, or financial restructuring) were assigned to the scope of policy loans to be negotiated with the World Bank.[28]

The macroeconomic policy content of the IMF programs with the Asian crisis countries was also a subject of controversy.[29] Here the criticism raised was that the IMF's monetary and fiscal policy advice was inappropriate for the new phenomenon of "capital account" crises that these countries were experiencing, as distinct from the typical "current account" crises of the past. The critics of the Fund raised essentially two concerns. One is that a policy of excessive fiscal retrenchment was advocated under the financial arrangements, which exacerbated the depressive effects of the crisis on output and employment. The second is that monetary policy was overly restrictive, resulting in exorbitantly high interest rates that threatened the solvency of banks, to defend unrealistic levels of the exchange rate.

The first criticism is only partially valid. While it is true that the IMF programs involved an initial fiscal stance that was somewhat restrictive, in most cases, a restrictive fiscal policy was not implemented, as originally intended. In evaluating the initial fiscal stance agreed for the program, it must be recognized that the Fund mission teams and the authorities were operating in conditions of great uncertainty about the likely course and impact of the crises that were unfolding. However, once the full dimensions of the crisis became clear, the initial plans for fiscal retrenchment were abandoned at the urging of the Fund, and fiscal conditions were significantly relaxed to allow automatic stabilizers to work. Program targets were adjusted, and in the end they did not operate as a binding constraint on government budgetary operations. The study of the Independent Evaluation Office of the IMF (IMF IEO 2003), which evaluated the Fund's performance in Indonesia and Korea, concluded that fiscal policy was not a factor in accounting for the severe economic downturn that was experienced in these countries.

In judging the appropriate stance of monetary policy, the authorities and the Fund were faced with a difficult dilemma. Because of the simultaneity of a banking and currency crisis these countries were facing, the appropriate monetary stance for one was in conflict with that for the other. In the case of a banking crisis, there needs to be liquidity support to the banking system and a policy of monetary ease. However, if the country was also experiencing a currency crisis, then an easing of monetary policy would exacerbate downward pressure on the exchange rate. In the case of a currency crisis, there needs to be a tightening of monetary policy to limit speculative demand for credit, to retain domestic financial savings, and to dampen the currency depreciation. However, if the country was also experiencing a banking crisis, a policy of monetary tightening, leading to a sharp increase in interest rates, would threaten the solvency of certain banks as the cost of their short-term term liabilities would exceed the earnings on their longer-term assets.

Faced with this dilemma, the authorities and the Fund tried to steer a middle course whereby currencies were allowed to depreciate if they were judged to have been overvalued, but some degree of monetary tightening was introduced to dampen the downward pressure on exchange rates and to prevent a complete collapse of the currency. Given the problem of "double mismatches" in these economies and the unknown degree to which a maturity mismatch or currency mismatch dominated the financial system in each country, the policy approach adopted seems to have been correct. The lesson for the Fund from these experiences was that much more attention needed to be given in future work in identifying with countries the balance sheet mismatches in their private corporate and banking sectors and taking preventive steps to eliminate these vulnerabilities.

The application of capital controls in Malaysia was also the subject of controversy. As a result of contagion effects, Malaysia's currency, which was pegged to the US dollar, was also attacked in early 1998, and was adjusted downward by the authorities. However, later that year, the authorities abandoned the kind of policy response that Thailand and

Indonesia attempted and introduced capital controls on a temporary basis to control further outflows and to give room for a more accommodating monetary and fiscal policy to support domestic economic activity. This action was strongly criticized by the international financial community.[30] On the part of foreign creditors and investors, the imposition of capital controls was seen as an arbitrary abrogation of an implicit understanding that limits on capital repatriation, which did not exist when capital flows entered the country, would not be imposed at a later date. The controls that Malaysia introduced were selective in nature and mainly were aimed at limiting speculative sales of the Malaysian ringgit in offshore markets. Those controls that were set on capital transfers abroad were limited to a term of eighteen months and then were phased out.

There is still some debate in the analytical studies of the Malaysian case as to the effectiveness of these controls, since they were introduced after a period in which Malaysia experienced significant capital outflows, but nonetheless they seem to have afforded the government more latitude for the conduct of domestic policy in support of economic recovery.[31] Since the time of the Asian crisis, reports of the Fund have taken a more tolerant view of the potential role of capital controls in the context of a policy program to deal with a financial crisis. The initial aversion to Malaysia's recourse to capital controls within the institution, even though they are still recognized as a legitimate policy instrument in the Fund Agreement, reflects the great change that had taken place in official circles from the time of the Bretton Woods system to the modern era of financial globalization. Under the earlier system, countries facing a problem of speculative capital outflows were authorized to impose capital restrictions, as reflected in the original wording of Article VI of the Fund Agreement that has remained unchanged since the time it was drafted.[32]

Access Limits under IMF Facilities

The issue of access limits under IMF borrowing facilities for crisis cases was the subject of intense debate during the second reform of the IFA. Before the crisis, under normal financing operations, countries were limited to borrowing the equivalent of 100 percent of their quota in the Fund in one year and 300 percent cumulatively during a consecutive three-year period. During the financial crises of the 1990s, as shown in table 5.2, these limits were ignored as the IMF attempted to provide the financing to stabilize countries' reserve levels and restore the confidence of foreign creditors that was needed on a case by case basis. In the first crisis case (Mexico), under strong pressure from the US government, access to Fund borrowing in 1994 was raised to 700 percent of its quota. Subsequently, the upper limit on access was raised to approximately 1,900 percent of quota for Korea in 1997, and around 2,500 percent in the case of Turkey in 2000.

These episodes represented a major expansion in the role of the IMF as an international lender of last resort (ILOLR) within the IFA. Consistent with that role, decisions were made during 1997 to shorten the maturity and increase the cost of "exceptional" access borrowing (under a new Supplementary Reserve Facility) in relation to the terms of regular IMF financing, in keeping with its emergency nature. However, much time was taken up during the reform debates on specifying the conditions for "exceptional" access to Fund financing to limit the extent of "moral hazard" involved in such lending. In February 2003, the IMF specified four conditions for exceptional access, which essentially defined the existence of a liquidity crisis, as distinct from a solvency crisis: (1) a country was confronting a sudden attack of capital flow reversals; (2) the country's external debt situation must be judged to be sustainable; (3) the country was expected to regain access to private financing under the period of Fund financing; and (4) the country's macroeconomic policy program was considered to have a high probability of success.[33]

In practice, very few countries facing crises in the late 1990s and early years of the current decade could be judged to have met these conditions, because of the difficulty of making a hard and fast distinction between problems of illiquidity and insolvency. Considering this problem, one prominent commission that was set up by the US Congress to recommend reforms to the IFA (Meltzer Commission) proposed in 2000 that all IMF lending be granted to countries that were judged to have met strict prequalifications (somewhat similar to those listed earlier). However, this proposal was seen as being too radical, as it would have denied IMF financial assistance to a potentially large share of the membership.

The experience of Brazil in the use of "exceptional financing" demonstrates the potential benefits of the Fund's ILOLR function in preventing a financial crisis that might have occurred in the absence of its intervention. During 2002, Brazil suffered strong, negative spillover effects from the financial crisis in Argentina, because of its large external debt burden, which were compounded by doubts among financial market participants about the resolve of a new left-of-center government to continue a fiscal consolidation program that had been put in place by a more conservative regime. The decision of the Fund in September 2002 to commit an exceptionally large financial arrangement (amounting to US$35 billion or 900 percent of Brazil's quota) provided strong support to the new government's declared program of macroeconomic and debt stabilization and helped to restore the confidence of international financial markets in Brazil's ability to maintain a viable external position. In the event, the government of Brazil exceeded its own fiscal and inflation targets and repaid its obligations to the Fund on an accelerated basis before the end of 2005.

The problem of potential moral hazard in exceptional financing packages of the IMF led to an important debate in the official community on the appropriate degree of burden sharing by private sector creditors in the resolution of financial crises (so-called private sector involvement or PSI). In most cases, the Fund plays a "catalytic" role through its lending to countries facing a balance of payments problem, whereby temporary financing from the Fund accompanied by appropriate policy adjustments will lead to a relatively quick resolution of payments difficulties and the resumption of normal private sector lending. In other cases, the Fund has attempted to exercise direct leverage over private creditors (through its major shareholders) to restore normal lines of credit (so-called concerted lending). As noted earlier, the IMF had adopted this approach during the debt crisis of the 1980s in making "new" or "fresh" money from the commercial banks a condition for its financial assistance to the indebted countries. This approach also was required in the case of Korea in 1997 when major shareholders in the Fund exercised leverage over banks in their countries to roll over short-term lines of credit with their correspondent banks in Korea, instead of withdrawing them, as they intended to do at the outbreak of the crisis in that country.

The most difficult case of private sector involvement arises in cases where countries are facing a potential or actual financial crisis because of an unsustainable external debt burden. This was the situation of Argentina toward the end of 2001. For most of the previous decade, Argentina had maintained an extreme form of exchange rate peg in the form of a currency board to limit inflation and provide a stable environment for economic growth. One of the problems that arose was that the government was not able to control the public finances and limit the growth of public sector debt. As the debt burden grew during the second half of the decade and Argentina began to lose external competitiveness because of the rigidity of its exchange rate regime, the risk premium on its foreign debt issued began to rise sharply.

During the period 2000–2001 when Argentina called on the IMF for financial support, the approach adopted under the Fund programs was that of a liquidity crisis instead of an insolvency crisis. Under this approach, in late 2001, the government reached an agreement with foreign creditors on a rescheduling of foreign lines of credit, which increased the cost of external financing, but stretched out the period of debt repayment to give time to the government to implement a program of fiscal consolidation. However, instead of debt refinancing, a program of debt restructuring was needed to reduce the burden of external debt through a partial write-down in the value of the debt. At the end of 2001, Argentina was unable to meet revised conditions for its financial arrangement with the IMF, and the Fund decided not to agree to a further revision of the policy program for the arrangement because of Argentina's poor track record. At this point, Argentina declared a default on its external debt and had to abandon its exchange rate regime. Because the domestic banks were heavily indebted with foreign loans, and were holding mainly local currency assets, these balance sheet mismatches created a banking crisis in the wake of the collapse of the exchange rate, in addition to the debt and exchange crisis (thus creating a triple crisis).[34]

Because of the crisis, Argentina entered into a period of very painful economic adjustment and a long process of debt restructuring. The debt renegotiation process was complicated by the fact that most of Argentina's external debt was in the form of bearer bonds that had been sold in numerous issues throughout the world. Thus it was extremely difficult to organize creditors into groups that could negotiate with the government. An organization such as the Corporation of Foreign Bondholders, which operated during the period of the gold standard, did not exist for Argentina. Eventually, a few ad hoc groups were assembled for most of the creditors, but the government of Argentina was not willing to enter into any negotiation, despite the urging of the IMF, which was providing a minimum line of credit to the central bank to facilitate some refinancing of Argentina's sizeable indebtedness to the Fund. Eventually, in 2004, the government announced a unilateral proposal for a new bond issue equivalent to 30 percent of the face value of the outstanding debt, on a "take it or leave it" basis. Seventy percent of the existing bondholders did accept the government's offer, which included some enhancements for higher interest payments in the event that the real growth of GDP exceeded a certain baseline trajectory (via GDP-indexed bonds). However, the indebtedness of those bondholders who did not accept the government plan was still unresolved as of early 2010, and Argentina remained in default.[35]

The Fund's Role in Sovereign Debt Restructuring

The experience of Argentina brought to light a major new problem for the IFA in regard to the handling of sovereign debt workouts with private bondholders. In late 2001, as the Argentinean crisis was reaching a climax, the IMF proposed the establishment of a Sovereign Debt Restructuring Mechanism (SDRM) to anticipate potential problems of debt defaults and facilitate debt restructuring. The SDRM was intended to be the functional equivalent of a national bankruptcy regime at the international level along the following lines. Countries facing debt difficulties could seek through the mechanism of the SDRM, which would be operated by the Fund, a temporary suspension or "stay" on debt service payments; the equivalent of "debtor-in-possession" financing would be provided by the Fund; creditors could agree by majority vote on the terms of a debt restructuring; and any dispute over the legitimacy of claims could be adjudicated by a dispute resolution forum attached to the mechanism.[36]

After much debate on this so-called statutory approach to debt restructuring, it was not accepted mainly because of opposition of the US government, which anticipated great difficulty gaining congressional support for an amendment to the Fund Agreement that would have been required to establish the SDRM. There was also some resistance from emerging market economies, which feared that the existence of the SDRM might lead to an increase in the risk premia on their debt in international markets. The US government also reflected the view of the private financial community, as voiced prominently by the Institute of International Finance (IIF), which emerged during the debt crises of the 1980s, as noted earlier, and has increasingly taken on the role of advocate for the interests of the major international banks in international policy debates on the IFA. Private lenders objected to the SDRM because they believed it might make debt restructuring too easy for creditors, thus weakening the sanctity of contracts. In their view, the difficulties involved in renegotiating debt should act as some deterrent on countries declaring a default in the first place. The private financial community also considered that there was a conflict of interest for the IMF in its position of a privileged creditor under the mechanism and administrator for the SDRM. In addition, it was feared that the IMF might encourage countries to access the mechanism in cases that were not warranted.

Instead of the SDRM, the IMF and the private financial community eventually endorsed in 2003 the adoption of a decentralized or "contractual" approach to debt restructuring involving the widespread use of "collective action" clauses in sovereign bond contracts. This approach might have facilitated negotiations in the case of Argentina, but obviously was not available in that case as Argentina's bonds were negotiated without such clauses. Before 2003, most contracts negotiated under New York law (governing the major financial markets of New York City) for sovereign bonds issued in the United States were based on "unanimous action" clauses (unlike the case of UK law governing bond issues in the major financial markets of London that typically include "majority action" clauses). The proponents of collective action bond clauses maintained that this approach would support three of the four functions mentioned earlier in the case of a bankruptcy proceeding (all except the provision for the adjudication of claims in dispute). In support of the contractual approach, the IIF promulgated a code of conduct for international borrowers, which lays out the principles of a voluntary, decentralized approach to debt restructuring ("Principles of Stable Capital Flows and Fair Debt Restructuring in Emerging Markets").[37] To date, virtually all debt contracts that have been issued in the United States contain collective action clauses. However, this system is largely untested by crisis, and thus it is unclear whether it can avoid the kind of bitter and protracted negotiations that occurred in the case of Argentina.

The SDRM debate was an important debate about institutional adaptations to the IFA. It was also the first time that major international banks (operating via the IIF) became significant participants in reform debates. Banks for many years had been an important pressure group within domestic politics on aspects of regulatory reform, but had not participated directly in debates on international financial reform until the IIF took on this role in the mid-1990s.

Crisis Prevention and the International Financial Architecture

At the same time that reforms were being made in the way the international community responded to financial crises through the IMF (crisis management), debates were taking place on the measures and safeguards that emerging market economies and the IFA could put in place to minimize the risk of future financial crises (crisis prevention). These debates focused essentially on four initiatives: the development of international standards and codes; improving the surveillance activities of the IMF and making them more visible; the establishment of a standing facility in the Fund that countries could access on a prequalified basis in the event of a financial attack; and the reform of the IMF Agreement to include capital account liberalization as part of the jurisdiction of the Fund along with current account liberalization.

The underlying premise of the approach adopted in the area of crisis prevention was that financial globalization was a beneficial force for most countries and needed to be accommodated, given the experience of the advanced countries since the first reform of the IFA. Accordingly, the focus was on what steps the developing and emerging market countries could take, with the assistance of the international financial community, to facilitate their integration into the international financial system. In view of the direction given to the reform effort by the G7, the intent was clear that the broader membership of the IMF should look to the experience of the advanced countries for guidance on capital account liberalization.

The approach to crisis prevention also relied heavily on more transparency in the operations of individual governments and the IMF to improve the flow of information for the guidance of financial markets to deal with the problem of asymmetric information as a cause for financial crises. The regular supply of information would not only improve the functioning of financial markets, but also act as a disciplining force on countries, as foreign creditors and investors would better be able to assess their performance and prospects and begin to take defensive action if adverse developments persisted.

Regulatory reform was also emphasized, but mainly at the national level where accountability and government control was strongest. Internationally, the G7 ministerial group established the FSF in 1999 to begin to coordinate the disparate elements of the IFA in the regulatory field that had developed since the end of the Bretton Woods system. As noted earlier, issues of financial system stability at the international level were identified as a public good, which the IFA needed to provide.

The Development of International Standards and Codes

The program of international standards and codes started as an initiative of the G7 in the wake of the Mexican financial crisis of 1994 with their call for the development of data dissemination standards to guide developing and emerging market economies on the scope, periodicity and timeliness of economic and financial statistics that they should publish to provide a regular and reliable flow of economic and financial information to financial markets. The pattern of dissemination of official statistics in the advanced countries was taken as the norm for this exercise. These standards were followed up in the Fund by the development of codes for monetary policy and fiscal policy transparency, which provided guidance to countries on good practice in the formulation and transparency of central bank and treasury operations.

Table 5.3 International standards and codes

Area	Standard	Year	Issuing Body
I. Data and Macroeconomic Policy Transparency			
1. Data Dissemination	Special Data Dissemination Standard	1996	IMF
	General Data Dissemination System	1997	IMF
2. Fiscal Policy Transparency	Code of Good Practices on Fiscal Transparency	1998	IMF
3. Monetary and Financial Policy Transparency	Code of Good Practices on Transparency in Monetary and Financial Policies	1999	IMF
II. Financial Regulation and Supervision			
4. Banking Supervision	Core Principles for Effective Banking Supervision	1997/2006	BCBS
5. Securities Regulation	Objectives and Principles of Securities Regulation	1998	IOSCO
6. Insurance Supervision	Insurance Core Principles	1999/2003	IAIS
III. Institutional and Market Infrastructure			
7. Insolvency	Insolvency and Credit Rights	2005	World Bank
8. Corporate Governance	Principles of Governance	1999	OECD
9. Accounting	International Accounting Standards	2002	IASB
10. Auditing	International Standards on Auditing	2002	IFAC
11. Payment and Settlement	Core Principles for Systemically Important Payment Systems	2001	CPSS
	Recommendations for Securities Settlement Systems	2001	CPSS/ IOSCO
12. Market Integrity	The Forty Recommendations of Financial Action Task Force	2002	FATF
	Nine Special Recommendations On Terrorist Financing	2002	FATF

Source: Financial Stability Board

When the FSF was established, it took control of this program and expanded its coverage to twelve core areas of data dissemination, policy transparency, financial system regulation, and market infrastructure. The list of these codes and the sponsoring agencies that developed them are presented in table 5.3, and they are briefly described in the appendix. These codes can be understood as providing guidelines for the effective operation of the infrastructure of financial markets, as regards their accounting, auditing, regulatory, corporate governance, informational and policy requirements, as well as the control of financial abuse through money laundering. The FSF was established to coordinate the work of national regulatory agencies in the G7 countries, the three G10 committees based at the BIS, the International Organization of Securities Commissions (IOSCO), the International Association of Insurance Supervisors (IAIS), and the International Accounting Standards Board (IASB). These organizations had all developed since the end of the Bretton Woods system and represented a mix of official and private sector entities involved in the specification of regulatory, accounting, and auditing standards to facilitate the development of the international financial system. Their membership was not universal, however, and represented primarily the interests of the advanced countries. The FSF also included representation from the major international institutions within the IFA, that is, the BIS, the IMF, World Bank, and OECD, as well as the ECB upon its creation. Since the G7 countries each had three representatives in the FSF (central bank, ministry of finance, and lead regulatory agency), they constituted a majority voice in the work of the FSF. The FSF was headed initially by the general manager of the BIS, acting in a private capacity.

The decision to locate the FSF in Basel reflected, in part, the important role that committees such as the BCBS (located at the BIS) had come to play in the international regulatory field. However, it also reflected an interest on the part of the G7 finance ministers in maintaining control of the standards and code initiative and avoiding disputes that might have arisen between them and the rest of the Fund membership over its scope and content. According to evolving practice in the Fund, decision making by the executive board has increasingly taken effect on a consensus-based approach, instead of strictly according to voting power for most policy issues.

The clubs and groups that are members of the FSF, along with the Financial Action Task Force (FATF), which acts in coordination with the OECD, reflect a growing influence of "soft" law in the international financial system. For the most part, they have less than universal membership and function with relatively little public accountability. Instead of legal decisions or formal rules embodied in treaty-based organizations, such as the IMF and the WTO, these entities adopt guidelines for international practice in areas of their specific functional expertise, which are then embodied in domestic law and practice of the countries that are members of the group. These guidelines in turn become "best practice" for other countries to adopt. The appeal of entities such as the FSF and the groups that it coordinates is that they can be constituted much more easily than treaty-based organizations and can come to agreement on technical issues of common interest much more quickly and with less political debate than would be the case in universal organizations. By the same token, however, these groups may be viewed as lacking legitimacy because of their limited representation and low level of transparency.[38]

Under the program of international standards and codes, the IMF and World Bank were asked by the FSF to monitor countries' progress in their implementation through the preparation of Reports on the Observation of International Standards and Codes (ROSCs). Initially, the advanced countries wanted these reports to be mandatory, but the developing countries resisted this approach, emphasizing instead that the standards and codes project should be seen as developmental, with the Bank and Fund providing technical assistance to allow countries to put in place the systems and procedures that would allow them over time to comply with their principles. Accordingly, the ROSCs were prepared on a voluntary and nonprescriptive basis, without any summary judgment or quantitative evaluation of the degree of country compliance with the standard being assessed. Most of the ROSCs have been published on the website of the IMF, with the agreement of the member involved, as part of a major change in the transparency of Fund operations in general.

Along with the program of standards and codes, the Fund and Bank also initiated, at the request of the FSF, a Financial Sector Assessment Program (FSAP) that countries would request voluntarily to assess the soundness of their banking systems and the effectiveness of their regulatory regimes. The FSAP included an assessment of the relevant standards and codes for each country's situation along with an evaluation of the vulnerabilities and risks to financial system stability that needed to be addressed. This program was intended to deal with exactly the kind of problems such as balance sheet mismatches, regulatory forbearance, and weak corporate governance structure that were important factors in the financial crises of the 1990s. To give more prominence to this exercise, it was decided that the results of the FSAP, which were presented in a Financial Sector Stability Assessment (FSSA), would be considered by the Fund's Executive Board at the same time as the annual Article IV consultation that was the main instrument of bilateral surveillance carried out by the Fund. As in the case of ROSCs, the FSAP received wide acceptance among the membership and has been viewed as a useful diagnostic tool for countries. Also, most countries have agreed to the voluntary publication of their FSSA report. Notably, however, the US government did not participate in the preparation of a FSAP report for its financial system and has only done so in the wake of the recent financial crisis.

Improving the Surveillance and Lender of Last Resort Functions of the IMF

Significant emphasis was given in the second reform of the IFA to expanding the focus of Fund surveillance to cover financial stability issues and improving the visibility of Article IV consultation reports. More disclosure of the Fund's country macroeconomic and financial sector assessments, along with improved data dissemination and policy transparency of individual countries, was seen as contributing to a better functioning of international financial markets. Before 1997, all Article IV consultation reports, along with letters of intent for financial arrangements, were considered confidential documents of the Fund, which were not made publicly available. Since that time, the Fund has moved to a position whereby there is a presumption of publication for all country documents, including the Summing-Ups of Board discussions at the completion of the Article IV consultation. As an exceptional matter, countries may object to the publication of one of its reports or insist on the deletion of market-sensitive information.

To improve the focus of Article IV consultation reports, it was decided to give more emphasis to the analysis of debt sustainability, macrofinancial linkages, and financial sector risk assessments in these reports. In addition, efforts were made to improve the coordination of bilateral surveillance with the Fund's main instrument of multilateral surveillance, the World Economic Outlook exercise. At the same time, it was also decided to initiate in 2001 a new surveillance exercise in the form of a Global Financial Stability Report to take up the issues of macro-prudential risk in the global financial system.

In the context of discussions on the Fund's role as an ILOLR, it was decided in 1999 to establish a Contingent Credit Line (CCL) that countries could access in the event of a financial crisis without the requirement of negotiating a letter of intent and seeking Board approval before the disbursement of Fund assistance. Instead, countries would be prequalified for access to the CCL on the basis of a favorable assessment in a recent Article IV consultation report and endorsement by the Fund (in a recent Summing-Up) of its macroeconomic policy program. A country would also be expected to be making good progress in meeting the Fund's Special Data Dissemination Standard. In principle, the idea of a CCL was an important adaptation of the Fund's financial facilities, as it would have created an insurance mechanism for countries to use in the event of a speculative attack, thus enhancing an ILOLR function under the IFA. However, the CCL was abandoned in 2003 in view of the fact that no country expressed interest in its use.

There were essentially two critical problems in its design. One was that the amount of unconditional access to IMF resources was relatively limited at the time a country made its initial request for activation. Further access was conditioned on the completion of a successful review by the Fund of the country's policy program and prospects. This restriction created some uncertainty among potential borrowers about continued access to CCL resources if appropriate understandings with the Fund could not be reached in the event of a speculative attack, once the facility was activated, or if eligibility was withdrawn. In this way, the CCL did not offer a clear enough alternative to regular Fund facilities. The other problem was one of perceived stigma in that eligibility might be interpreted as a perverse signal of potential vulnerabilities that market participants were not aware of.

It would take another decade before a suitable multilateral insurance scheme could be created in the IMF. In the meantime, two developments transpired. One was the creation of regional reserve pooling mechanisms such as the Chiang Mai Initiative (CMI) among the East Asian countries, beginning in 2000. The CMI had initially been suggested by the Japanese government as a regional defense fund during the height of the Asian financial crises, but both the US government and the IMF discouraged its formation, as they believed crisis management responsibilities should be concentrated in the IMF. The other response to the lack of a credible insurance mechanism at the international level was the pattern of self-insurance that many emerging market countries exhibited in the immediate aftermath of the Asian financial crisis. Once the recovery was underway, countries such as Korea, Thailand, and Malaysia, began to accumulate foreign reserves in their central banks, taking a lesson from the fact that those countries that had been spared the effects of contagion by the crisis each had significant levels of foreign reserves.

Debate also focused on the appropriate exchange rate arrangement that emerging market countries should maintain as a defense against financial crisis. Given the moral hazard associated with the maintenance of a de facto pegged exchange rate regime among all the crisis countries, the view developed that countries should adopt a "two-corner" solution if they were going to be able to accommodate financial globalization in a viable manner. One alternative would be to pursue a purely free floating exchange rate policy, under which borrowers would have to consider any exchange risk involved in foreign borrowing, thus limiting their imprudent behavior. Under this solution, large reserve holdings would be unnecessary, as the exchange rate would serve as a shock absorber in the event of any speculative attack. The other alternative would be to pursue a policy of a "hard" peg regime, such as a currency board or the adoption of a common currency as in the case of the EMU, in which case the government would effectively surrender its discretion to conduct an independent monetary policy (according to the impossible trinity).[39]

Notwithstanding the economic logic behind the two-corner solution, experience would show that it was too simplistic a guide for emerging market countries. On the one hand, the experience of Argentina showed that even a hard exchange peg could not provide any protection against a financial crisis, if there was a fundamental problem in the management of the public finances. On the other hand, the experience of the Asian countries following the regional crisis demonstrated that even these countries were not prepared to renounce the use of discretion in managing their exchange rates, given their reliance on an export-led development model. This resistance to the implementation of a flexible exchange rate policy came to be known as "fear of floating."[40] This tendency was illustrated in particular, in the case of China, and would be a factor that led to the problem of global imbalances that preceded the current financial crisis. Thus, self-insurance continued to be a common practice of the emerging market economies in the lead-up to the current global crisis.

The Proposed Capital Account Amendment to the IMF Agreement

The remaining important issue taken up in the debate on crisis prevention during the second reform of the IFA was the appropriate pace of capital account liberalization for developing and emerging market economies. Given that all the financial crisis cases had embraced capital account liberalization in one form or another, the obvious question to be answered was what flaws existed in the way in which this policy was implemented. In some cases, the preconditions for capital account liberalization had not been satisfied in terms of a sound banking system and independent regulatory function. In other cases, there were clear problems in the sequencing of capital account liberalization with the liberalization of short-term capital flows (the most volatile element of capital flows) preceding that of long-term capital movements (such as direct investment and long-term portfolio capital flows that were more stable and persistent).

Before the Asian financial crisis, the IMF had not adopted a formal policy on capital account liberalization, in part because this was not part of its jurisdiction. However, as noted before, the issue was taken up in individual cases in the context of Article IV consultation discussions. At the urging of the advanced countries, the Executive Board of the IMF began to discuss in the mid-1990s whether the Fund Agreement should be amended to include capital account liberalization as one of the purposes of IMF membership, along with current account convertibility. The idea of giving the Fund jurisdiction in this area would have filled a gap in the IFA in that no international institution had jurisdiction in this area that would justify its surveillance of the ways in which countries managed the process of capital market integration. In 1997, the Executive Board approved a decision to recommend such an amendment to the IMF Board of Governors, which was endorsed by the IMFC in September of that year. The timing of this decision, however, proved to be problematic. Even though the Board of Governors recommended that work begin on preparing such an amendment, it was resisted by many governments because of the capital account crises that were occurring in Asia. Such an amendment was also criticized by many outside the Fund because it was interpreted (inappropriately) as a signal that the Fund would force countries to liberalize their capital accounts prematurely. In the light of this controversy, debate on this amendment was never concluded.[41]

In the wake of the Asian financial crises, much policy and analytical debate was devoted to the question of what benefits, if any, accrued to developing countries from capital account liberalization. There has been further discussion on the preconditions of capital account liberalization and its proper sequencing over time. These issues are explored in more detail in chapter 6.

A related issue that has received much policy and academic debate is what kind of capital account restrictions may be appropriate for minimizing disruptive capital flows and limiting speculative capital inflows of a short-term nature. The experience of Malaysia in imposing capital controls at the peak of its financial crisis has motivated much of this debate. The consensus that seems to have emerged is that direct, quantitative controls should be avoided, but that indirect, price-based controls such as nonremunerated reserve requirements on banks or firms may be effective in limiting short-term capital inflows by increasing their cost. The case of Chile has shown that indirect, cost-based controls can be effective in influencing the maturity of capital inflows, if not their total volume.[42]

Summary and Conclusion

The second reform of the IFA focused specifically on the needs of developing and emerging market economies in meeting the challenges of financial globalization. Unlike the first reform that addressed issues of international monetary reform and the interests of both advanced countries and developing countries, the second reform focused on the needs of developing economies in responding to the growth of financial globalization as reflected in a series of devastating financial crises that threatened the stability of the international financial system. The reform essentially tried to address the question of how the risks of financial globalization could be minimized for these countries through improvements in the capacity of the IFA to handle crisis management and crisis prevention. As in the first reform, the IMF was at the center of debate on how the IFA should be reformed. The creation of the FSF was an important innovation within the architecture that was intended to strengthen the regulatory and other infrastructural foundations of the international financial system. The G7 ministerial group guided the process of reform and formed a new group (the G20) in 1999 to include the largest emerging market countries in a common forum that could advise on certain aspects of reform.

The approach adopted in the second reform of the IFA was one of "adaptive incrementalism" rather than major architectural redesign. Changes were made in the operations and coordination of existing institutions with a view to minimizing the risk of future financial crises and improving the capacity of the Fund to manage them. In the area of crisis management, the Fund's role as an international lender of last resort was considerably expanded. Access limits on the use of Fund resources were substantially increased in response to the needs of each crisis case as it unfolded during the second half of the 1990s. This action by the Fund led to an active debate on how to deal with the potential problem of "moral hazard" in IMF lending. One result was a clarification of the conditions in which "exceptional access" lending would be provided. In this connection, the nature of Fund conditionality in its crisis lending was also examined, especially as regards the scope and content of structural conditions attached to Fund financial arrangements. The other response was to clarify expectations about the burden sharing of private creditors (so-called private sector involvement or PSI) in each case in which the IMF was providing "exceptional access" financing. One aspect of this response was a reexamination of the arrangements for sovereign debt workouts with private creditors, which traditionally have been managed in an ad hoc, informal manner without significant involvement of the official sector. Initially, the G7 authorities were open to the idea of establishing within the IFA a formal mechanism to handle debt problems, and a formal Sovereign Debt Restructuring Mechanism operating in association with the IMF was actively considered. However, with resistance from private sector creditors and lack of enthusiasm from the US Treasury, this proposal was rejected in favor of a continuation of an ad hoc informal approach.

In the area of crisis prevention, the approach adopted by the G7 was to improve the flow of information to financial market participants and the financial conditions in emerging market economies with a view to making the international financial system operate more effectively. In this respect, financial crises were viewed as a manifestation of information asymmetries in the international financial system and structural weaknesses in the financial sectors of those countries wishing to participate in the global financial system. To deal with the first issue, efforts were made to improve the transparency of IMF surveillance through the publication of its country reports and to establish standards for the timely publication by countries of essential statistics regarding their economic and financial position. IMF surveillance was expected to be improved by a sharper focus on the policy and structural deficiencies in member countries' financial sectors and a new focus on global financial stability. To guide countries in the improvement of their financial sectors, the FSF was created in 1999 to work with the IMF and World Bank and a number of Basel-based organizations on the development and implementation of twelve core standards and codes to improve policy transparency and financial market integrity, in particular in the emerging market countries.

The second reform of the IFA did not address directly the gap in the architecture as regards oversight of the international financial system. The proposed capital account amendment of the Fund Agreement would have placed that responsibility formally within the IMF, but this constitutional change was seen as premature in the light of the financial crises that were occurring at the time of its consideration. The IMF and BIS would continue to share informal responsibilities in this area, along with the newly established FSF. However, a clear division of labor and lines of decision making were left unspecified.

CHAPTER 6

The Challenge for Developing Countries in a World of Financial Globalization

The expansion of financial globalization to encompass a number of middle-income countries after the mid-1980s has raised a number of challenges not only for those countries, but also for other developing countries that have not participated in this expansion. The onset of financial globalization has also posed a challenge for the role of official development finance, as private flows to developing countries since the early 1990s have risen to a level well in excess of ODA flows from bilateral and multilateral sources. Within the IFA, the role of official development finance is to fill a missing market in the channeling of financial resources to those developing countries that do not have access to international capital markets. This gap has been filled predominantly by the World Bank, along with other multilateral development banks, and by official bilateral aid flows. The IMF has also been called on to play a role in development finance, although its net contribution has been relatively small in relation to other institutional players. This chapter examines first the changing pattern of private capital flows to developing countries and then the challenge for low-income countries and the official aid community arising from the growing influence of private capital flows.[1]

The Rise of Private Capital Flows to Developing Countries

The previous chapter highlighted the dramatic surge in private capital flows that occurred during the 1990s following the resolution of the debt crises of the 1980s through the use of securitized finance that opened the door to foreign bond placements by emerging market countries. That experience revealed a continuing characteristic of private capital flows to developing countries regarding their volatility and procyclicality, which were often associated with devastating financial crises in recipient countries.

Through the end of the Bretton Woods era, capital flows to developing countries were dominated by official loans and bilateral aid. This pattern was abruptly changed during the second half of the 1970s with a surge in private banking flows to many developing countries with the recycling of petrodollars, as discussed in the previous chapter. This was the first big wave of private capital flows to the developing countries, but 80 percent of these flows were accounted for by only fifteen countries, mainly in Asia and Latin America. During the 1980s, capital flows to developing countries were roughly evenly divided between private and official flows, as banks began a period of withdrawal from the practice of general purpose lending to sovereigns (figure 6.1). As a result, the main component of private flows was foreign direct investment. Compared with private portfolio flows, foreign direct investment has been much more stable in its rising trend over time. However, it has been heavily skewed in favor of the large middle-income countries; during the 1990s, the top ten recipients received, on average, around two-thirds of total FDI flows, while Brazil, China, and Mexico accounted for roughly half. Six of the ten largest recipients of FDI were also the largest in terms of FDI flows relative to GDP, while seven of the ten were among the largest developing country exporters.[2] However, during the most recent surge in private capital flows to developing countries since 2002, FDI flows began to spread more widely among developing countries.

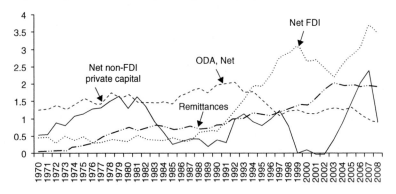

Figure 6.1 Flow of private capital, official aid, and remittances to developing countries (as percent of GDP)

Source: World Bank, World Development Indicators (WDI); OECD.stat

During the 1980s and 1990s, two distinct patterns of FDI flows to the large middle-income countries could be detected. The first, which was typical of East Asia, was "efficiency-seeking" and involved the development of export platforms for large multinational corporations in high-technology industries such as electronics and telecommunications. East Asian countries were particularly successful in integrating with the global economy through their participation in large, vertically integrated production or marketing chains, which have come to dominate global trade and production. Their success represents a challenge to other developing countries in view of the first-mover advantages that they have gained from the development of local technological capabilities and technology clusters, which act as a magnet for continued, strong FDI inflows.

The other pattern of FDI flows, which was typical of Latin America, was "market-seeking" and related to the development of a large domestic presence by multinational corporations in local consumer markets or the exploitation of natural resources. Much of this FDI took the form of mergers and acquisitions, as distinct from "greenfield" investment in new activities, and was motivated by a wave of privatization and the lifting of restrictions on foreign bank activity and investment in natural resources that took place in the wake of the debt crisis of the 1980s. After 1994 and the finalization of NAFTA, Mexico diverged from this regional pattern and began to benefit from efficiency-seeking investment of North American multinationals in its automobile and electronics sectors.

The pattern for other non-FDI flows to developing countries has been similar to that of FDI, in that a major share (approximately 75 percent) of these flows has been allocated to the same ten largest recipients of FDI, given their larger market size and stronger investment climate. However, they have been far more volatile than FDI flows to developing countries, as reflected most recently in their surge during the years before the recent global financial crisis and their sudden drop during late 2008 and 2009.

Since the early 1990s, it is also important to note the emergence of remittances as a new form of cross-border resource flow to developing countries, along with the rising weight of private capital flows. During the period 2005–7, the flow of remittances was roughly equivalent to the flow of private capital, although the distribution of these two resource streams is quite distinct. Remittances have also grown to a large multiple of official aid flows in recent years. Remittances represent a major source of foreign exchange receipts for many developing countries and thus provide an important private safety net that has helped to alleviate poverty in recipient countries. They also constitute a form of private social insurance for countries that have been afflicted by economic and financial crises.[3] However, remittances have also provided an important mechanism for financing terrorism and money laundering that have received increased attention after 2001 by the Financial Action Task Force (FATF), which was set up in Paris at the OECD in 1989 to coordinate activities at the national level to limit financial transactions in support of drug trafficking and terrorist financing. Since the terrorist attacks of 2001, countries have been strongly encouraged under the international standards and codes initiative of the FSF to adopt the recommendations of the FATF on anti-money laundering and combating the financing of terrorism in regard to the operations of both banking institutions and informal remittance-service providers.

The problem of financial crises in the 1990s and the failure of the proposed capital account amendment to the Fund Agreement in 1997–98 have engendered an active research program on the costs and benefits of financial globalization for developing countries and the appropriate sequencing of capital account liberalization. The simple fact that most poor countries have capital account restrictions and most advanced countries do not have suggests that there are certain advantages from financial globalization that accrue to countries at a certain stage in the process of development. These can be deduced from certain tenets of neoclassical economic theory, as discussed in chapter 2 of this book. A good example of the literature on the benefits of financial globalization is a book by Frederick Mishkin (2006) entitled *The Next Wave of Globalization: How Disadvantaged Countries Can Harness Their Financial Systems to Get Rich*. He points to three benefits in particular: one is that financial integration lowers the cost of capital that promotes investment that, in turn, leads to higher growth; a second is that the entry of foreign capital and financial institutions can improve the allocation of capital within the recipient country; and third, the globalization of the domestic financial system promotes the development of stronger property rights and institutions that helps the financial system to function more effectively. In addition, one can point to the potential transfer of technological know-how through financial integration, which can yield benefits in terms of productivity gains.

Notwithstanding these potential benefits of financial integration, there is little systematic empirical evidence on the benefits of capital account liberalization for developing countries that has been able to validate the theoretical claims advanced in its favor. In one recent survey of the literature by Kose et al (2009), the authors concluded that there is no robust evidence on the positive association of financial globalization and economic growth among developing countries. They also could not find any evidence of international consumption risk-sharing arising from the increased trade in financial assets by developing countries, as the volatility of consumption in relation to aggregate income increased for this group of countries during the 1990s. This same study did show that among the developing countries, those countries that were more financially integrated tended to exhibit higher rates of economic growth than those that were less financially integrated. However, in the case of more financially integrated countries, the authors of the study concluded that it was difficult to reject the case of reverse causality, as high growth countries may simply choose to be more financially integrated. In any event, it is clear from the experience of China and India that substantial integration with international capital markets is not a necessary condition for rapid economic growth.

On a more disaggregated basis, it is possible to detect certain benefits from financial integration on economic growth arising from the liberalization of foreign direct investment and domestic equity markets, although the strength of these effects may be contingent on a certain threshold of financial or institutional development. In the latter case, for example, there is clear evidence that when developing countries liberalize portfolio flows into their local stock markets, the cost of capital falls and investment increases along with the growth rate of GDP per capita.[4] Another variant on the studies cited earlier is that the benefits of financial integration on economic growth in developing countries may be more indirect in that they operate through certain "collateral" effects of improved governance and institutions, as well as enhanced discipline over macroeconomic policies, which themselves have been shown to be determinants of economic growth.[5]

In any event, the experience of financial crises in the 1990s and the subsequent academic literature have yielded a consensus view that there are certain preconditions for capital account liberalization that developing countries should satisfy for the benefits of financial globalization to be realized. These can be expressed in terms of a reasonable degree of macroeconomic stability and a sustainable fiscal position, a sound financial regulatory regime, and strong property rights. There is also now a strong presumption in favor of sequencing capital account liberalization, beginning with the liberalization of foreign direct investment, followed by the opening of local equity markets and freedom of other long-term portfolio inflows. The liberalization of outward capital flows by local residents and short-term capital movements should come at a final stage when the domestic financial system is well developed and a robust regulatory regime is in place.

In this context, the experience of China and India is instructive. Both countries have followed a gradual process of domestic financial liberalization and integration with global financial markets, which has shielded them from the severe contagion effects of financial crises in the 1990s and the global financial crisis of 2008-9. China has been a strong magnet for foreign direct investment that has supported the integration of its local manufacturing into international production chains. Both countries began a process of financial opening in the late 1980s on a gradual and calibrated basis, but they remain still below the average of emerging market economies in terms of de facto measures of financial globalization. However, they are above the average for that group in terms of the share of FDI and portfolio equity liabilities in total external liabilities. Foreign capital outflows by domestic residents and businesses are more tightly controlled than corresponding inflows.[6] Only recently have these countries permitted the entry of foreign banks into local financial markets.

The development of local financial markets is one of the most important steps developing countries can take to promote sound economic development and to prepare the ground for their eventual integration with international financial markets.[7] At the early stages of the development process, financial systems in developing countries are predominantly bank-centered. Banks play an essential role in mobilizing financial savings and in identifying and monitoring worthwhile projects for investment in conditions of weak information and control mechanisms that make it difficult for savers and investors to come together directly through equity placements and bond contracts. The problem of asymmetric information, which is inherent in financial markets, biases financial markets in developing countries toward debt and away from private equity and toward bank debt as distinct from other forms of debt contracts such as bonds, notes, and commercial paper. It also biases debt contracts toward short terms of maturity, which limit the risk exposure of banks and other investors.[8]

Governments have an essential role to play in promoting sound banking systems through the support of the necessary infrastructure in the form of accounting, legal, and corporate governance arrangements and the development of an effective regulatory and supervisory regime. In this connection, the joint IMF-World Bank Financial Sector Assessment Program (FSAP), which was initiated in 1999 with the second reform of the IFA, has played a beneficial and useful role in promoting improvements in the banking and financial systems of a large number of developing countries. During the first decade of its existence, 108 developing countries had participated in the FSAP, which provided an assessment of the financial risks and vulnerabilities in these countries, as well as an evaluation of the degree to which domestic regulatory regimes complied with the core international standards and codes listed in table 5.3 that were developed as a result of the second reform of the IFA. These assessments have triggered in most cases follow-up technical assistance from the Bank and Fund in areas of bank supervision or financial market infrastructure.[9]

Governments also have a critical role to play in promoting broader financial market development through the establishment of stable macroeconomic conditions and the pursuit of sound public finance. More specifically, the promotion of a market for government bonds in such conditions can spur the development of a local private bond market, as the yields for different maturities of government debt can serve as benchmarks for the pricing of corporate debt. With time, the development of local bond markets can attract foreign investors, thus allowing countries to escape the problem of "original sin," which was identified in the previous chapter as one of the causes of the financial crises of the 1990s. The Asian Bond Initiative, supported by the Asian Development Bank, provides a successful example of this approach, through which many central banks in the East Asia and Pacific region created a pool of reserves to invest in local currency sovereign debt in eight regional markets.[10]

Within the last decade, bond markets in emerging market economies have grown rapidly, with the outstanding stock of domestic bonds reaching the equivalent of approximately US$6 trillion at the end of 2008, compared with US$1 trillion in the mid-1990s.[11] More than 95 percent of the debt outstanding at the end of 2008 was denominated in local currency. In this connection, it is also interesting to note that emerging market economies have also increased the share of local currency-denominated debt in their international bond placements, even though these amounts are relatively small in relation to local bond placements. According to BIS statistics, of the total bonds and notes issued internationally by emerging market economies outstanding at the end of 2008, around 16 percent or US$157 million was denominated in local currency.

The Role of Official Development Finance in a World of Financial Globalization

Given the highly skewed nature of financial flows to developing countries and the concentration of FDI in the middle-income countries, what is the appropriate role for official development finance? More broadly, what role can the IFA play in promoting sound development of low-income countries and in facilitating their gradual integration in global financial markets?

Globally, it is essential that the IFA foster stability of the global financial system and an effective balance of payments adjustment mechanism among systemically important countries to support a sustained expansion of world trade and foreign investment flows that are conducive to the sustained growth of developing countries. At the same time, procedures and safeguards need to be in place to minimize the possibility of financial crises, which have been highly costly for developing countries in terms of output loss and public debt burdens. But these efforts alone will not be enough to ensure the full integration of low-income countries into the globalized economy. Targeted assistance through official aid is required to alleviate poverty and to help developing countries foster the conditions that would attract foreign direct investment and other long-term capital flows. Given the growing size of private financial flows to developing countries in relation to official flows, the burden on the effectiveness of development assistance is even greater.

Unfortunately, the overall record of development assistance has not been a positive one. Notwithstanding the large cumulative amounts of official aid that have been provided to developing countries since 1960 (around US$2 trillion according to the OECD), it is difficult to establish empirically any positive association between development assistance and economic growth.[12] (By contrast, high rates of economic growth have been shown to be strongly correlated with significant poverty alleviation.) One of the more recent attempts to find a link between aid and growth (Rajan and Subramanian 2008) shows that the finding of no link is robust across a number of empirical specifications and controls. There may be a number of reasons that can account for this result. One is that not all aid is given for economic development purposes; some of it is humanitarian or for reconstruction, while other cases show that it has been given for political reasons to support a regime that is favorable to the donor country. In addition, there are many cases where development loans have been provided to countries, despite a poor track record of performance, in part to enable the repayment of past loans. These are the cases that have qualified for official debt cancellation from the IMF and World Bank under the Multilateral Debt Relief Initiative of 2005 (see the following text). More specifically, Rajan and Subramanian show that development assistance in a number of cases has been associated with an overvaluation of a recipient country's currency, thus frustrating export development, which can be a powerful inducement to growth.

Another recent empirical finding that has cast doubt on the effect of development assistance is that many of the high-growth success cases in economic development have not been heavily reliant on foreign capital inflows, be they private or official, as they have been able to generate high levels of domestic savings during the development process.[13] Many of the high growth cases of East Asia (including China) come to mind in this context, which pursued an export-led development strategy that made them less reliant on external financing than countries in Africa and Latin America. This result suggests the implication that in many developing countries the constraint on economic development is not so much the availability of domestic savings, but rather limits on investment. In cases where domestic savings has not been a constraint on development, the provision of foreign financing or development assistance has simply led to an increase in consumption and higher imports or a rapid expansion in domestic credit for speculative activity, which often laid the ground for a financial crisis.

As a result of these kinds of studies, which have cast serious doubt on the effectiveness of past development assistance, an active debate has been running within the official and academic communities on the right approaches to development and the appropriate conditions for successful development. One manifestation of this debate is the dispute between development aid advocates such as Jeffrey Sachs, who strongly recommend a top-down or "planners" approach to economic development, and development skeptics such as Bill Easterly who advocate a bottom-up or "searchers" approach to development.[14]

An example of the former approach, in Easterly's view, was the U.N. Millennium Development Goals (MDGs) of 2000. Professor Sachs has been a passionate advocate of scaled-up assistance to support improvements in health and education levels in poor countries, as called for in the MDGs, for these countries to break out of their "poverty trap."[15] On the opposite side, Easterly argues that the top-down approach of the MDGs is simply one more example of failed attempts at development planning, which foreign aid has supported in the past with demonstrably poor results, as discussed earlier. Dambisa Moyo in her popular bestseller, *Dead Aid*, makes a similar case. Instead, Easterly recommends a more limited, bottom-up approach in support of "searchers" or development entrepreneurs in low-income countries who initiate changes at the grass-roots level to empower poor people and enable them to improve their livelihoods. Muhammad Yunus, the 2006 Nobel Peace Laureate who started a revolution in microcredit in Bangladesh, and Greg Mortenson, the founder of the Central Asia Institute that supports girls' education in poor communities of Afghanistan and Pakistan, come to mind as examples of development "searchers."[16]

Development aid critics such as Easterly and Moyo would argue that much of the development assistance generated through World Bank loans and grants, IMF concessional lending, and bilateral aid programs in the post–World War II era has been characterized by top-down approaches with largely failed results in terms of gains in per capital income for the recipient countries. However, such a critique ignores the positive results of development assistance that has supported sustained income gains and poverty alleviation in many Asian countries through macroeconomic policy reforms, the application of the "green" revolution, and investment in critical infrastructure (port facilities, power generation, and transportation networks). In addition, development aid has supported successful campaigns to eradicate river blindness in Africa and polio in Latin America, while major progress is being made in the control of malaria in many poor countries with the support of private and official sources of aid. Nevertheless, there is also clear evidence of development aid failures, for example in countries such as Zaire and Zambia, where development assistance was provided on a continued basis to governments that had a poor record of policy reform, or in conditions where aid funds were wasted through corruption and mismanagement.

To some extent, the mixed record of development assistance reflects significant changes in official views of major development institutions such as the World Bank about the critical ingredients for successful development outcomes. Initially, in the early post–World War II period, the theory of the "Big Push" was popular, which assigned a key role to government action in promoting public investment in physical infrastructure and in helping to overcome coordination problems in private investment. This led to an important emphasis in Bank lending on basic infrastructure projects and the support of investment in new plant and equipment, which came to be associated with the idea of "capital fundamentalism."[17] Later in the 1960s, the focus of Bank policy and lending shifted to the agricultural sector and the challenge of rural poverty as key bottlenecks in the development process. With the emergence of the international debt crisis in the early 1980s, as noted in chapter 5, the emphasis in Bank lending and policy shifted to an emphasis on macroeconomic fundamentals ("getting the prices rights") and structural adjustment, as defined by the "Washington Consensus." More recently, at the turn of the century the focus of the Bank's development policy lending has shifted to good governance and sound institutions (e.g., the protection of property rights) as critical features of the development process, consistent with a reorientation of academic development studies toward an emphasis on the "deep determinants" of growth.[18] Each of these shifts in development practice was marked by the recognition that the prevailing view of development priorities was incomplete and inadequate in eliminating the obstacles to economic growth of low-income countries.[19]

Along with these paradigm shifts guiding development practice, one can also trace a marked evolution of thinking in academic and official circles about the appropriate roles of the state and the market in the development process. Initially, in the post–World War II era, problems of market failure were seen as the major obstacle to the economic development of poor countries, which could be overcome only by significant government intervention, for example in helping to coordinate private investment. A benevolent view of government activism was grounded in the experience of the Great Depression, wartime planning, and early industrialization under Soviet planning. Beginning in the 1970s, a counterrevolution began to emerge, based on studies of East Asia's export-led growth experience, which argued that government failures were more important than market failures and that government policy itself had often been an obstacle to development. Over time, this thinking was crystallized in the principles of the "Washington Consensus" that envisaged a much-reduced role for government in the development process in favor of greater weight for the role of market forces in guiding economic development.[20] This shift was also supported by the "public choice" school of economic thinking, which changed the idealized view of government as a detached, rational actor in decision making to one in which government decisions were significantly influenced by private agents and institutions. The concept of "rent-seeking" as an outcome of private-public interaction is an example of this approach.[21]

More recently, something of a synthesis in thinking about the roles of the state and market can be seen in the World Bank's approach to economic development. Instead of a view of the state and marketplace in conflict, this view recognizes that both must be seen as complements. This idea is most fully articulated in a book by Nicholas Stern, who was chief economist of the World Bank during 2000–2003, entitled *Growth and Empowerment*, which identifies the promotion of human development and a sound investment climate as critical objectives for the Bank's policy work and lending. This simple conception of the development challenge combines the critical role of the government in promoting a sound institutional framework for private initiative and investment and the effective delivery of basic social services to improve the welfare and capabilities of poor people.

As approaches to development practice have evolved in institutions such as the World Bank, its views about development policy have become somewhat less prescriptive. One example of this tendency is an important study by the Bank published in 2005 on *Economic Growth in the 1990s: Learning from a Decade of Reform*. In that study, the Bank concluded that the uneven growth record in low-income and transition countries since the late 1980s demonstrated that the general principles that guide development policy and practice do not translate directly into positive development results, and that these principles need to be adapted to specific, local conditions, often in an experimental fashion. This study was followed up by a three-year exercise sponsored by the Bank under the so-called Growth Commission, which comprised a panel of prominent officials from leading developing countries and a few academic experts, to determine the key ingredients of successful development outcomes. The commission examined the development experience of thirteen countries (mostly from the East Asian region) that had sustained the longest record of high growth in per capita income (in excess of 5 percent in real terms). In its final report released in 2008, the commission essentially endorsed the agnostic approach reflected in the 2005 study cited earlier and refrained from any strong prescriptive recommendations on economic development. It identified many common elements among the strong growth performers, such as an emphasis on educational attainment, export orientation, sound finance, and effective public administration, but did not attempt to provide specific approaches or roadmaps for replicating their experience.[22] On the basis of these studies, one can conclude that, in a world in which each country must find its own path to development, there is clearly much room for "searchers" or development entrepreneurs.

A parallel shift from top-down to bottom-up approaches can also be detected in the field of development research. Often in the past, guidance on development policy was drawn from aggregate level, macroeconomic growth studies, which examined the association between the level or growth in per capita income among a cross-section of countries and various explanatory variables such as trade openness, financial depth, and institutional strength. The results of such research have guided some of the shifting focus of development practice in institutions such as the World Bank, for example in its emphasis on improving the investment climate and the effectiveness of government institutions. More recently, however, the validity of this research has been questioned because of the large number of explanatory variables under study and the difficulties of establishing causality in a statistical model. An alternative methodology, which was pioneered by the MIT Poverty Action Lab (that was established in 2003), has emphasized a more microeconomic or bottom-up approach of using randomized control trials (RCT) in the design of social policy interventions, for example, to improve local schooling and health conditions in low-income countries. This new approach was inspired by the practice of randomized trials, comparing control and treatment groups, by government agencies such as the Food and Drug Administration in its approval of new drugs for the US market.

There has been some experimentation in the World Bank in the use of this new approach to the design of certain social assistance programs, such as conditional cash transfer programs in Latin America. Under these programs, which were pioneered in Mexico, cash assistance grants to poor families are conditioned on evidence that parents have met certain requirements regarding school attendance and preventive health care for their primary school age children. These programs, which have been widely replicated throughout Latin America, have benefited from the initial use of RCT to confirm that such interventions, with careful preparation and monitoring, can increase school enrollment, while improving preventive health care and raising household consumption.

The use of RCT in development studies is not without its critics in the academic community, as evidenced by a recent conference volume of the Brookings Institution (Cohen and Easterly 2009). But both the positive results on the ground and the attention that some of the main proponents of RCT, such as Esther Duflo (the codirector of the Poverty Action Lab), have received suggest that this approach has been a positive innovation in development economics.[23]

At a more global level, the technique of RCT can be applied to the design of programs to achieve some of the MDGs. The achievement of universal primary education in developing countries, for example, needs to be mediated through specific experiments that show positive results at reasonable cost. Project design based on RCT has demonstrated the positive impact on school attendance of certain interventions associated with the supply of free meals, textbooks, or basic immunization.

The evaluation of aid and lending programs can also benefit from the use of RCT. Often in the past, aid effectiveness has been determined on the basis of goods and services delivered to schools and clinics or the fulfillment of certain prescribed procedures, without consideration of the direct effect of aid on educational and health outcomes of poor families. With guidance from trained academics and financial assistance from abroad, staff from local nongovernmental organizations (NGOs) in developing countries could be employed in conducting such evaluations.

On the basis of the above consideration of top-down and bottom-up approaches to development, it would appear that there is some merit in trying to combine both approaches in an effort to improve development assistance. The identification of the MDGs was certainly a worthwhile endeavor in forging a universal consensus on appropriate goals to be achieved in the international effort to reduce severe inequalities among countries and deep poverty in the global economy. At the same time, it should be recognized that implementation of the MDGs will be enhanced if efforts are made within aid-recipient countries to identify development entrepreneurs at the local level who are able to devise practical and effective ways of improving the livelihoods of poor communities. In addition, aid effectiveness can be improved if sufficient resources are allocated to impact studies that make use of RCT and other evaluative techniques to determine the success or failure of aid efforts at the local level.

New Approaches to Official Debt Restructuring

Another area of active controversy in development assistance has been the issue of official debt relief, which has focused prominently on the work of the Paris Club. As noted in chapter 5, during the first thirty years of its existence, the Paris Club approach to sovereign defaults of official debt (both ODA and non-ODA) was to offer so-called classic terms of rescheduling of interest and principal repayments during a period of up to two years covered by an IMF financial arrangement. With the emergence of the "Brady Plan" of discounted debt exchanges for commercial bank loans in arrears, the Paris Club began to experiment with debt cancellation arrangements, first in regard to debt service payments during the period 1988–91 and then for the stock of debt beginning in 1994. As in the case of commercial bank indebtedness, there was a gradual realization among the G7/8 leaders and Paris Club creditors that debt rescheduling of official credits was insufficient to restore economic viability to many of the low-income countries, and that debt restructuring (including debt cancellation) was required.

In 1996, a further bold departure was agreed at the Lyons G7 Summit to introduce the HIPC (Heavily Indebted Poor Country) Initiative for forty-one of the most severely indebted poor countries (mostly in Africa), which included debt reduction on Paris Club credits of up to 90 percent. In 1999, this initiative was linked to a major revision of IMF and World Bank concessional lending to low-income countries under the Poverty Reduction and Growth Strategy (PRGS). The development of the PRGS within the Bank and Fund was a recognition of the failure of much of their concessional lending during the previous two decades. It also marked a reorientation of their lending to poor countries to focus on cases where governments demonstrated clear ownership of economic development programs and a broad participatory process was pursued to establish national commitment to the program. Debt relief under the enhanced HIPC Initiative was directly linked to the development of Poverty Reduction Strategy Papers (PRSPs) by low-income debtors that became the basis for determining IMF-World Bank financial support based on a careful assessment of debt sustainability and a comprehensive policy program to support long-term development objectives.

This new approach to debt sustainability for low-income countries was expanded in 2005 with the Multilateral Debt Relief Initiative (MDRI) agreed to at the Gleneagles G8 Summit that led to agreement in the IMF and World Bank (as well as the African Development Bank and the Inter-American Development Bank) to cancel, for the first time, up to 90 percent of their claims on the forty-one countries included in the HIPC initiative. The losses from these debt operations would be covered by a portion of the profits arising from the sale of some of the Fund's gold reserves and by a combination of special donations and profit transfers in the case of the World Bank.

The Future of Development Assistance

Given the World Bank's central role in development assistance within the IFA, it is worthwhile considering the implications of the foregoing discussion for its operations. It is the largest multilateral development institution in terms of its loan portfolio and is the largest single source of official development finance within a complex array of bilateral and multilateral development institutions.

Aid coordination has been a continuing concern within the field of development assistance and has become much more difficult with the proliferation of donor agencies, both public and private. Poor coordination among donors and the associated burden on recipient countries must be seen as one reason for the weak results of aid disbursements, noted earlier. At the multilateral level, the Bank has wholeheartedly embraced the MDGs as a modus vivendi for its operations, but in each of the eight targeted areas of the MDGs, the Bank is executing programs that have significant overlap with activities of other UN agencies such as FAO, ILO, UNESCO, and WHO. At the very least, there should be an interagency task force among these bodies that helps to ensure effective coordination in program design, implementation, and evaluation. Each of these agencies should also be represented in the Development Committee, and the work of the UN System in supporting the MDGs should be given more attention in its deliberations.[24]

At the country level, coordination of aid activities has been assisted by the development of PRSPs since 1999, noted earlier, as a framework supporting all IMF-World Bank lending to poor countries, not only those covered by the HIPC initiative. The PRSP process has significantly raised the expectations on developing countries in terms of country ownership and local participation with respect to previous experience to improve development outcomes. The PRSPs are intended to be fully linked with the MDGs, and thus can provide a convenient umbrella under which other donor agencies can coordinate their activity. The Bank should seek to strengthen its role as a coordinator of donor activity that it has been doing with the formation of country-level donor assistance groups and the development of sector-wide approaches to lending programs that seek to incorporate financing from other agencies in the design of its own development assistance. A particular challenge for the Bank in this regard is the growth of South-South lending by countries such as China, which has grown rapidly in recent years, in particular in the African region. In these cases, the Bank should develop cofinancing arrangements where it would be able to bring its technical expertise and country knowledge to bear to improve the targeting and coordination of this new form of development assistance.

Given the special needs of low-income countries and the increasing access of middle-income countries to private financial flows, the Bank should reduce the share of its lending to the latter group and increase the size of its loans and grants to the former group. During the first half of the last decade, nearly 70 percent of the Bank's regular lending was allocated to nine of the largest developing economies such as Brazil, China, India, Mexico, and Turkey. Many of these same countries were also accumulating large foreign asset positions abroad during this period, which also raises questions about the appropriateness of such lending. Some continued involvement of the Bank in these countries can be justified because of the importance of poverty reduction programs in many of these countries and the volatility of private capital flows.

As a complement to its conventional lending, the Bank should do more to help mitigate the risks for developing countries arising from volatility associated with terms of trade shocks, natural disasters, and disruptions in global credit markets. Although it is the primary role of the IMF to provide liquidity in the face of capital flow reversals, the Bank could help to mitigate the procyclicality of private financial flows by adopting a countercyclical role for its lending by offering loans with state-contingent disbursements.[25] The Bank has experimented with the use of loans with a deferred drawdown option as a contingent line of credit, which could be expanded. The Bank should also be expanding its work in developing countries to assist with the development of local currency bond markets as a hedge against the risk of borrowing in foreign currencies ("original sin"). One promising initiative in this area, which should be expanded, is the World Bank/IFC-sponsored Global Emerging Market Local Currency Bond Market Fund (GEMLOC) that is composed of a portfolio of local currency sovereign and corporate bonds from a number of merging market economies. The Bank could also help to develop a market for GDP-indexed debt for developing countries, which would allow interest rates to vary in line with terms of trade shocks or deviations of GDP growth from some normal trend.

Another area where the Bank should be refocusing its lending practices is in the area of financing for global programs, in particular for disease eradication, environmental protection, and climate change mitigation. In recent years, a proliferation of separate trust funds (around 200) have been established in the Bank by different donors to deal with specific aspects of these issues without clear direction or priority-setting by the management and Board of the Bank. Some of these funds could be consolidated, and a strategy for the Bank's involvement in the financing of global programs should be established with clearer links to the Bank's more traditional country assistance strategies. More generally, the expansion of trust funds, which number in excess of 1,000, that are administered by the Bank on behalf of a number of donor countries and agencies to support specific programs in developing countries provided disbursements prior to the recent global crisis that were equivalent to around one-third of normal IBRD/IDA disbursements to these countries. The proliferation of these funds runs the risk of increasing problems of coordination and fragmentation within the Bank's lending activities with low-income countries.[26]

In the light of concerns raised about aid effectiveness and the evaluation of development assistance in the previous section of this chapter, the Bank should be devoting more time and resources to the issue of program evaluation and impact assessments in the design of social assistance. With the development of new approaches such as RCT in the design of social assistance programs, more efforts should be made to strengthen the role of impact evaluation in Bank projects. Generally, the Bank has been faulted over the years for its culture of lending that has emphasized loan disbursements over program monitoring and evaluation.

The Bank has its own in-house evaluation office (Independent Evaluation Group-IEG) that does a range of long-term assessments of Bank programs, but the independence of this group can be questioned given its reliance on regular Bank staff for the conduct of its work and its practice of reviewing draft assessments with concerned staff and country authorities before conclusion. Because of these limitations, there has been a strong call from many participants in the development community for an outside evaluation group to assess the effectiveness of Bank lending programs.[27] Such a group would not be a substitute for in-house assessment work to develop good practice guidelines for various kinds of development programs based on Bank experience or the use of RCT in the design of lending programs.

Closely related to the evaluative function within the Bank is its role in research and technical assistance. The Bank prides itself on being a "knowledge bank" and plays a major role in shaping national and international debate on development issues through its research, advisory, and training functions. Since 1978, its flagship publication, the World Development Report, has been a principal instrument for shaping official views on key aspects of the development agenda. Some of these reports have been widely praised for their pioneering efforts in developing new benchmarks for cross-country comparisons, for example, in the measurement of poverty or the business and investment climate in developing countries. However, in a major external review of its research work, the Bank was criticized for erring too much on the side of policy advocacy in some of its research work, for example, on aid effectiveness, even when the empirical methods and results of that work were open to serious question and challenge. This same evaluation criticized the Bank for not devoting adequate resources to the analysis and evaluation of its own lending programs to determine what works and does not work in development practice.[28] The Bank's IEG has raised similar concerns about weak monitoring and evaluation of the Bank's analytical and advisory services (economic and sector work and nonlending technical assistance) and its training activities.[29]

To strengthen effectively the role of the World Bank in development assistance, serious attention also needs to be given to its governance arrangements, as regards political oversight, leadership selection, and power sharing within the institution. These issues apply as well to the IMF, given the similarity of their governance arrangements. Governance reform of the Bretton Woods institutions is a key aspect of the current reform of the IFA, which is taken up in chapter 9 of this book.

Given the primary and dominant role of the Bank in development assistance, it is appropriate to ask what role, if any, the IMF should play in this area. Even though the IMF has been involved in development assistance since the first reform of the IFA, there is good reason to question whether this is an appropriate role for the central monetary institution in the global system. The Fund's primary responsibility lies in the area of bilateral and multilateral surveillance and oversight of global financial stability. Net disbursements of long-term concessional lending by the IMF through its Poverty Reduction and Growth Facility have been relatively modest in recent years, especially in comparison with those of the multilateral development banks, and could be easily absorbed by the World Bank whose primary mission is development assistance.[30] Pressures for financial involvement of the IMF in developing countries have arisen mainly from the desire of other agencies to have the Fund's endorsement of a developing country's macroeconomic policy framework, which has usually been signaled by its approval of a financial arrangement for that country. However, with the development of the Policy Support Instrument in 2005, the Fund began to provide its imprimatur for a country's macroeconomic policy framework in a formal way without entering into a long-term financial arrangement. Developing countries needing temporary assistance from the Fund because of terms of trade shocks or natural disasters could also access the Fund's Exogenous Shocks Facility, which was established in 2005 and was further modified in 2008 and 2009 to increase its flexibility of use and ease of access. In addition, short-term balance of payments assistance could still be provided by the Fund to low-income countries on concessional terms.[31]

Summary and Conclusion

Since the late 1980s, financial globalization has extended to a number of developing countries, particularly in East Asia, Central and Eastern Europe, and Latin America. This trend was dramatized by a number of spectacular financial crises in the 1990s among the main emerging market economies, as recounted in chapter 5. This trend has also been reflected in a sharp rise in foreign direct investment that has exhibited much less volatility than other forms of private capital flows, which were the trigger for those crises. However, the availability of these flows has tended to be concentrated in a number of large, middle-income countries, which poses a challenge for other developing countries and for the official development agencies that exist to assist them in taking advantage of the benefits of globalization.

The empirical literature on the experience of capital account liberalization of developing countries strongly suggests that this process must be managed in a cautious manner and conditioned on a number of domestic economic and financial reforms. This conclusion is buttressed by the fact that heavy reliance on external finance has not been a necessary ingredient in the experience of the high performing emerging market economies. This evidence also suggests that policies to promote domestic savings and sound local financial markets are more important at early stages of development than efforts to attract large private capital inflows. China and India provide examples of this gradualist approach, while benefiting from significant inflows of foreign direct investment.

The challenge for the official aid community is how to channel its development assistance in a way that supports the integration of the poorer countries into the global economic and financial system. Unfortunately, the record on aid effectiveness is mixed, at best. The increasing official debt burden for a number of developing countries during the last quarter of the previous century is testimony to this fact. Broad international agreement on the MDGs at the beginning of the new century, linked to Poverty Reduction and Growth Strategies supported by the IMF and World Bank and comprehensive debt relief for the most heavily indebted low-income countries, has provided a coherent framework to guide development assistance. However, this assistance needs to be well coordinated, targeted, and subject to careful evaluation, if it is to be effective.

The World Bank, as the premier development agency within the IFA, has a key role to play in helping to fulfill the promise of the new development framework just cited. Given the Bank's technical capacity to deal with a broad range of development challenges, its ability to mobilize financial resources on a large scale to fund its operations, and its in-depth knowledge of developing countries, it is in a unique position to catalyze and coordinate bilateral and other multilateral development assistance. The proliferation of donor country trust funds in the Bank, which involve a multiplicity of donors, recipients and development objectives, poses a particular challenge for the Bank in its coordination of development assistance. Other challenges for the Bank are to find the right balance in its operations with middle-income countries, which can access the international capital markets, and low-income countries that can not to the same degree, and the integration of its funding for so-called global programs (disease eradication, environmental protection, and climate change mitigation) with country-based lending. Another important area where improvements can be made is in linking the Bank's formidable research capacity to its operational work with a view to generating useful lessons from its development activities, through the greater use of impact evaluation studies using randomized trials and other empirical techniques.

CHAPTER 7

Financial Globalization and the Onset of the Global Financial Crisis of 2008–9

This chapter focuses on the antecedents and causes of the current financial crisis that erupted in the United States in mid-2007 and was then transformed into a global financial and economic crisis in September 2008. After the cascade of emerging market financial crises during 1994–2002 and the events surrounding the terrorist attacks of September 11, 2001, there was a period of relative calm in international financial markets. In this environment, a new wave of financial globalization unfolded that would intensify financial linkages among the advanced countries, as well as those between the advanced and emerging market economies.

These linkages spanned the entire spectrum of financial instruments, but were particularly strong in the case of banking system flows and trade in derivatives and structured financial products or securitized debt instruments. This period was also characterized by a sharp increase in the size of gross capital flows among the advanced countries, which represented a process of international portfolio diversification on the part of corporations, financial institutions and households, which was particularly dramatic in the case of the United States (figure 7.1). The development of the single financial market in the European Union beginning in 1999 unleashed a strong growth in cross-border financial flows in that region. On a global basis, cross-border capital flows rose from US$3 trillion in 2002 (around 8 percent of global GDP) to US$11 trillion in 2007 (21 percent of global GDP), of which more than half in the latter year were in the form of cross-border lending and deposits by banks, largely for maturities of less than one year.[1]

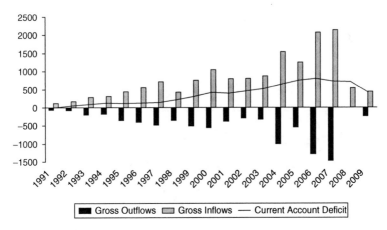

Figure 7.1   US Gross financial flows and current account deficit (US $ billions)
Source: US Bureau of Economic Analysis

Significantly, these developments in international investment were facilitated by an unprecedented growth in the cross-border activity of large bank holding groups, or large complex financial institutions, which operated across a range of financial services. In the United States, the emergence of these financial conglomerates can be traced to the Gramm-Leach-Bliley Act of 1999 that repealed the restrictions on commercial banks engaging in investment banking activities that had been in place for the previous sixty-six years. As a result, there was a growth in both the size and concentration of large financial service institutions: the share of total banking system assets controlled by the top three banks in the United States rose from approximately 10 percent in the mid-1990s to 40 percent by 2008.[2] A similar trend can be observed in Europe following the emergence of the single financial market in 1999.

This phase of financial globalization was also unique in that there was an unprecedented net flow of capital from developing to advanced countries, as several large industrial countries (in particular, the United States) increased their reliance on foreign borrowing to the highest level in relation to GDP during the post–World War II era. These various linkages described earlier were reflected in an unprecedented expansion of global imbalances from around 3 percent of global GDP in 2001 to nearly 6 percent in 2007 (see figure 2.4).

During the period 2003–7, the number of financial crises (involving a banking, currency, or sovereign debt crisis) averaged around 3 per year, compared with around 17 per year during the period 1990–2002.[3] In regard to emerging market economies, the sharp reduction in the number of financial crises after that of Uruguay in 2002 until the outbreak of the current global crisis in the last quarter of 2008 can be attributed to a number of factors. One was the relatively benign conditions in the global economy as reflected in subdued inflation, low real rates of interest, and a decline in the volatility of indices of both real and financial activity. The decline in the volatility of macroeconomic aggregates such as real GDP, unemployment, and inflation in the advanced countries was in evidence since the late 1980s, but was particularly strong in the last decade. This phenomenon (the so-called great moderation) has been the subject of much debate, as to whether it reflected the absence of major shocks to the global economy (e.g., large spikes in the price of oil before 2008), improved macroeconomic policy implementation associated with the adoption of inflation targeting by independent central banks and fiscal rules in many countries, or better techniques of inventory management that have reduced the volatility of inventory investment.[4] The decline in indices of financial volatility in regard to short-term interest rates, equity values, and bond prices was particularly pronounced in the last decade. This behavior appears to have been related, in part, to the "great moderation," as well as to the manifestations of greater financial market resilience in the form of deeper and more liquid markets, the availability of derivatives to hedge risk, and the presence of large well-diversified institutional investors.[5]

A second factor that can account for the absence of financial crises in the period since 2002 is the widespread practice of "self-insurance" on the part of emerging market economies through the accumulation of large foreign reserve positions. As noted earlier, one of the lessons from the Asian financial crises was that those countries that escaped contagion from the financial turmoil in Thailand, Indonesia, and Korea were ones that had accumulated relatively large central bank foreign reserve positions, such as Hong Kong, Singapore, and Taiwan. After the crises subsided, countries in the East Asian region began to accumulate official foreign reserves as a form of defense against possible future speculative attacks. This behavior was repeated among emerging market economies in Eastern Europe and Latin America. Gross official foreign reserves of developing and emerging market economies rose from US$747 billion at the end of 2001, or around 4.5 percent of aggregate GDP, to US$4.7 trillion at the end of 2007 equivalent to 11.5 percent of GDP, thus accounting for nearly four-fifths of the growth in global reserves during this period[6] (figure 7.2). This was an unprecedented development in the international monetary system, as it represented a massive intent on the part of developing countries to establish an insurance mechanism against the risks of capital flow volatility, but in a manner that was costly for the

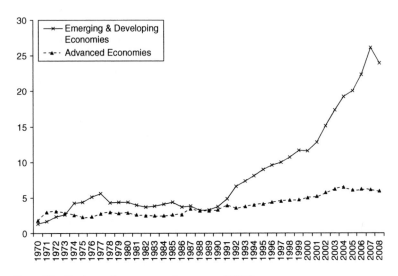

Figure 7.2 Foreign exchange reserves (as percent of GDP)

Source: IMF, International Financial Statistics; IMF, World Economic Outlook (April 2000 and October 2009 vintage)

countries involved and globally inefficient. One by-product of this behavior has been the rise in the number of sovereign wealth funds outside the advanced countries, which were created mainly to diversify the investment allocation and improve the yield of official reserve assets.[7]

Many studies have tried to explain the self-insurance behavior of emerging market economies and whether it can be rationalized in terms of conventional models of optimizing behavior. Before the impact of financial globalization, developing countries typically sought to maintain official reserves equivalent to around 3 to 6 months of import payments, as a precautionary balance against periods of temporary illiquidity. After the crises of the 1990s, it was suggested that emerging market countries needed to maintain external reserves equivalent to the value of their short-term external debt on a rolling, forward-year basis (the so-called Guidotti-Greenspan rule). However, actual reserve levels of a number of East Asian countries have exceeded levels that could be predicted by this rule. More recently, a study by Obstfeld, Shambaugh, and Taylor (2008) demonstrated that the observed levels of official reserves in relation to GDP can be explained statistically by cross-country differences in the degree of financial openness (as measured by an index of freedom for foreign capital flows), financial development (as reflected in the ratio of M2 to GDP) and exchange rate variability. The implication of this study is that countries with relatively large stocks of liquid domestic liabilities, high exposure to foreign capital flows, and less flexible exchange rate regimes (because of the phenomenon of "fear of floating") tend to have higher levels of foreign reserves. According to the study just cited, these factors can account for approximately two-thirds of the current estimated stock of "precautionary" reserves of developing countries (on the order of US4–4.5 trillion).

A third factor that may help to explain the decline in the incidence of financial crises in the emerging market economies after 2002 is the widespread effort to improve financial market regulation and conditions in these countries. As noted in chapter 6, one of the major initiatives of crisis prevention during the second reform of the IFA was the implementation of international standards and codes and the Financial Sector Assessment Program (FSAP) of the IMF and World Bank, in which around two-thirds of the Fund's membership have participated. Notably, however, within the G20, Argentina, China, Indonesia, and the United States had not participated in the FSAP before the recent financial crisis.

A further development that has helped to strengthen financial markets in developing countries was the strong growth in the presence of foreign banking institutions since the late 1990s. Bank deposits and loans represent the largest share of financial assets in emerging market and developing economies. Foreign direct investment in the banking systems of emerging market economies and the internationalization of financial services was fostered by the GATS agreement of 1997 and a sharp rise in bilateral investment treaties thereafter. As measured by the growth in foreign mergers and acquisitions of financial institutions in the advanced countries, this activity was particularly strong in Eastern and Central Europe and Latin America. Generally, the expansion of foreign bank activity in these markets has helped to strengthen competition, improve the delivery of financial services, and promote better management and risk practices within local banking cultures. However, one other by-product of this trend in international banking has been an increase in the transmission of business cycle impulses from the advanced to developing countries, which was in evidence during the recent global financial crisis.[8]

Causes of the Crisis in the United States

Much has been written about the antecedents of the current financial crisis, which can be summarized under the headings of macroeconomic, microeconomic, and ideological factors.[9] Although these factors fostered the unique conditions that gave rise to the crisis at a given point in time, it is also important to note that the current crisis exhibited many of the same general features of financial crises in the 1990s, associated with rapid capital inflows, which afflicted the emerging market econo-mies. The only difference was that this time the crisis originated in the advanced countries, and in particular in the country that had the repu-tation for the deepest, most liquid and diversified financial markets in the world. The classic features of a financial crisis, associated with major capital inflows, are lax monetary policy, regulatory ease, and speculative lending activity fed by herding behavior of investors and a bubble phe-nomenon (mania), which are then followed by a collapse of asset values, de-leveraging, and panic. All these features were present in the financial crisis that played out in the United States during 2007–8.

Macroeconomic Factors

One of the macroeconomic factors that helped to create the conditions for the crisis was the phenomenon of the Great Moderation noted earlier. In the benign macroeconomic and financial conditions that preceded the crisis, the assessment of risk by financial institutions in future investment oppor-tunities was minimized and the models that institutions used to evaluate the vulnerability of asset portfolios and the adequacy of net worth were calibrated on the basis of data reflecting benign conditions in the financial markets. In this environment, one must also factor in the behavior of the central banks in the main financial center countries, which adopted a very relaxed monetary policy stance in the wake of the 9/11 terrorist attacks. While this policy stance was appropriate at the time it was implemented, it was maintained for too long a period of time and was reversed only when the manic phase of the financial crisis was well advanced.[10] From November 2001 through December 2004, the short-term policy interest rate in the United States (the federal funds rate) was held below 2 percent, and from June 2003 to June 2004, it was below 1 percent. For much of this period, short-term interest rates, adjusted for the rate of inflation, were negative.[11]

An environment of extremely low, short-term policy rates and a flat yield curve led investors to seek higher returns in nonfinancial invest-ments such as commodities and real estate, using relatively low-cost finan-cial instruments as leverage. The housing market in the United States and a number of European countries was already in an upswing since the late 1990s, but housing prices began to rise more sharply in the period after 2002 in the light of the substantial easing of monetary policy.[12]

The other important macroeconomic factor supporting the crisis was the phenomenon of "global imbalances" that has been mentioned a num-ber of times in previous chapters. These imbalances were reflected in per-sistent current account surpluses of a number of East Asian high export economies (notably China), oil exporters and Germany, on one side, and persistent current account deficits of certain advanced countries (notably the United States), on the other. The episodic nature of current account deficits on the part of the United States has been a problem for the stability of the international monetary system in previous periods, in particular leading up to the breakdown of the Bretton Woods system. Beginning in the early 1980s, the US current account deficit reemerged (except for a brief reversal in 1992), and its net international investment position became negative for the first time in the late 1980s. However, the current account imbalance of the United States and its net international liability position increased substantially after the turn of the current century, reflecting a major expansion in both government expenditure and private consumption (figure 7.3). By contrast, China, which together with the United States accounted for approximately one-half of global imbalances during the last decade, exhibited a large and rising external current account surplus and a growing net international asset position.

In a basic macroeconomic context, these imbalances reflected a fundamental disequilibrium between national savings and investment in the surplus and deficit countries mentioned earlier. In the case of China, national savings exceeded investment, and net exports needed to be positive to offset relatively low consumption and bring about macroeconomic balance. The opposite was true for the United States, as national savings was very low (and domestic consumption was very large). The persistence of these imbalances represents a problem for the international adjustment mechanism and the exchange rate system. Under the gold standard, such imbalances would not persist for long, as countries were required to make

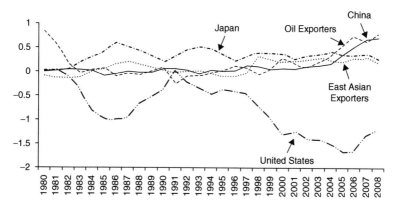

Figure 7.3 Current account imbalances (as percent of World GDP)
Source: IMF, International Financial Statistics

adjustments in domestic expenditure to maintain fixed exchange rates in terms of gold that served to reduce external imbalances over time. During the Bretton Woods system, the reluctance of the United States to make adjustments to its domestic expenditure to deal with a growing current account imbalance, and of European countries to allow an appreciation of their currencies, ultimately led to the breakdown of that system. In a world of flexible exchange rates, currency depreciation would help to reduce domestic demand (and the savings-investment gap) in countries with large current account deficits, while currency appreciation would help to increase domestic demand in countries with large current account surpluses. Over time, the combined effect of these imbalances would tend to diminish, if market-induced changes in exchange rates were reinforced by adjustments in domestic expenditure.

In the period leading up to the current crisis, this process of exchange rate adjustment only was evident in the case of the United States, as the real effective exchange rate for the United States depreciated by around 20 percent from the end of 2001 through 2007, whereas the real exchange rates for China, the rest of East Asia (excluding Japan) and the oil exporters, showed little or no change; most of the burden of exchange rate appreciation was carried by the euro zone during this period, which did not exhibit a marked imbalance in its current account transactions (table 7.1). The exchange rates of the major surplus countries tended to remain unchanged in real effective terms as they continued to peg their currencies to the US dollar. In the case of high export economies in East Asia, the maintenance of a low value for their currencies was considered essential to

Table 7.1 Changes in real effective exchange rates, December 2001–December 2007 (percentage change – minus sign equals depreciation)

Currency	REER Change
US Dollar	-20.9
Euro	22.5
Japanese Yen	-22.3
Chinese Renminbi	-7.8
East Asia Exporters[a]	8.1
Oil Exporters[b]	0.6
Memorandum Item	
International Oil Price in Real Terms[c]	153.2

[a] Includes Hong Kong, Indonesia, Korea, Malaysia, Philippines, Singapore, Taiwan, and Thailand. Regional combined REER change is weighted by 2007 GDP at PPP.
[b] Includes Bahrain, Iran, Nigeria, Saudi Arabia, and Venezuela. Group combined REER change is weighted by 2007 GDP at PPP.
[c] U.K. Brent petroleum price in US$/barrel, deflated by U.S. CPI.
Source: BIS; IMF WEO; IMF International Financial Statistics

sustain the export-led growth model that has characterized their postwar development experience. This was particularly true for the case of China. Given its dominance in the region, other exporters in East Asia feared a loss of competitiveness if they allowed their currencies to appreciate, while the value of the Chinese renminbi remained largely unchanged. The maintenance of relatively unchanged exchange rates by East Asia emerging market economies was also consistent with their desire for self-insurance through reserve accumulation, as explained earlier.

The undervaluation of exchange rates of the Asian export economies created a problem for their major foreign market in the United States in that it artificially withdrew demand from that market which required a compensating increase in domestic expenditure in the US economy to maintain macroeconomic balance and a minimal gap between its actual and potential output. The flow of funds and capital inflows from current account surplus countries to the United States provided the financing to cover its current account deficit and the gap between its domestic expenditure and income. Given the reputation of the United States for the soundness of its financial system, its financial markets were a natural destination for countries seeking investment outlets for official reserve assets and sovereign wealth funds. The increase in global savings originating in East Asian export economies and oil exporters, which was intermediated through the US financial system, lowered the long-term real interest rate in global capital markets and facilitated an expansion in domestic consumption and housing investment that was encouraged by relaxed monetary and fiscal policies in the advanced countries.

Microeconomic Factors

In addition to the macroeconomic factors noted earlier, one can also point to other microeconomic factors that fostered a boom in housing construction and finance, in particular in the subprime housing market of the United States. These related to regulatory gaps and flaws, the development of new structured finance and derivative products, and distorted incentives in mortgage finance, rating agencies and compensation schemes for financial institutions, which ultimately had global ramifications.

On the regulatory side, financial institutions took advantage of a number of gaps in the coverage of financial supervision to establish what has been called a "shadow banking system" that operated largely outside the normal scope of prudential regulations and minimum capital requirements that apply to the traditional banking system. This parallel financial system comprised money market funds, hedge funds, insurance companies, investment banks, and off-balance sheet operations of commercial banks (or Structured Investment Vehicles—SIVs), which relied mainly on wholesale funding from the capital markets as distinct from retail deposits of the traditional banking system. Total assets managed by these institutions increased by around 350 percent from the end of 2001 to the end of 2007, and they represented close to 50 percent of total financial system assets in the latter year.[13] Along with the growth of the "shadow" banking system, there was an enormous expansion in the issuance of credit derivatives, or credit default swaps, which are a form of insurance for securitized and other kinds of financial instruments, in over-the-counter (OTC) transactions outside the regulated exchanges for derivative trading. From the first half of 2001 through the first half of 2007, the value of credit default swaps grew from less than US$1 trillion to more than US$60 trillion.[14] In an environment of easy money, low-cost financing, minimal capital requirements, and high risk tolerance, hedge funds, investment banks, and SIVs could achieve capital leveraging of 20 or even 40 to 1, well in excess of the asset-capital ratio of around 12.5 to 1 implicit in the minimum capital requirement of 8 percent under the Basle capital adequacy standard for traditional banking operations. In terms of both an easy money policy linked to foreign capital inflows and a weak regulatory environment, the United States replicated many of the conditions that gave rise to the emerging market financial crises in the 1990s.

In addition to the development of a "shadow" banking system, the pattern of mortgage finance operations was changed in a fundamental way from that of traditional banking operations. Traditionally, community-based banks would fund their credit operations with a variety of short-to-medium term (retail) deposits from their local customer base and provide long-term mortgages to credit-worthy borrowers who could satisfy certain minimum income and balance sheet requirements. Banks would typically hold these mortgages to maturity or refinance some of them through an asset sale to the large Government-Sponsored Enterprises (Fannie Mae and Freddie Mac), which supported the mortgage finance market in the United States. The proceeds from such sales would provide additional funding to banks to enable them to finance additional mortgages. This pattern of traditional mortgage finance was called the "originate to hold" model.

With the development of new structured finance instruments and derivative products, this model was changed to one of "originate to distribute." The repackaging of mortgage loans originated by banks into mortgage-backed securities (MBS) and collateralized debt obligations (CDOs) had already started in the 1990s, but took off in a major way after 2001 as the housing cycle went into the full swing of its manic phase. The securitization of financial assets, whether in the form of traditional mortgages, credit card receivables, or student loans, was a major financial innovation as it allowed the original holders of these instruments to diversify their portfolios and disperse risk throughout the financial system among those institutional or wealthy individual investors who were considered best able to manage it. Securitization was a particularly appealing device for banks to transform subprime or risky mortgage credits into financial assets that could be attractive to financial institutions throughout the "shadow" banking system. During the period 2001–06, subprime and other nonprime (so-called Alt-A) mortgage credits grew from around 8 percent of all mortgages originated in the housing finance market to around 34 percent.[15]

The essential appeal of structured finance products such as ABS, MBS, and CDOs was that marketable securities could be created with higher credit ratings than the average rating of the underlying pool of assets. Subprime mortgages were the equivalent of "junk" bonds, but could be combined with other conventional mortgages with lower probabilities of default and sold in separate tranches of the underlying pool of assets. A senior tranche could be structured with a preferred claim on the payments from the underlying assets and could be marketed separately as a security that was less risky than the underlying bonds.[16] In an environment of rising housing prices and little history of default on mortgage-backed securities, the major credit rating agencies (Standard and Poors, Moodys, and Fitch) were prepared to give many of these securities AAA ratings. By 2007, roughly 60 percent of global structured finance products were rated AAA, compared with only 1 percent of corporate bond issues.[17] In an environment of low interest rates, these securities, which carried relatively attractive yields, were actively acquired by banks and other investors. In the case of banks, they would have carried a lower capital charge, because of their AAA rating, than an individual mortgage credit, thus enhancing their appeal as an investment.

Within the system of "originate to distribute," the structure of incentives became misaligned with perverse results. Unlike the "originate to hold" model in which a local bank originated a mortgage and typically held it to maturity, the other model separated the various procedures involved in the traditional bank operation and allocated them to different entities, each of which had no permanent stake in the transactions they performed. Mortgage originators initiated and underwrote mortgage contracts, which were financed by banks or household finance agencies, which then sold these contracts to other banks or broker-dealers, which in turn repackaged these contracts with other mortgages and sold them as separate tranches of MBS or CDOs to individual and institutional investors, including SIVs. In a rising housing market in which there was little expectation of a significant decline in housing prices, this process was vigorously applied to subprime or Alt-A mortgages involving first-time home buyers who could not qualify for standard mortgage contracts involving strict income requirements and higher downpayment obligations. In a chain of procedures, in which no individual entity had an incentive to monitor the activities of others with whom it engaged, some of whom were not subject to any regulatory oversight, the normal process of monitoring and control broke down, and fraud and abuse set in.

This process of securitization was further enhanced by the operations of the large credit rating agencies, which bestowed unrealistically high ratings on most of the tranches derived from MBS and CDOs. Since credit rating agencies were paid by the investment firms that created the securitized instruments being traded, they had an incentive to give them a favorable rating if they wanted to maintain an active business relationship with that firm, apart from the results of flawed mathematical models they may have used to calculate the probability of default. Then, if MBS and CDOs were given AAA ratings, banks and other financial institutions had an incentive to acquire them since they would incur a lower capital charge than for other forms of private credit. If in addition, large insurance companies such as AIG were prepared to offer credit default swaps (CDS) in the OTC market[18] as a form of insurance against the possibility of default on these securities, which were not subject to the normal prudential requirements that apply to other insurance operations, their marketability was further enhanced. Finally, if banks could shift these securities to an off-balance sheet SIV for which little or no capital position would be required if the SIV maintained a line of credit with its parent institution, banks could actively trade in these securities with funding generated by short-term repurchase agreements (REPOs) or commercial paper sold to money market funds, which were attracted by the AAA rating of the assets they were backing.

Within the traditional banking system, it has long been recognized that perverse incentives, or moral hazard, for banks can arise from the fact that their retail deposits are insured by the government to minimize the possibility of depositor panic in the event of distress in the banking system. In the absence of sound regulation, the access of banks to a government safety net can induce risky behavior on the part of bank managers seeking high returns for themselves and the bank's shareholders. Within the "shadow" banking system, where deposit insurance was less of a factor, there may have also been an implicit expectation, especially among large financial institutions, that they too could have access to the federal safety net if they were considered "too big to fail" or "too important to fail." This certainly turned out to be the case for the two large GSEs (Fannie Mae and Freddie Mac), which were widely perceived to carry an implicit guarantee on their debt instruments and invested heavily in the acquisition of mortgage-backed securities.[19] In September 2008, this implicit guarantee was honored by the US government, as these institutions were considered "too big to fail" because of their substantial weight in the mortgage finance market in the United States and the worldwide distribution of their AAA debt instruments. Other large private institutions, such as Citigroup and AIG, may have also been viewed as "too big to fail" by market participants, because of their large balance sheets, diversified activities, and extensive international operations. The implicit expectation of the managers of these institutions and their creditors that they could have access to the federal safety net in the event of financial market distress would have created a condition of moral hazard that would have added to the other factors supporting the upswing of the financial cycle, in addition to the competitive advantage they may have enjoyed from a lower cost of borrowing vis-à-vis smaller financial institutions.[20] The fact that these institutions were recognized as "too big to fail" by the US regulatory authorities in September–October 2008 obviously gave credence to this view.

The high degree of leverage that could be achieved within the "shadow" banking system was directly related to its reliance on wholesale, market-based funding for its liabilities. This reliance on short-term market-based instruments, instead of retail deposits typical of the traditional banking system, also created a significant degree of liquidity risk for the institutions involved. This funding was based primarily on the issue of short-term commercial paper or repurchase agreements (REPOs) using MBS or CDOs as collateral. Many of the REPOs issued were of an overnight maturity, which exposed the originating institution to significant funding risk in the event of market turbulence.[21] This source of market-based funding grew substantially after 2001, from around 25 percent of the stock of M2 in the traditional banking system to around 80 percent in August 2007, just as the first tremors from turmoil in the subprime mortgage finance market were beginning to be felt.[22]

As an example of the kind of leverage that could be achieved in the "shadow" banking system, consider the case of REPO financing in which typically a discount or "haircut" is applied to the value of the securities used as collateral to determine the amount of borrowing or funding that can be generated by the institution issuing the REPO. If the discount is 2 percent, which might apply in normal times, a portfolio of securitized assets worth 100 would generate 98 in funding liabilities, which implies that the borrowing institution would need an equity base of 2. The resulting leverage in this case is 100 divided by 2, or 50 to 1.[23]

Compensation schemes for financial institution CEOs have been identified as a particular problem that exacerbated the upswing of the recent financial cycle. The narrow focus on the next quarter's financial results and the linkage of managers' financial rewards to recent earnings reports with an emphasis on promoting stockholder value created perverse incentives to take on more risk in the search for higher financial returns. The oft-quoted statement by Charles "Chuck" Prince, the former CEO of Citigroup, captures the kind of herd behavior that is difficult to stop and the pressures top managers are under to deliver strong financial results during the boom phase of a financial cycle. In an interview with the *Financial Times* on July 9, 2007 regarding the ongoing boom in structured finance, he was quoted as saying that "When the music stops, in terms of liquidity, things will get complicated. But as long as the music is playing, you've got to get up and dance. We're still dancing." The problem of executive compensation is properly more of a concern for corporate governance than it is for public policy and needs to be remedied by greater shareholder involvement in the selection of corporate boards, a larger role for independent directors, and the reinforcement of risk management systems within financial institutions. Nevertheless, supervisory authorities need to ensure that appropriate internal safeguards and mechanisms are in place to align executive compensation with the long-term viability of the financial institutions they manage.

Executive compensation schemes can be seen as a factor imparting a procyclical bias to the upswing of a financial cycle, which is augmented by the effect of mark-to-market accounting and capital requirements. In times of economic boom, the valuation of bank assets improve and earnings increase along with the value of bank capital, thus allowing banks to expand their leverage through more borrowing. Conversely, during times of economic decline, bank asset valuations weaken, loans become impaired and capital write-downs increase, thus reducing the scope for banks to lend and reinforcing the decline.

Ideological Factors

In addition to the macroeconomic and microeconomic causes for the crisis that have been mentioned, one must recognize the role played by certain ideological factors. These can be identified most simply as a belief system based on the "efficient markets" theory of finance and confidence in the ability of markets to regulate themselves. Both of these presuppositions have proven to be unwarranted in the current crisis, even though they had strong support among many policy makers and academic experts.[24]

The efficient markets theory of finance postulates that the current price of a financial asset traded in competitive markets will reflect all the relevant information about current conditions and future prospects for the asset, and thus its price is not subject to any misalignment between its current and "true" underlying value that could give rise to profitable trading. A more general variant of this thesis is that consumers and investors operate in financial markets as "representative agents" on the basis of "rational expectations" about the future, and therefore would not be "fooled" by bubble phenomena and speculative activity driving the value of assets away from their fundamental value. In a world of efficient markets and rational expectations, there are no frictions in financial markets and financial cycles of boom and bust should not exist. Financial markets in the efficient markets framework would tend toward equilibrium and would only deviate from equilibrium in the event of random shocks. Clearly, the events of the last few years have undermined the credibility of this framework and have shown that financial markets are inherently unstable and that asset prices can deviate substantially from their fundamental or intrinsic value. Obviously hedge fund managers and many professional investors understand that financial markets experience periods of euphoria and panic during which asset prices deviate from their fundamental or underlying value, thus creating opportunities for profitable trades, but many policy makers, regulators, and academic economists were wedded to a view of efficient markets in which this behavior would not occur.

In relation to the current crisis, one off-shoot of the efficient markets hypothesis was the development of value-at-risk (VAR) models for assessing the riskiness of financial institution portfolios. Similar models were also used by the credit rating agencies in determining the quality and safety of privately traded financial assets, such as asset-backed securities, and were endorsed by the regulatory authorities in their supervision of large bank holding companies. VAR models are based on the assumption that the risk of an asset follows a normal distribution with relatively "thin tails" for extreme events, based on a traditional bell-shaped curve that underlies conventional probability theory. Behavioral finance theorists, however, have argued that the behavior of financial markets does not follow a normal distribution of possible outcomes as regards the likelihood of extreme events such as those that occurred in September–October of 2008. Instead, the distribution of possible outcomes for financial markets may exhibit "fat tails," with a higher probability of extreme events than suggested by a normal distribution.[25] Behavioral finance experts also have shown that investor behavior is clearly subject to irrational elements such as herding and panic because of the inability of individuals to process continuously all the relevant information bearing on their investment decisions.[26]

The application of VAR models in risk assessment of financial institutions and rating agencies turned out to be severely biased if they were based on the relatively benign behavior of financial markets that preceded the crisis, as noted earlier, and an expectation that housing prices would continue on an upward trajectory. In this way they gave rise to unrealistically optimistic assessments of capital requirements for financial institutions and the risk of securitized assets that formed a large share of financial portfolios, both domestically and internationally. It is estimated that roughly 40 percent of the structured finance instruments related to mortgage finance were held by foreign financial institutions, mainly in Western Europe (and Germany and the United Kingdom, in particular).[27]

An additional ideological bias that was pervasive among policy makers and regulators in the main financial center countries was a belief in the self-regulating power of markets and a view that free markets could operate effectively with a minimum of regulation. As applied to financial markets, this view was at variance with the basic lessons of economics as regards the necessary institutional foundations of competitive markets in terms of property rights, contract enforcement, and regulations to ensure the quality of products and services provided by firms. Nevertheless, this view was sustained by the notion that full disclosure of information by financial firms, coupled with the importance firms attributed to their "reputational" capital, would reinforce the self-disciplining power of free markets. Perhaps the most dramatic admission of this bias was that of Alan Greenspan, former Chairman of the Federal Reserve, in testifying before a congressional committee in late 2008 that the emergence of the crisis shattered his confidence in the ability of financial markets to monitor themselves.[28] Without an appreciation for this bias, it is hard to understand the benign view adopted by most policy makers and regulators about developments that were taking place within the shadow banking system before the crisis.

The Emergence of a Global Financial Crisis

What was the chain of events that transformed a crisis in the subprime mortgage market in the United States into a global financial crisis? The evolution of the crisis can be broken down into three phases: the first phase started with the turmoil in money markets in the summer of 2007 arising from a spread of defaults on subprime mortgages through February 2008; the second phase began with the demise of the Bear Stearns investment firm in March 2008 and ran through mid-September with the collapse of Lehman Brothers and the rescue of Merrill Lunch and AIG; the third and global phase began in late September and persisted through late March 2009 at which point financial markets began to improve.

The trigger for the first phase was the leveling off of housing prices in 2006 and the beginning of a decline in prices later that year that began a sequence of defaults on subprime mortgages. Homeowners who had entered into jumbo mortgages at initial low "teaser" rates, in the expectation that they could refinance those loans against a higher value of their homes in the future, suddenly found themselves holding debt for more than the value of those homes. Unable to refinance or pay the higher interest on their mortgages, they defaulted. Certainly one of the factors helping to bring about a change in the direction of housing prices was the policy of the Federal Reserve to raise short-term interest rates by 300 basis points from late 2004 until June 2006. This increase in short-term rates put upward pressure on longer-term mortgage rates and raised the cost of liquidity financing for many investment banks and SIVs involved in the trading of MBS.

An increase in the rate of defaults on subprime mortgages called into question the valuation of mortgage-backed securities, and their trading values began to decline. Given the high leverage with which many institutions in the shadow banking system were operating, their capital positions came under threat along with their access to short-term funding that was backed with the collateral of mortgage-backed securities. To meet funding requirements at a lower capital base, institutions were forced to sell securities in a market, where buyers were rapidly disappearing, which further depressed their value. This process of "de-leveraging" and increased perceptions of counterparty risk on the part of money market funds and other purchasers of asset-backed commercial paper led to turmoil in the money markets and ultimately to the demise of Bear Stearns. In March 2008, that firm had to close two of its hedge funds that had experienced substantial losses from their investments in MBS.

With the collapse of Lehman Brothers and government intervention in AIG in September 2008, financial markets entered a panic phase globally given the extensive placement of mortgage-backed securities among international banking institutions and the uncertainty about counterparty risk involved in credit default swaps issued by AIG and other financial institutions. Wholesale funding for the "shadow" banking system dried up, as perceptions of counterparty risk rose dramatically, and banks curtailed credit as their capital positions weakened with the loss in market value of their MBS holdings. One by-product of the process of securitization was that holdings of MBS in the "trading book" of the banks was subject to mark-to-market accounting conventions that required downward adjustments in the value of assets and capital with a loss in the market value of MBS. In the traditional ('originate to hold") banking system, individual mortgages held in the "loan book" of the bank were subject to historical cost accounting less any amount of amortization.

With the collapse of the housing market and severe distress in the "shadow" banking system, equity markets also began to weaken in the expectation of a curtailment of credit for business and households. The collapse of financial wealth then fed into a decline in consumption and investment. The one unanticipated event in the last quarter of 2008 was the strengthening of the US dollar. In the financial crises of the 1990s, emerging market currencies suffered dramatic declines as investors withdrew funds from these markets. In the case of the United States, given its primary reserve currency role and the safety and liquidity of its government debt, the dollar strengthened as investors sought a "safe haven" once funding was withdrawn from the "shadow" banking system.[29]

The flight to safety of US short-term government debt, however, severely affected the financial position of emerging markets, as investors once again withdrew funds from emerging market stock and bond holdings in a generalized environment of high risk aversion. Thus began the severe downturn of the third cycle of capital flow volatility for emerging market economies that began in the 1970s with the private bank financing of the oil crisis and was followed by the private investment boom of the 1990s. The current crisis was particularly unfortunate for emerging market economies, as many of these countries had fortified their monetary and fiscal systems, and had avoided many of the excesses revealed in the operations of the "shadow" banking system.

According to estimates of the McKinsey Global Institute, the impact of the crisis on global private wealth and capital flows has been dramatic. In 2008, the total value of global financial assets is estimated to have fallen by the equivalent of US$16 trillion to US$178 trillion. During 2008 and the first half of 2009, the decline in private equity and household wealth amounted to US$28 trillion, or the equivalent of close to 50 percent of global GDP. Global capital flows are estimated to have dropped from around US$10.5 trillion in 2007 to US$1.9 trillion in 2008.[30] In economic terms, the impact of the financial crisis has been equally dramatic. According to World Bank data, in 2008 global GDP declined for the first time since World War II, by 2 percent, while global trade volume contracted by 14 percent, the most in 80 years.

Summary and Conclusion

The global financial crisis of 2008–9 followed a period of unprecedented expansion in financial globalization, as the network of financial linkages among the advanced countries and between advanced and emerging market economies was further intensified. During the period

2000–2007, the stock of international claims and liabilities among the advanced countries nearly doubled in relation to GDP. These linkages reflected a rapid growth in the cross-border activity of international banks, in particular large complex financial institutions (LCFIs), and a significant expansion in derivative trading, including for credit default swaps, a relatively new form of credit derivative. Reflecting relatively benign conditions in the global financial system, the incidence of financial crises after 2000 fell sharply with respect to the previous decade.

Developing countries as a group experienced a major new wave of private capital inflows after 2000, as many emerging market economies were viewed as attractive outlets for investment in the light of reforms that had been undertaken to improve their macroeconomic policy and financial regulatory regimes. Many of these reforms were prompted by efforts to implement international standards and codes that had been promoted in the context of the second reform of the IFA. Along with these reforms, developing countries also engaged in a massive program of self-insurance against the risk of financial crises by expanding substantially their foreign reserve positions. The generation of large external savings represented an unprecedented flow of foreign capital from the developing to the advanced countries.

The origins of the financial crisis of 2008–9 within the subprime mortgage market of the United States have to be understood within the classic dynamics of financial crises associated with lax monetary policy, a weak regulatory framework and easy access to foreign capital inflows, which give rise to bubble phenomena. These are the same ingredients that were present in the financial crises of the 1990s. Financial innovation in the form of securitized instruments, or structured finance products, and credit derivatives also played an important role in propelling a boom in the housing market by expanding the scope for mortgage financing beyond the limits of traditional banking institutions.

A number of different factors can be identified as playing a role in the development of the crisis. On the macroeconomic front, a period of benign economic and financial conditions in the United States created an environment in which the volatility of financial markets was reduced and perceptions of risk were minimized. This environment, together with a very relaxed stance on monetary policy in which short-term interest rates were negative in real terms for an extended period of time, led to an increased investment in nonfinancial assets, such as housing and commodities, and an expansion in household consumption. The increase in consumption, along with an expansion of fiscal policy, led to a widening of the current account deficit of the United States, which was financed by large external savings of oil exporters and dynamic export economies of East Asia.

Within the benign economic environment prevailing in the United States, a bubble in the housing market was fed by a combination of specific factors that fostered speculative activity within a segment of the financial sector that operated largely outside the normal prudential restraints on the traditional banking system (so-called shadow banking system). The transformation of traditional mortgages, including those for high-risk, low-income borrowers, into structured financial products such as MBS and CDOs, which were insured by credit default swaps and highly rated by the credit rating agencies, facilitated a wide distribution of high-risk financial assets throughout the financial system of the United States and that of many countries in Western Europe. This process would not have unfolded without a flawed system of incentives in which normal standards for the origination of mortgages were relaxed because lenders did not maintain a financial stake in the mortgages they created; risk management of financial institutions was reduced because of poor risk valuation models and distorted executive compensation schemes; and rating agencies failed to assess appropriately the risk of securitized instruments because of conflicts of interest with the firms they were advising in the development of such instruments. In the case of LCFIs, perceptions of moral hazard may have also played a role in speculative activity, as these institutions were viewed as having access to the government's safety net because they were deemed "too big to fail."

The crisis was also fostered by certain beliefs on the part of policy makers and regulatory authorities as regards the efficiency of financial markets and their ability to maintain equilibrium and stability through the discipline of informed investors and the self-interest of financial institutions to protect shareholders' equity. In an environment of flawed incentives, weak disclosure and moral hazard, such a belief in the self-regulating power of financial markets proved to be severely deficient.

Once the housing bubble had peaked, the process by which a crisis in the subprime mortgage market of the United States was transformed into a global financial crisis can only be explained by the widespread distribution of securitized instruments supporting that market, the unstable sources of liquidity that were supporting investment in these investments, and the financial distress of two LCFIs (Lehman Brothers and AIG) that were highly interconnected with international financial markets. Doubts about the extent of counterparty risk for highly leveraged financial institutions amidst a collapse in the prices of securitized mortgage instruments led to widespread panic in international financial markets and a credit crunch as investors and financial institutions sought safe-haven investments.

CHAPTER 8

The Role of the International Financial Architecture in Crisis Prevention and Crisis Management

The emergence of the global financial crisis in 2008–9 was clear evidence of a system failure of the IFA in terms of crisis prevention. Although some policy analysts and institutions were raising concerns about the build-up of risk within the "shadow" banking system and the sustainability of global imbalances, most policy makers in the advanced countries were not prepared for the severity and swiftness of the events that transpired in the final quarter of 2008. Why then was the IFA unable to prevent the outbreak of crisis, given its responsibility for maintaining global financial stability? Once the crisis erupted, how has the IFA responded in terms of crisis management? These are the major questions that this chapter attempts to address.

These questions are particularly relevant in view of the fact that the second reform of the IFA was focused on improving its crisis prevention and crisis management capabilities. This was true certainly with respect to the problem of crises in the emerging market countries, which was the main focus of official attention at the time. While that reform was guided principally by the advanced countries, it was never clearly contemplated at that time or in the lead-up to the recent crisis that serious threats to global financial system stability would emerge within the major financial center countries.

The International Financial Architecture and Crisis Prevention

In attempting to identify the problems of crisis prevention, one can point to at least four failures in the functioning of the IFA, related to: (1) the workings of the international adjustment mechanism; (2) the oversight of global financial system stability; (3) the coordination of international financial regulation; and (4) the international lender of last resort mechanism. Defects in these four areas bear directly on the provision of essential public goods for which the IFA is primarily responsible.

The International Adjustment Mechanism

As noted in the previous chapter, the persistence of global imbalances is prima facie evidence of a breakdown in the international adjustment mechanism. In each of the four periods of international monetary arrangements described in chapter 3, the international system has grappled with the problem of establishing a workable system for the resolution or elimination of payments imbalances among countries. During the gold standard, given collective attachment to the rigors of fixed exchange parities in terms of gold, large payments imbalances were diminished over time through adjustments in domestic expenditure induced by movements in gold (to which domestic money supplies were fixed) or short-term capital or both. During the Bretton Woods system, this adjustment process was expected to work through periodic adjustment in fixed exchange rate parities, if domestic expenditure policies produced systematic imbalances among countries, although in practice countries relied mainly on adjustments in domestic expenditure to maintain external balance. By contrast, during the post-Bretton Woods era, the adjustment mechanism was expected to be reliant on both the flexibility of exchange rates and adjustments in domestic policy to bring about viable payments positions over time.

One of the virtues of the gold standard as a commodity-based reserve system was that pressures for the adjustment of international payments imbalances were in principle symmetric for both surplus and deficit countries. The British proposal for establishing an international reserve currency system (based on the Bancor) at the Bretton Woods Conference and the debates of the Committee of 20 during the first reform of the IFA on establishing an SDR-based reserve system would have preserved that principle of symmetry in the adjustment mechanism. However, in the current system of flexible exchange rates and dominant reserve currencies, there have been two constraints on the international adjustment process. One is that the United States as the leading reserve currency country in the system faces little pressure to make external adjustments as long as its currency is in demand as an international store of value, the major vehicle currency in international trade, and the supplier of international liquidity needed to sustain international transactions over the long term. Thus, the United States has been able to maintain a current account deficit and sustained increase in its international debt position almost continuously since the early 1980s. This behavior constituted the "exorbitant privilege" which French authorities complained about during the period of the Bretton Woods system.[1]

The second problem in the current regime of flexible exchange rates is that the burden of adjustment on deficit and surplus countries (other than the United States) is asymmetric. Countries running balance of payments deficits will gradually tend to encounter resistance from foreign creditors to unlimited financing and will be forced by financial market pressures to adjust. By contrast, countries experiencing balance of payments surpluses can resist pressures to allow their currencies to appreciate, at least for a considerable period of time. This delay, however, will require compensating action on the part of monetary policy to absorb or sterilize the expansion in the domestic money supply associated with the accumulation of foreign reserves through the issue of domestic securities. Such action ultimately will entail a significant cost for the central bank or treasury, which has to pay the interest burden on this debt.

Since the end of World War II, the IMF has been at the center of the international monetary system with primary responsibility for facilitating the international adjustment mechanism through an effective system of exchange rate arrangements. With the end of the Bretton Woods system, the Fund essentially has had two instruments for carrying out this responsibility. One is the application of conditionality regarding the use of its financial resources, and the other is its surveillance function. The former instrument is only relevant in the case of countries facing an external payments deficit that do not have recourse to external financing other than from the Fund and is therefore inherently asymmetrical and selective. Through the application of conditionality, the IMF is able to exercise discipline or leverage regarding the policy adjustments that a government makes to bring about the restoration of a viable balance of payments position. By contrast, the impact of surveillance relies upon the persuasiveness of the Fund in presenting its views and a country's willingness to cooperate with the Fund in finding a solution to its payments difficulties.

In the lead up to the recent crisis, the IMF was certainly aware of the potential risks to the international system arising from the problem of global imbalances and was making those views known through both its bilateral and multilateral surveillance exercises. In a number of the semiannual WEO reports, the IMF had called attention to the risks for the global economy of the problem of global imbalances and their unsustainability, which have in effect been validated by the recent crisis.[2] These views were generally endorsed by both the IMF Executive Board and the IMFC during 2005–6, along with the broad outline of a strategy to address these imbalances. However, in neither body was any consensus reached on the necessary policy coordination that would be needed to implement the strategy. To a large extent, this situation reflects inherent limitations in the structure and functioning of these consultative bodies. The Board of the Fund essentially is comprised of mid-level Finance Ministry or Central Bank staff, which do not carry decision-making authority in their capitals and cannot make policy commitments on behalf of their governments. The IMFC is only an advisory body of the IMF and has not been used by its members, who are in fact the finance ministers or central bank governors of the countries represented, for policy coordination. As noted earlier, among the advanced countries, efforts at policy coordination via a peer review mechanism have been restricted to fora such as the G7 or the OECD, which are inappropriate for the resolution of the problem of global imbalances as they exclude some of the key countries involved, such as China and Saudi Arabia, which need to play a part in their resolution.

It should be noted that expert opinion outside the Fund had been divided on the risks and problems posed by the phenomenon of global imbalances, before the recent crisis. On one side, economists such as Alan Greenspan and Professor Richard Cooper of Harvard have argued that global imbalances were the natural outcome of important investment portfolio shifts taking place among different groups of countries in an era of increased financial globalization.[3] As US-based firms and households sought to diversify their financial portfolios through the acquisition of foreign assets, emerging and developing countries revealed a preference for investing in US financial assets given the depth and diversity of investment opportunities in that market. Those sympathetic to these views tended to see a limited role for coordinated policy intervention to influence global imbalances. Other academic analysts, however, such as Ken Rogoff of Harvard and Maurice Obstfeld of Berkeley, cautioned against such a benign view of the problem of global imbalances. In their view, the growing current account deficit of the United States, which reached 6.5 percent of GDP in 2007, coupled with the long-run steady increase in its net international debt position, could not be sustained over the long term as countries would lose confidence in the ability of the United States to reverse that course.[4] Over time, countries would become increasingly reluctant to accumulate further US debt obligations, which would bring about a collapse of the US dollar and a significant increase in the risk premia on US public debt. These predictions, based on the experience of emerging market economies during the 1990s, obviously did not play out during the recent crisis, as the dollar strengthened and the value of US government securities rose as global investors viewed US public debt as a "safe haven" investment during a period of financial crisis. However, with the deterioration in the fiscal and debt position of the United States as a result of the crisis, the future risks for the US dollar and interest rates still remain.

In addition to the multilateral surveillance of the WEO exercise, the Fund initiated in 2006 an unprecedented multilateral consultation exercise specifically focused on the problem of global imbalances. This exercise brought together representatives of the United States, the euro region, Japan, China, and Saudi Arabia in an effort to reach common ground on a framework of coordinated policy adjustments to address the problem of global imbalances. Initially, teams of Fund staff prepared different scenarios for each participant's macroeconomic and external prospects over the medium-term, along with options for policy adjustment to bring about a sustainable position. Then, in a second round of discussions led by the managing director of the IMF, an effort was made to agree on a single policy program for each of the five participants that were mutually consistent. However, each participant essentially reiterated policy pronouncements they had already announced in the context of their national policy setting, thus resisting any effort to reconcile these positions with a common external objective developed through the IMF.[5] The IMFC in its review of the exercise simply called attention to the valuable exchange of information which it provided, without any commitment to the monitoring of future policy actions of the five participants.[6] The exercise essentially lapsed at about the time that early tremors of the current crisis were beginning to be felt. Once again, as in the case of the WEO exercises, an opportunity was missed to use the Fund as a forum for the identification and resolution of important global financial issues.

Questions have also been raised as to whether the Fund was exercising firm surveillance over the exchange rate practices of its members in its bilateral surveillance during the period leading up to the current crisis. In the case of China, for example, the IMF in its annual consultation exercises with China was reluctant to declare the Chinese renminbi to be overvalued or to be misaligned, even though such a view has been widely held among experts outside the organization.[7] During the period from mid-2005 to July 2008, the Chinese authorities were in principle pursuing a flexible exchange rate policy for the Chinese currency vis-à-vis the US dollar, but in practice the real effective value of the renminbi only appreciated by a relatively small amount, during a period in which the People's Bank of China (PBC, the central bank) was accumulating massive amounts of foreign exchange (see table 7.1).[8] These foreign currency inflows reflected a growing external surplus for China on both its current and financial accounts which, together with the large foreign reserve accumulation of the PBC, represented clear prima facie evidence of an undervalued currency. During this time, the IMF's main recommendation was that the authorities should allow more flexibility in the management of the renminbi.

The effectiveness of the Fund's surveillance over exchange rate policies of its members was the focus of a recent review by its Independent Evaluation Office, which was concluded in 2007. That study criticized the institution for the quality of its exchange rate advice and the ineffectiveness of its policy dialogue with advanced and emerging market economies on exchange rate issues.[9] At the end of June 2007, the Executive Board in one of its periodic reviews of surveillance procedures decided to revise its guidelines for exchange rate management to give more guidance to members on currency misalignments and to allow for more critical assessments by the Fund of the exchange rate policies of its members that were deemed to be "fundamentally misaligned." Unfortunately, this recent revision of surveillance procedures has not lead to a clearer assessment by the Fund of China's currency arrangement. For a period of two years, the Chinese authorities refused to conclude the Article IV consultation discussions with the Fund, in part because of its concern that the IMF was being unduly influenced by the views of its largest shareholder (the United States) in its determination to take a tougher stance on currency misalignments. (During this period, bilateral economic discussions between the United States and China had not been able to reach any satisfactory understanding on an upward adjustment to the value of the renminbi.) In its conclusions of the 2009 Article IV consultation in July 2009, the Executive Board simply expressed support for the increased role of market forces in determining the value of the Chinese currency and the real appreciation that had taken place since 2005, without expressing a clear view on the appropriateness of the current exchange rate level or its future evolution.

This recent experience in the exercise of the Fund's surveillance mechanism reflects two underlying weaknesses in the structure of the Fund. One is that the large countries have not been willing to give the Fund the authority it needs to help bring about coordinated policy adjustments for the stability of the global economy. This reluctance of the advanced countries to have the IMF play a direct role in their policy coordination can be traced back to the decision of the G7 finance ministers to exclude the IMF managing director from direct participation in their peer review exercises beginning in the late 1970s, as discussed in chapter 4.[10] The other weakness is that the asymmetry of power within the Fund between the advanced countries and large emerging market economies has weakened the legitimacy of the institution and the stakeholder commitment that the latter countries are willing to make to the institution. Basically, these weaknesses reflect a problem of governance within the Fund, which is taken up in the next chapter of this book.

The Oversight of Global Financial System Stability

Although responsibility for oversight of the international adjustment mechanism within the IFA has been centered in the IMF, responsibility for global financial systemic stability has been shared among different institutions. This division of labor among essentially three institutions (the BIS, Financial Stability Forum [FSF], and IMF) has not been well coordinated and has resulted in a "silo" approach to the exercise of this responsibility.

Attention to financial system stability, or macroprudential risk, came more directly into the purview of the IFA with the second reform of the late 1990s in the wake of a series of financial crises in emerging market economies. It is separate from the traditional regulatory approach to microprudential risk, which looks at the factors bearing on the soundness and solvency of individual financial institutions. The focus on financial system stability at the national or global level is intended to identify the interconnections among large financial institutions with significant cross-border activities and the financial linkages among systemically important countries that can give rise to systemic instability in the event of financial distress at the individual institutional or national level.[11]

At the national level, attention to financial system stability issues has not been uniformly pursued among all the advanced countries. This is an important consideration in understanding any failings at the international level. In the UK, the authority for macroprudential regulation has been vested in the Bank of England which, among other things, has published a semiannual financial system stability report since 1999. This responsibility was in addition to that of its inflation-targeting regime. In the United States, however, in part because of the highly fragmented nature of its financial regulatory structure, financial system stability was not formally assigned to the Federal Reserve Board, nor to any other agency within the US government. Instead, the Federal Reserve has pursued mainly its dual mandate of price stability and full employment, with little or no focus on systemic or macroprudential risks.

At the international level, as noted earlier, responsibility for global financial stability has essentially been shared among three institutions, with overlapping and somewhat competing mandates. The BIS has for many years been a strong advocate for a macroprudential approach to financial supervision and has served as a center for discussion on international monetary and financial issues since its emergence as a venue for G10 discussions in the early 1960s.[12] As discussed in earlier chapters, it also provides a secretariat function for three G10 committees dealing with international payments and settlements, banking supervision, and developments in the global financial system, which have a bearing on global financial system stability. In addition, the BIS has been the primary disseminator of data on international banking activity and an important forum for discussion on international financial issues through its research function and various publications. As a central banking institution, the BIS work program overlaps to a significant degree with that of the IMF, and yet there is no formal coordinating arrangement between the two institutions, although IMF staff participate in many of its meetings.

In the years preceding the crisis, the G10 Committee on the Global Financial System had undertaken studies on selected aspects of the international financial system including developments in the global housing finance market and the role of private credit rating agencies in the evaluation of structured finance products. In the former study, the committee came to a relatively benign view of the potential systemic risk arising from mortgage securitization and generally highlighted the benefits of greater reliance on capital market funding of household finance (CGFS 2006). In the latter study, the committee did not see any conflict in the role of credit agencies as advisors to the firms designing securitized instruments that they would be rating, which was different from their traditional role in the rating of bonds. In both cases, it was believed that reputational credibility would be a strong force in favor of sound judgment.[13] In retrospect, this turned out to be a flawed conclusion, but one that was probably consistent with the views of the national authorities represented on the committee.

The Annual Report of the BIS has for many years provided an important assessment of global economic and financial conditions. In the years preceding the current crisis, it was clearly identifying potential risks associated with the accumulation of global imbalances and the underpricing of risk in private markets for derivatives and securitized instruments. However, these reports, as authoritative as they are, do not support a process of policy deliberation or decision making within the organization. The BIS is essentially a central bankers' organization, and a selective one at that, with only fifty-six members, including of course the central bank governors of the G10. As a nonuniversal institution, it does not have a clear international mandate for oversight of the global financial system and does not include the political representation (i.e., ministers of finance) with authority to act in this area.

The FSF which was created with the second reform of the IFA in 1999 is a much more informal body than either the BIS or IMF. Before 2009, it was dominated by its G7 representation, which controlled the majority of its membership. Without a formal secretariat, it has relied on the staff support of the BIS, and its current and former chairman have been senior central bank officials from one of the G7 countries. Given that the IMF, along with other international institutions, including the BIS, OECD, ECB, and World Bank, were also represented in the Forum and its direct reporting status with the G7 Finance Ministers and Central Bank Governors, it could be viewed as the primary body responsible for global financial system stability, even though it shared some of that responsibility with the IMF. Thus, at meetings of the IMFC, it was the chairman of the FSF, rather than the managing director of the IMF, who was authorized to address issues of financial system stability in its deliberations, while the Fund's views were reported separately through the conclusions of its Global Financial Stability Report, in which the FSF had no input.[14]

However, the FSF does not have any executive authority or decision-making function within the IFA, as does the IMF. Before the outbreak of the recent crisis, it had only commissioned two specific studies on issues related to the global financial system and existed primarily as a forum for the exchange of information on international financial issues among representatives of the central banks, regulatory agencies, and finance ministries of the advanced countries. Before the recent crisis, it met twice a year to consider vulnerabilities in the international financial system and to exchange information on developments in regulatory practice in the advanced and main emerging market economies. However, its vulnerability assessments were not coordinated with those undertaken by G7 country authorities at the national level.[15]

The primary focus of the FSF in the years leading up to the current crisis was in the area of international financial regulation and in monitoring the program of international standards and codes, which was implemented primarily by the IMF and World Bank. None of the FSF's semiannual communiqués issued in the three years before the crisis identified any area of collaboration with the IMF other than that of the FSAP exercise and the ongoing review of offshore financial centers. Similarly, in its reports to the IMFC before the recent crisis, no specific issues of systemic risk were raised by the FSF.[16]

Since the second reform of the IFA, the IMF has shared responsibility with the FSF for the oversight of global financial system stability, with a primary focus on its macrofinancial dimension. However, this responsibility is not formally established in the Articles of Agreement of the Fund, which (as a result of the second amendment) limits the formal mandate of the IMF to surveillance of the international monetary system. In addition, until recently, the division of labor between the IMF and FSF on global financial stability issues had not been clearly established, and the coordination between the two bodies was relatively restricted, as just discussed.

The main instrument of the Fund for assessing global financial stability has been its semiannual Global Financial Stability Report (GFSR) which, together with the WEO, forms part of the Fund's multilateral surveillance function.[17] Before 2007, these reports had a significant emphasis on developments in emerging market economies, which was consistent with the Fund's interest in working with these countries to reduce the vulnerabilities that gave rise to the financial crises of the 1990s. This emphasis was also consistent with the attention being given in the Fund's bilateral surveillance to specific vulnerabilities arising in emerging market economies from, for example, "double mismatches" in the balance sheets of local firms and financial institutions.[18]

Nevertheless, the GFSR clearly reinforced the message of the WEO on the need for a coordinated response to the problem of global imbalances and called attention to the risks associated with developments in the subprime mortgage finance market of the United States and the rapid growth in household financial debt. However, as in the case of the WEO, these signals did not translate into a focused discussion at the level of the Executive Board or the IMFC on the need for a policy response.

The GFSR fully described the ongoing rapid expansion in securitization of mortgage finance and credit default swaps in OTC markets, but consistent with the conventional wisdom at the time it adopted a relatively favorable view of the benefits of structured finance for the financial system. In the GFSR of April 2006, the IMF asserted that "[t]here is growing recognition that the dispersion of credit risk by banks to a broader and more diverse group of investors, rather than warehousing such risk on their balance sheets, has helped make the banking and overall financial system more resilient . . . The improved resilience may be seen in fewer bank failures and more consistent credit provision. Consequently the commercial banks may be less vulnerable today to credit or economic shocks."[19] In retrospect, this assessment, while widely shared in academic and policy circles, was incorrect. Instead of dispersing risk, the process of securitization ended up concentrating risk in the banking system, as many of these securities ended up being held by banks, either directly on their balance sheets or in off-balance sheet SIVs.

A similar weakness of IMF procedures to focus a policy response on emerging problems can be seen in the results of the annual surveillance exercises with the advanced countries. In its latest review of surveillance in September 2008, the Fund staff identified a number of examples where potential problems and risks in financial markets of the advanced countries had been identified by IMF missions that later revealed themselves in the crisis. However, in a number of cases, these references are located in special studies attached to the main report for the Article IV consultation and did not carry over into the conclusion or Summing-Up of the Executive Board's discussion, which represents the official view of the institution of a member's policies and prospects.[20]

Even where financial problems are clearly identified by the Fund staff, there is a tendency in the Executive Board, because of its consensus style of deliberation, for serious criticisms of countries to be blunted or resisted especially in the case of the advanced countries. In this regard, it is instructive to consider the views expressed by the UK Financial Supervisory Authority in its review of the financial crisis (The Turner Review), which examined the work of the IMF in its oversight of global financial stability before the crisis. It concluded that, notwithstanding the correct identification of unsustainable risks in many cases by the Fund staff, "these warnings were often ignored, in particular by the rich developed nations. And IMF reports, which can be agreed in a somewhat politicized process of review by national directors and the board, can be subject to influence to fit in better with dominant intellectual assumptions and to avoid overt criticism of major powers."[21] Such a criticism calls for a much more independent role of the IMF in assessing financial risks in the future and tends to confirm a view of many authorities from emerging market economies that the Fund has not been even-handed in its surveillance of the advanced countries.[22]

One particular gap in the IMF's surveillance work can be identified in the coverage of the FSAP exercise. Since this was a voluntary program, not all members of the IMF have participated. Notably, Japan resisted participation until 2002–3, at the end of a decade of financial problems. In addition, as noted earlier, four other members of the G20 had not participated in this assessment before the recent crisis: the United States, China, Argentina, and Indonesia. Whether an FSAP exercise for the United States would have identified the problems that led to the emergence of the crisis will never be known. However, such an exercise would have probably identified the severe gaps in the US regulatory framework and its fragmented structure and the need for more attention to the "shadow" banking system, in which the seeds of the recent crisis took root.

In the final analysis, the failings of the IFA in the oversight of global financial stability have to be traced to the work of the G7 finance ministers and central bank governors that effectively function as the steering committee for the BIS, FSF, and IMF. In none of the communiqués of the G7 before the outbreak of the crisis is there any signal of concern over the conditions that created it, apart from the need to address the problem of global imbalances for which the G7 was not the appropriate venue. This conclusion is not surprising given the relatively benign views of the financial authorities in the advanced countries on the power of market discipline, the risk management practices of private financial firms, and information disclosure to minimize the need for regulatory oversight. Such an assessment is fully consistent with the views expressed in the Turner Review of the UK Financial Supervisory Authority, cited earlier, which attempted to account for the regulatory failures in the United Kingdom that helped to give rise to the crisis.

International Financial Regulation

In addition to flaws in the oversight of global financial stability, there were weaknesses in the microprudential aspects of international financial regulation related to capital adequacy standards under the so-called Basel accords. The Basel I accord, which was developed by the Basel Committee on Bank Supervision in 1988, established for the first time a uniform standard for capital adequacy requirements for commercial banks that has been widely adopted by governments across the globe. As noted earlier, that accord established broad categories of bank loans and assets that could be differentiated according to their risk weighting for the calculation of capital requirements. However, in the late 1990s, work began on a revision of the 1988 accord that would allow for a more refined classification of risk weightings within the broad categories identified in the first accord. Final agreement was reached on a revised Basel Capital Adequacy Accord in 2004 (Basel II), which was in the process of being implemented in the advanced countries at the time the current crisis erupted. By 2007, it was broadly in effect within the major European countries as a result of its incorporation in the EU capital adequacy accord. In the United States, as of April 2008 it was beginning to be phased in for the fifteen or so largest, internationally active banks. The crisis, however, has revealed serious flaws in the application and design of the two accords.

One flaw in the Basel I standards, which has been recognized for some time in academic discussion of financial regulation, is their procyclical bias that tends to exacerbate the upswing of the financial cycle during its expansion phase and then to reinforce the downturn of the cycle during its reversal.[23] As noted earlier, during times of economic boom the valuation of bank assets as sources of collateral improves and earnings increase, thus allowing banks to increase their leverage. Conversely, during times of financial bust, bank assets become impaired and charges against capital increase, which may lower bank capital below minimum requirements, thus limiting the scope for banks to provide new credit and reinforcing the downturn of the cycle. The application of "fair value" or mark-to-market accounting rules to the determination of the capital adequacy of financial institutions that were active in the trade of securitized instruments would have exacerbated this procyclical bias.[24]

Another flaw in the existing capital adequacy standards is that they encouraged banks to transfer securitized assets such as MBS and CDOs to off-balance sheet entities (structured investment vehicles or special purpose vehicles) where they would be subject to very low capital charges. Initially, under the Basel standards, a zero risk weight (or no capital charge) was assigned to assets held in SIVs, as well as to so-called liquidity enhancements, or short-term lines of credit that sponsoring banks issued to SIVs to maintain their financial integrity in the event they were unable to roll over their funding in the capital markets. Subsequently, in 2004, regulatory authorities in the United States ruled that off-balance sheet assets supported by a liquidity enhancement would be subject to a conversion factor of 10 percent for purposes of calculating capital charges, which implied that such assets would carry a capital charge equivalent to only one-tenth of that which the same asset would carry on the balance sheet of the bank.[25]

In general, the Basel II accord gave more favorable treatment to mortgage securities with respect to their treatment under Basel I, which the recent crisis has shown to be unwarranted. Under the revised Basel standard, the risk weight for securitized assets such as MBS and CDOs that were held on the "trading book" of the bank's balance sheet was only 20 percent if that security carried a AAA rating, even though the underlying mortgage credits if held on the "lending book" of the bank would have carried a risk weight of 50 percent, compared with 100 percent for other consumer loans.[26]

An additional problem in the existing capital adequacy standards is the overall design of the Basel II accord. It is based on a so-called three-pillar approach that the crisis has shown to be severely flawed. The three pillars involved the following: (1) minimum capital requirements which, in the case of large banks, would be determined by their own internal risk models; (2) supervisory review of these requirements; and (3) public disclosure by banks of their financial positions and risk exposures to allow private market monitoring to operate as a discipline on bank behavior. In effect, this framework changed the basic approach of regulation from one that was solely reliant on the supervisory process to one which would rely on the combined forces of bank owners and their risk managers, supervisors, and market forces.[27] Such a change was fully consistent with the ideological biases examined in the previous chapter, which emphasized the self-regulating ability of markets and the reputational credit of financial institutions as deterrents to excessively risky behavior.

In the determination of minimum capital requirements, the revised accord recognized that most banks would not have the resources to develop their own internal risk models, in which case they would follow a so-called standardized approach in which risk weights were aligned with the ratings provided by credit rating agencies, where applicable, to the loans and securities held by the bank. The general effect of this new approach to capital requirements was effectively to lower minimum credit requirements with respect to Basel I and to introduce a competitive advantage in favor of the large financial institutions, which generally relied on some variant of VAR methodology for their internal risk modeling. The accord also recognized for the first time an official role for the private credit rating agencies in the regulatory process.

None of the innovations of the Basel II accord explained above operated effectively in the period preceding the current crisis. Internal risk models based on VAR calculations severely underestimated capital requirements for the large banks; the rating agencies provided unrealistically positive valuations for many of the structured finance products that were being traded among banks; and the transparency of bank reporting was severely limited, especially as regards their off-balance sheet (SIV) transactions and the extent of their leveraged positions.

The process by which this approach was embodied in the Basel standard represents a classic example of regulatory capture by the major international banking institutions, operating within an intellectual environment that minimized the need for financial regulation and promoted the self-regulating power of financial markets. In part, this result is inherent in the workings of the Basel Committee itself which, before the crisis, was limited to its G10 membership (plus Luxembourg, Spain, and Switzerland) and could be expected to be responsive to the interests of the large banks operating in their territories. It also represents an interesting case of the role played by private institutions within the IFA. By tradition and longevity, the private credit rating agencies (Fitch, Moody's and Standard and Poors) have come to play a powerful role in the determination of risk weights that national regulatory bodies use in assessing capital adequacy requirements and the creditworthiness of sovereign governments around the world. Since 1975, they have been given the status of Nationally Registered Statistical Rating Organizations (NRSROs) by the US Securities and Exchange Commission which simply recognized their established market status, but effectively granted them exclusive authority for the valuation of traded financial instruments and government bonds. However, before the recent crisis, the NRSROs were not supervised by the SEC, nor were they required to disclose the methodologies they used in their rating assessments. As noted earlier, they also operated with clear conflicts of interest vis-a-vis their main clients.

The other private entity, which has gained influence in deliberations on the IFA, is the Institute of International Finance (IIF). As discussed in chapter 5, this institution was formed in 1982 to assist the commercial banks in their debt workouts with developing countries following the outbreak of the international debt crisis. During the second reform of the IFA, the IIF played an important role in the debate over the Sovereign Debt Restructuring Mechanism and presented a strong voice opposing its creation on behalf of its major bank shareholders. During the debates within the Basel Committee on Bank Supervision, the IIF acted as a strong lobbyist for the internal risk model approach adopted in the Basel II accord.[28]

An International Lender of Last Resort Mechanism

The lack of an international lender of last resort mechanism for the IFA was revealed most clearly in the years preceding the current crisis by the pattern of self-insurance that many emerging market economies had exhibited in their large accumulation of foreign reserves. As noted earlier, efforts by the Fund to create a Contingent Credit Line were not successful during the early years of the last decade because of certain limitations in the design of the facility. These countries have also viewed large foreign reserve positions as a preferred alternative to the use of conditional resources from the Fund. In addition, in certain regions, there has been an effort to establish reserve-pooling mechanisms in the absence of an international facility, such as the Chiang Mai Initiative involving the ASEAN countries plus China, Korea and Japan, noted earlier.[29]

In the wake of the global crisis that erupted in October 2008, it is striking to note that even these reserve defenses were inadequate to withstand the severe downward pressure on emerging market exchange rates arising from the cessation and withdrawal of capital flows during the last quarter of 2008. Thus began a third wave of capital flow volatility for the emerging market and developing countries, which has continued to present a problem for the IFA.

The growing phenomenon of self-insurance on the part of the emerging market economies reflected a fundamental problem in the IFA in that there has been no central insurance pool or effective international lender of last resort mechanism at the global level that would obviate the need for large reserve accumulation by individual countries. Such behavior is clearly inefficient for the global system and represents a large cost for the countries involved in terms of foregone investment and yield. One of the failures of the second reform of the IFA was not to put in place an emergency liquidity facility in the IMF, which countries could access in the event of a speculative attack. The establishment of a Contingent Credit Line in the IMF was not successful because countries saw relatively little difference between the CCL and access to regular facilities of the Fund. In addition, countries in East Asia, if not elsewhere, have been reluctant to use the regular facilities of the IMF under its "enlarged access" policy because of the stigma associated with such borrowing and the concerns expressed over the burden of structural conditionality imposed during the financial crises of the 1990s.

The International Financial Architecture and Crisis Management

Initially the response to the global financial crisis, given the rapid and unexpected pace of events, was handled at the level of individual governments in the advanced countries in close consultation with each other. Subsequently, the G20 was called into action, both at the ministerial and at the heads of government level, to act as a coordinating mechanism for the IFA. The initial policy responses were focused primarily on a substantial easing of monetary policy, official support for the financial sector, and countercyclical fiscal policy. Through mid-2010, the role of the IFA in crisis management can be viewed to have been very effective.

In the area of monetary policy, central banks in the United States, the United Kingdom, and euro area quickly instituted a sequence of policy rate reductions in September 2008 that was followed later in the year by a policy of "quantitative easing" by which substantial liquidity was made available to the financial sector after policy rates had been reduced to extremely low levels (near zero in the case of the United States). Under the latter framework, central banks expanded the size of their balance sheets by providing additional liquidity facilities to nonbank financial institutions and acted as a "market-maker of last resort" for financial assets for which trading had come to a virtual halt. In terms of both the range of financial institutions involved and the size of asset purchases, the balance sheet operations of the major central banks were unprecedented. The pace and depth of these actions differed across the three monetary policy areas given different policy mandates and frameworks for policy action. Action by the ECB, both before and after September 2008, tended to lag that of the United States and the United Kingdom given its exclusive mandate for controlling inflation and somewhat slower perception of the impact of the financial crisis on the European economy. Through June 2009, the amount of liquidity support provided by the central banks of the advanced countries amounted to US$2.5 trillion, or an average of nearly 7 percent of respective GDP.[30]

In the area of financial sector support, less consistent policies were followed. In the area of deposit guarantees, for example, early action by some countries (e.g., Ireland) to establish full backing of banking system deposits was not coordinated with other European countries that created tensions and panic in those countries that did not follow suit. Liquidity support mechanisms were established by several central banks at the national level, without consideration of the potential need for international coordination of dollar swap arrangements to deal with a surge in demand for US dollar assets as the crisis deepened.

In the case of failures by certain large globally active financial institutions, actions taken by the home country were not coordinated with that of the host countries where the financial institution had operations. Conflicts between home and host country supervisors over the burden sharing of insolvency led to a "ring-fencing" approach of segmenting the asset and liability positions of foreign bank branches or subsidiaries in host country jurisdictions to protect host country depositors. The failure of two large banks domiciled in Iceland in late 2008, which had large operations in the United Kingdom and the Netherlands, has led to a protracted conflict among the three countries over financial responsibility for their failure. In the case of the failure of Lehman Brothers, an attempt by Barclays Bank to acquire the US investment bank prior to its bankruptcy was not successful, in part because of weak consultation between the US and UK regulatory authorities. Subsequently, the decision of the US authorities to let Lehman Brothers go into bankruptcy was not coordinated with major European countries whose financial institutions were significantly involved with it. As a result, the UK and other European authorities "ring-fenced" Lehman's assets in their countries to protect its depositors in that country that conflicted with the bankruptcy procedures being pursued by the US authorities.[31] Similar problems were experienced in handling the resolution of insolvencies among European governments, for example, in respect of the Fortis bank group.[32] Experiences such as these have pointed to significant gaps in the IFA with respect to a cross-border resolution mechanism for large globally active financial institutions, as well as in the coordination of supervision for such firms.

Notwithstanding these problems of coordination, beginning in late 2008, governments across the advanced countries initiated a broad-based program of capital injection, asset purchases, and loan guarantees to support their financial sectors which, as of mid-2009, cumulated to an amount of US$7.7 trillion, or the equivalent of around 25 per cent of GDP, on average, for the G20 countries.[33] Notably, during this period of financial turmoil, the basic infrastructure of payment, clearing and settlement systems for foreign exchange and securities transactions operated without major disruption.

The third area of policy response to the crisis in respect of fiscal policy was also characterized by an initial lack of international coordination, notwithstanding early calls by the IMF for such action.[34] A political consensus on the need for fiscal policy stimulus in the United States was demonstrated by an initial effort of the Bush administration in mid-2008, which was followed by a much larger fiscal support package in early 2009 as one of the first actions of the new Obama administration. By contrast, there was much more skepticism about the need for fiscal stimulus within Europe, and early resistance to such action by Germany, which was perhaps best placed to implement fiscal expansion given its sound fiscal position before the crisis. Ultimately, a coordinated European fiscal response was engineered by the European Commission in early 2009, which was weaker than that of the United States. Again, as the spread and depth of the crisis became widely perceived, governments in the advanced countries shifted to a policy of significant fiscal ease. According to data compiled by the IMF, overall government deficits for the G20 countries deteriorated by around 6 percent of GDP in 2009 with respect to precrisis levels in 2007, on a weighted average basis; of this amount, 2 percent of GDP reflected discretionary fiscal action to deal with the effects of the crisis, apart from measures to provide financial sector support noted earlier. Most of the remaining effect on the fiscal deficit (of around 4 percent of GDP) reflected the impact of automatic stabilizers.[35]

Although fiscal actions to support the financial sector and stimulate economic recovery have generally been effective, they have resulted in a heavy debt burden for the advanced countries. According to IMF estimates, the average debt burden for the G20 advanced countries will deteriorate by approximately 40 percentage points of GDP with respect to precrisis levels to reach 118 per cent of GDP by 2014. By contrast, the average debt burden for the G20 emerging economies will remain largely unchanged at approximately 36 percent of GDP over the same time period. The challenge of restoring fiscal sustainability in the advanced countries will remain one of the enduring legacies of the global crisis (IMF FAD 2009).

The international effort to involve the machinery of the IFA in crisis management was initiated with a call by the European governments to organize a series of meetings of the G20, at the level of both heads of state and finance minister/central bank governors. The first of these took place in November 2008 (in Washington, DC), which was followed up by meetings in April 2009 (London), September 2009 (Pittsburgh), and June 2010 (Toronto). Following the heads of government meeting in November 2010 (Seoul), the G20 Summits will revert to their annual cycle, while the finance ministers and central bank governors will continue to meet on a quarterly basis. The call to action of the G20 was highly significant for the IFA, as it was a recognition on the part of the advanced countries that the G20, rather than the G7, was the appropriate steering committee for managing the global response to the financial crisis. Since November 2008, the G7/8 have not made any pronouncements on the management of the crisis, nor on reform of the IFA in deference to the preeminent role of the G20. This action is significant in that the G7 ministerial group had been acting as the steering committee for the IFA since the mid-1970s and was the principal coordinator of the international response to the financial crises of the 1990s.

As noted earlier, one of the outcomes of the second reform of the IFA was the creation of the G20 in 1999 as a consultative group involving the G7 and the main emerging market economies, at the finance minister/central bank governor level. Such a grouping was seen as appropriate given that the main thrust of the second reform was directed at the emerging market economies. Before the current crisis, the G20 had kept a relatively low profile in relation to the G7. There was little publicity about their annual meetings, communiques were limited to a brief discussion of the topics on the Group's agenda, and policy recommendations were not generated from their deliberations. Very little information about the work of the group was provided on the Group's website (www.G20.org). The current crisis has elevated the G20 to a significantly higher level of importance. More than anything else, this change is a reflection of the growing importance of the large emerging market economies, such as Brazil, China, and India, in the international economic and financial system, which is likely to have implications for the governance of IFA as examined in the next chapter. The new role of the G20 in global economic governance was confirmed in the communiqué of the Leaders' Summit in September 2009 when they declared that the G20 was "the premier forum for international economic cooperation."

In calling the G20 to action, political leaders have been clearly aware of the problems that a lack of policy coordination created for the recovery from the Great Depression of the 1930s, to which the current crisis has been often compared. The effects of that crisis on the global economy would not have been as deep nor as long had there been a successful effort to coordinate national policy responses. In this connection, the essential role of the G20 has been to ensure that policy responses of countries are broadly consistent and that policies such as competitive exchange rate devaluations and trade restrictions, which exacerbated the impact of the Great Depression, are avoided. In this policy coordination role, the G20 has helped to avoid a "free rider" problem, which can frustrate effective collective action in the absence of a monitoring mechanism.

The G20 process has essentially pursued three tracks in its response to the global crisis: one was to identify appropriate policy responses and to monitor progress in implementation; the second was to mobilize financial support to ease the global liquidity strains of the crisis; and the third was to chart the main reform effort to improve the IFA in regard to its crisis prevention and management capabilities for the future. The effort in the third area just mentioned will give rise to the third reform of the IFA, once again driven by crisis. Both the IMF and FSF have played key roles in supporting the G20 process.

Setting the Policy Agenda

On the policy front, the G20 has consistently supported a four-pronged approach among its membership to deal with the global crisis. The first was related to crisis containment by means of direct government action to stabilize national financial systems through central bank liquidity provision, loan and deposit guarantees, and the recapitalization of financial institutions. The second was to reinforce actions already being taken by the advanced country central banks in the area of monetary expansion through a reduction in policy rates and actions to expand their balance sheets. The third prong was support for a policy of fiscal stimulus to bolster aggregate demand in the face of sharp declines in private consumption and investment. Finally, the G20 played a useful role in limiting national efforts at trade protectionism and in mobilizing support for a renewed commitment to the Doha round of trade talks.

In this activity, the IMF has played a key role as an informal secretariat for the G20. The IMF has taken the lead in quantifying the magnitude of the fiscal effort required to sustain the global economy in the wake of the financial crisis and in estimating the magnitude of financial sector losses for the most affected countries that would need to be addressed through public and private capital injections. The Fund has also prepared regular, periodic updates for the G20 on changes in the global economic outlook and prospects. In this connection, the Fund has been active in monitoring the implementation of policies of the G20 governments in the three areas noted above.

Mobilizing Additional Financing for the Global Economy

Special financing arrangements to deal with the global financial crisis have come in the form of an activation of an international lender of last resort (ILOLR) mechanism operating through the combined efforts of the major financial center central banks and the IMF, temporary additional resources to support IMF lending operations, and a new SDR allocation. Resources under these three mechanisms have amounted to the equivalent of around US$1.5 trillion.

The US Federal Reserve assumed the lead in activating an ILOLR mechanism in view of a global demand for US dollars, which emerged in the second half of 2008, to fill funding gaps of financial institutions arising from heightened counterparty risk and a flight to "safe haven" dollar-based assets. Initially, in December 2007, the Federal Reserve put in place modest foreign exchange swap facilities with the Swiss National Bank (US$4 billion) and the European Central Bank (US$20 billion). Beginning in September 2008, with heightened turmoil in interbank money and foreign exchange markets, these facilities were substantially expanded in size and number. By end-October, reciprocal currency arrangements had been put in place with nine central banks, including for the first time, those of Brazil, Korea, Mexico, and Singapore (each for US$30 billion), while the limits on existing lines with the Bank of Canada, the Bank of England, the European Central Bank, and the Bank of Japan were removed. By early February 2009, the Federal Reserve's swap network had been expanded to include the central banks of Australia, Denmark, New Zealand, Norway, and Sweden, bringing the total bilateral lines of credit to fourteen. In certain cases, these swap facilities were reinforced by additional bilateral lines of credit in other currencies to the Bank of Korea from the Bank of Japan, to the central banks of Hungary and Poland from the ECB and Swiss National Bank, and to the central bank of Iceland from the three Scandinavian central banks, bringing the total network to twenty-two.[36] While this swap network played a vital role in easing pressures in international money and foreign exchange markets, it is not clear what criteria were used to select the countries involved or to determine the limits of the swap lines.

Given the acute shortage of dollars that was manifested in the international banking system among the advanced countries, total drawings on the Federal Reserve reached a peak of US$583 billion in December 2008 that were then reduced to US$50 billion by October 2009 and fully repaid by February 1, 2010.[37] This was an unprecedented action on the part of the Federal Reserve as an ILOLR in size and scope, which was critical to the containment of the crisis and the stabilization of short-term money and foreign exchange markets. During the 1960s, the Federal Reserve had played a similar role to defend the Bretton Woods system.

At the end of October 2008, action was taken by the IMF to create a Short-term Liquidity Facility (SLF) in an effort to supplement the ILOLR initiated by the Federal Reserve with a view to providing short-term financial assistance to countries that were not included in the central bank swap network discussed earlier. This was the second attempt by the Fund to create an ILOLR mechanism following the failure of the CCL in the early years of the decade. Unlike regular financial arrangements from the Fund, access to the FSL would be determined on the basis of certain eligibility criteria related to the strength of their macroeconomic policy framework and external prospects. Access was limited to the equivalent of 500 percent of a member country's quota for a maximum period of three months.

Unfortunately, for a second time, these terms were not attractive to the membership, and there were no requests for access. In March 2009, it was decided to liberalize significantly potential access under such a facility (which was relabeled the Flexible Credit Line) by increasing the access limit to ten times a country's quota and extending the time period for drawings up to a limit of three years. With this revision, three emerging market countries (Mexico, Colombia, and Poland) signed up for the facility for a total access of around US$80 billion. Such an amount committed most of the notional amount that the IMF had committed for such financing in late 2008 when the global crisis erupted.[38]

In addition to these efforts, the IMF became active in the negotiation of regular financial arrangements with a number of emerging market economies, in particular Eastern and Central European and CIS countries that had been highly dependent on foreign bank financing from commercial banks in the euro zone. Between September 2008 and May 2009, the Fund approved financial arrangements with fifteen countries directly affected by the crisis for a cumulative amount of US$82 billion. Access under some of these arrangements was similar in relation to IMF quotas to those approved during the 1990s, as noted in table 5.2, although conditionality was more streamlined and simplified. As in the case of financial crises in the 1990s, many of these arrangements were supported by parallel financing from other official sources, including both the European Union (US$21 billion) and individual European governments (US$26 billion) for the countries of Eastern and Central Europe, and the World Bank (US$11 billion) in other cases.[39] Similarly, in May 2010, the IMF coordinated with the EU in providing a combined three-year line of credit equivalent to US$145 billion for Greece, which represented the largest commitment of IMF resources in relation to quota (3,200 per cent), although not the largest commitment in monetary value.

In view of the pressure these lending operations were placing on the total resources of the IMF, in April 2009 the G20 decided to support a substantial increase in IMF resources temporarily from US$250 billion to US$750 billion through an augmentation of borrowing arrangements under the New Arrangements to Borrow (NAB) and a new program of bilateral borrowing from selected central banks.[40] In addition, the G20 agreed to a new allocation of SDRs for an amount of SDR162 billion (or around US$250 billion) to further increase the availability of international reserves in the international financial system. This allocation was the first one since the period 1979–81. At the same time, the G20 endorsed an expansion of US$150 billion in resources for the World Bank and the regional development banks to support an increase in trade financing. In addition, the Bank increased its lending operations from around US$24 billion a year during fiscal years (ending June) 2005–8 to an average of US$53 billion during the last two years, in response to the withdrawal of private financing from developing countries.

Preparing for the Postcrisis World

Since its first meeting in November 2008, the G20 has given particular emphasis to the lessons of the crisis for regulatory reform, the role of macroeconomic policy, and reform of the IFA. In the first area, the role of the FSF has featured prominently. In April 2008, it was asked by the G7 to conduct a thorough stocktaking of regulatory failures that had helped to foster the crisis and to begin the process of charting a path of reform (Financial Stability Forum 2008a and 2008b). Since late 2008, it has been active in coordinating with the BCBS on revisions to the Basel capital adequacy accord, the development of guidelines on executive compensation for financial service firms, and the preparation of a new framework for the regulation of large complex financial institutions and their resolution in the event of crisis. Broadly speaking, four areas of reform in national financial regulation are likely to emerge. One is that the perimeter of financial regulation will increase beyond the traditional banking system to include all financial institutions that may pose a potential risk to the financial system. A second set of reforms is under way to strengthen the Basel II capital adequacy standard which, among other things, will introduce an overall leverage ratio and liquidity requirement to complement higher capital requirements in limiting excessive leverage of financial institutions, as well as some form of dynamic provisioning and capital buffers to limit its procyclicality. A third change, which has been given strong endorsement at the international level, is the identification of a systemic regulatory agency within each national system to cover macroprudential risk. Finally, procedures will be put in place to facilitate the resolution of large financial institutions in cases where they cease to be viable without significant injections of government assistance. In this connection, colleges of national supervisors have been established in the advanced countries to allow for closer cooperation and information sharing in the supervision of large, complex financial institutions.

In the area of macroeconomic policy, the G20 has focused essentially on two issues: one is the timing and pace of withdrawal of monetary and fiscal stimulus and the exit strategy for this withdrawal, and the other is a plan to prevent the reemergence of the problem of global imbalances. In the second area, the G20 have committed themselves to a Framework for Strong, Sustainable, and Balanced Growth for 2010 and beyond, which will be a "mutual assessment" or "peer review" process of policy coordination in which the IMF will play a key advisory role. In this connection, the IMF was asked to provide an evaluation of the consistency of policy programs prepared by the G20 governments in January 2010, which the IMF evaluated in follow-up meetings at the ministerial and leaders levels of the G20 in April and June. In the second half of the year, a range of policy adjustments were proposed by the IMF to national economic programs, as warranted, for further consideration by governments in November.

This exercise holds out the prospect of a more effective process of policy coordination than that which resulted from the Fund's multilateral consultation procedure of 2006–7, although it has been complicated by inconsistent policy actions among the main surplus and deficit countries that need to adjust to bring about a global rebalancing. It also represents the first time that the G7 authorities, operating now within the G20, have acknowledged formally an important monitoring and surveillance function for the IMF in their policy discussions.

In respect of reform of the IFA, the G20 has focused its attention primarily on the work of the FSF and IMF. In April 2009, the G20 endorsed the conversion of the FSF to the Financial Stability Board (FSB) and an expansion of its membership to include representatives from all the G20 governments. As a Board, the FSB would have its own (small) secretariat, but would still fall short of constituting a new institutional arrangement within the IFA. It also has been given an expanded list of responsibilities that may go beyond its limited capacity to deliver (see chapter 9), including closer coordination with the IMF in carrying out the oversight of global financial system stability. To this effect, the FSB and IMF have been asked to prepare for the IMFC joint "early warning exercises" of emerging risks and vulnerabilities in the global financial system, the first of which was considered in October 2009.

In regard to the IMF, the G20 has recognized the need for reform in its governance arrangements, but has not spelled out a clear vision for the role of the IMF in the future of the IFA. This task is attempted in the next chapter.

Summary and Conclusion

The transformation of a financial crisis in the United States into a global financial and economic crisis during the fall of 2008 represented both a failing and a challenge for the IFA. The eruption of the crisis reflected a failure of crisis prevention on the part of the IFA, whereas management of the crisis has introduced new challenges for the architecture. As in the past, the magnitude of this crisis has made it clear that further reforms of the architecture are needed to deal with the problems of global finance. This process, which will be ongoing for the next few years, will constitute its third reform.

The inability of the IFA to forestall the recent crisis reflected problems in the functioning of both the international monetary system and the international financial system. Within the international monetary system, the problem of global imbalances, which helped to foster the lax monetary conditions that contributed to the crisis, reflected a fundamental flaw in the international adjustment mechanism. In this connection, the rigidity of exchange rates for persistent surplus countries in the global economy and the inability of the IMF to act as an effective forum for international policy coordination are important defects that need to be addressed in the third reform of the IFA. Both the bilateral and multilateral surveillance mechanisms of the IMF need to be strengthened to reinforce the international adjustment process. Similarly, the pronounced tendency on the part of developing countries since the time of the second reform of the architecture to accumulate high levels of foreign reserves as a form of self-insurance against financial crises reflects a fundamental weakness in the ILOLR mechanism within the architecture. Again, the IMF is the logical place in which to establish such a mechanism, at least for the developing countries, but it has been hampered by an insufficiency of financial resources and governance problems that limit its effectiveness and legitimacy.

At the level of the international financial system, the recent crisis has clearly revealed problems in the coordination of international financial regulation, in both its macroprudential and microprudential dimensions. In regard to the former dimension, the oversight of global financial stability during the past decade was split across at least three entities, the BIS, the FSF, and the IMF, with insufficient coordination among the three. Although both the BIS and IMF were carrying out periodic assessments of the global financial system, these analytical reviews did not identify specific vulnerabilities in the advanced countries and did not support a decision-making process in which vulnerabilities, if identified, could be addressed. The FSF was intended to foster coordination among disparate elements of the IFA, but it has been hampered by the fact that it has no executive or decision-making authority and has only served as a forum for information sharing among its constituent members. Nor was it given a mandate to play an independent role in monitoring national regulatory practices in the G7 countries. In addition, the simple fact that none of the G7 members, except Canada and Italy, participated in an FSAP exercise with the IMF in the three years (2005–7) preceding the crisis deprived it and the IMF of one important diagnostic tool that might have revealed potential risks for global financial stability.

As regards microprudential regulation, the main focus at the international level since the second reform of the IFA was the revision of the Basel Accord on capital adequacy standards. The crisis has revealed fundamental problems with the conceptual approach adopted for the revision of the Basel Accord, which was in the process of being implemented among the advanced countries at the time the crisis erupted. The so-called three-pillar approach of Basel II involving, among other things, the use of internal risk models for the large banks, increased reliance on risk weights linked to the evaluations of the major credit rating agencies, and greater reliance on information disclosure to market participants provided a very weak environment for regulating financial institutions before the crisis. Both the internal rating models based on VAR calculations and the ratings provided for securitized instruments have proven to be highly flawed. In addition, banks concealed from both investors and the regulators the true extent of their balance sheet risk because of extensive reliance on off-balance sheet transactions by means of SIVs. Both Basel I and Basel II were also problematic in the lead up to the crisis in that they assigned inappropriate risk weights to securitized products and virtually eliminated capital requirements for off-balance sheet transactions of the banks; they also exhibited a procyclical bias that contributed to the speculative phase of the housing bubble in many countries.

In its management of the recent crisis, the IFA has responded well and has helped to forestall a repeat of the Great Depression, which was greatly feared at a time of international financial panic during October 2008. The central banks of the major financial center countries, following the lead of the Federal Reserve, initiated an aggressive, coordinated response to the crisis of confidence in the international financial system during the last quarter of 2008 by reducing sharply policy interest rates and by providing substantial liquidity facilities and asset market support for a wide range of financial institutions. The major central banks also put in place by early 2009 a large network of swap facilities, mainly for the advanced countries, which provided an important ILOLR mechanism on a temporary basis. In March 2009, this network was supplemented by a new emergency credit line of the IMF (the FCL) for certain prequalified emerging market economies, while access and conditionality under normal Fund arrangements was substantially eased for a number of other developing countries most affected by the crisis.

In late 2008, the G20 at both the ministerial and heads of government levels was called into action to function as a coordinating body for crisis management. The transfer of this responsibility from the G7 to the G20 was significant for the governance of the IFA, as it recognized the important role that the main emerging market economies needed to play in the management of the international financial system. The IMF carried out an important supporting role for the G20 in establishing the need for coordinated fiscal action to mitigate the effects of the crisis on the global economy (through fiscal stimulus) and to rehabilitate the financial sector in the main industrial countries. The G20 also provided important political support for a temporary augmentation of the Fund's financial resources to allow it to contribute to the ILOLR mechanism noted earlier.

Notwithstanding efforts of the G20 to coordinate national responses to the global financial crisis, some degree of "financial protectionism" was clear in the actions of national regulators in dealing with the effects of the financial crisis. The timing and scope of deposit guarantees that governments put in place varied across countries, which added to financial stress in certain jurisdictions, while ring-fencing of asset and liability positions of large financial institutions with multicountry operations was common. These latter actions complicated the process of government intervention in failing institutions and pointed to problems in the sharing of regulatory information and the absence of arrangements for burden sharing in the event of insolvency of large multinational financial firms.

CHAPTER 9

The Third Reform of the International Financial Architecture

The current global financial crisis has revealed clear problems in the functioning of the IFA, mainly in respect of crisis prevention. An international effort spear-headed by the G20 has been under way since late 2008 to address some of these problems, but it is not yet clear how far this process will go. The purpose of this chapter is to examine the broad scope of the global reform effort that is needed and to consider alternative proposals for addressing specific aspects of the reform agenda. In this commentary, areas where the reform considerations of the G20 fall short are identified.

The reform of the IFA needs to be premised on a vision of how the international financial system should function for the benefit of advanced and developing countries alike and of what public goods are essential for its effective functioning. Once having established the key public goods that are required to support the proper functioning of the international monetary and financial system, the mandate and governance of the key institutions within the IFA need to be addressed. The recent financial crisis has made it clear once again, as in past financial crises, that problems in the functioning of the international financial system can threaten the prosperity of individual countries and undermine the stability of the global economy. These problems can be identified as (1) the tendency of the system to support bubble phenomena across borders through the persistence of global imbalances; (2) the volatility of private capital flows to developing countries that have a pronounced procyclical character and can have highly disruptive economic effects; (3) the development of large, complex financial institutions (LCFIs) with significant cross-border activities that are "too big to fail" and can threaten financial system stability; (4) and the "perverse" flow of capital from developing to advanced countries for self-insurance purposes.

These problems again point to the need for certain public goods that the IFA should provide, which were identified in chapter 2. One is an effective international adjustment mechanism to avoid the problem of global imbalances. A second is an effective international lender of last resort or global insurance mechanism, which would minimize the need for self-insurance against the threat of private capital volatility. A third is effective oversight of global financial system stability to detect excessive leverage and concentrations of financial risk and identify vulnerabilities in the international financial system. A fourth is a system of international financial regulation to deal with the problem of financial institutions that are "too big to fail" and to mitigate the procyclical tendency of private capital flows. Finally, there needs to be a system of development finance to ensure a minimum flow of development capital to developing countries that do not participate fully in the global financial system and a sovereign debt workout mechanism for countries with unsustainable debt burdens.

The main contours of the reform effort under way suggest a reinforcement of existing institutional arrangements with a strengthening of the FSF (now FSB) in the field of international financial regulation and an enhancement of the IMF's financing and surveillance functions to support global financial system stability. These two institutions encompass the global equivalent of the regulatory, policy, and financial aspects that a central bank and regulatory agency provide at the national level, but without the full supranational authority implied by that analogy.

Notwithstanding this reinforcement of existing structures, it is clear that overlapping and duplicative arrangements continue to exist within the IFA. The work of the BIS has a significant degree of overlap with that of the IMF in their policy, research, statistics, and financial activities. In the area of surveillance for the advanced countries, there is obvious duplication in the work of the IMF, OECD, G7, and EU. In addition, there has been a proliferation of informal bodies involved in the transgovernmental aspects of the IFA that have promoted cooperation, information exchange, and the development of "soft" law for the global financial system, which need to be coordinated.

In the light of these considerations, the most important issue facing the IFA is its governance structure, in particular as regards power-sharing, lines of authority, and accountability arrangements. This issue is taken up first in the remainder of this chapter, followed by a consideration of the main problems in the delivery of public goods for the global financial system dealing with the workings of the international adjustment mechanism, a lender of last resort mechanism, the oversight of global financial stability, international financial regulation, and sovereign debt restructuring.

Governance Arrangements

One of the key defects in the governance of the IFA, which the current crisis has revealed, is the absence of a central consultative and policy-making body to coordinate decisions regarding its operations. On a de facto basis, this has been handled by the G7 and now the G20, but these are not universal bodies. Although the G20 is far more representative than the G7 of the preponderant weight of economic power in the global financial system, it still excludes the representation of most countries in the global economy. Moreover, it is a self-appointed body without any established criteria or system of rotation for its membership, which weakens its legitimacy. In the light of these considerations, some analysts have recommended the creation of a Global Economic Security Council operating within the United Nations to oversee all aspects of the international economic and financial architecture, including official aid, trade issues, and finance.[1] However, such a body would have a highly complex portfolio and would require the coordination of many different ministerial functions at the national level in its governmental representation and a host of institutions at the international level. Alternatively, it has been suggested that the G20 could be replaced by a similar grouping of countries representing the largest shares of global population or GDP, which could be seen as reasonably objective criteria for membership and would allow for some rotation as these shares change over time. For example, using the threshold of a share of global GDP or population larger than 2 percent as criteria for membership would result in a list of sixteen countries that would be more representative and somewhat smaller than the current G20, which in fact has begun to exceed that numerical limit with the inclusion of the Netherlands and Spain because of their insistence on membership.[2]

Within the IFA itself, one group that could also serve as its steering committee is the IMFC, which oversees the work of the IMF. It has the virtue of being a committee of universal membership, based on the constituency system of the IMF. Up until now, the IMFC has operated only as an advisory body on behalf of the Board of Governors of the IMF, which are generally finance ministers of the 187 governments that constitute the shareholders of the institution. Under the existing Fund

Agreement, it could be converted into a decision-making IMF Council; alternatively, the IMFC could be reconstituted as an International Monetary and Financial Council, which could provide more legitimacy than the G20, if certain changes are made in the governance of the IMF itself that are discussed below. The point of such a conversion would be to identify a clearer locus of political authority for the management of the IFA within a strong institutional basis, and as such it should exercise oversight of not only the IMF, but also the FSB.[3] Such an arrangement would make sense given the primary responsibility that the IMF and FSB in effect share for the oversight of global financial system stability and the need to enhance coordination between the two bodies. Linking the FSB to the IMFC would suggest changing the country membership in the FSB over time to a constituency system or one of rotating regional members to improve its representation and legitimacy. In addition, the IMFC should become the focal point for discussion and decision on issues relating to crisis prevention and crisis management within the international financial system.

Some further attention needs to be given to the division of labor between the IMF and the FSB. In November 2008, the heads of these two bodies signed an aide-memoire that established for the first time an understanding about the respective roles of the two bodies regarding global financial system stability. Accordingly, the FSF was to take the lead in overseeing and coordinating the regulatory aspects of the international financial system, while the IMF was to monitor the macrofinancial aspects of the global financial system. Together, they would prepare a joint "early warning exercise" on vulnerabilities and risks to the global financial system twice a year for the consideration of the IMFC.

In April 2009 when the FSF was converted to the FSB and its membership was expanded from the G7 (plus Australia, Hong Kong, Singapore, and Switzerland) to the G20, the Charter that was devised by the G20 for the FSB considerably expanded its scope and responsibilities.[4] As part of its mandate, for example, the FSB will "assess vulnerabilities affecting the global financial system, . . . promote coordination and information exchange among authorities responsible for financial stability, . . . and monitor and advise on market developments and their implications for regulatory policy."[5] The significant expansion in the mandate of the FSB raises two problems and concerns: one is whether it will have sufficient technical staff to carry out these functions, as at present it is expected to have a secretariat of only around a dozen or so staff; and the other is whether some of its new responsibilities might better by carried out by the IMF.[6] Thus, the division of labor between these two bodies needs to be revisited, with a clearer demarcation for oversight of international financial regulation residing with the FSB, joint responsibility of the IMF and FSB for oversight of global financial stability (e.g., through the preparation of joint EWS exercise, among other things), and global surveillance and financing responsibilities in the IMF.

A reconstituted IMFC will not carry the authority and legitimacy it deserves without further governance reform of the IMF itself. Such reform is essential to restore the effectiveness of the IMF as the central, universal institution within the IFA. These issues relate to country representation ("voice and vote"), leadership selection, and the role of the Executive Board. The reform of IMF governance has been debated extensively for most of the period since the second reform of the IFA without significant advance, but the current crisis has given renewed attention to such reform at a higher political level, including the Leaders' Summits of the G20.[7] Given the strong parallelism in the governance structure of the IMF and World Bank, the three issues noted above also need to be addressed within the latter institution as well.

Under the quota-based determination of voting power, access to IMF financial resources and SDR allocations, it is important that quotas be revised regularly to ensure that relative county shares are realigned with shifts of relative economic strength among the Fund membership. Even though there is a procedure for the revision of quotas on a five-year basis, shifts in the relative power between advanced and developing countries have been slow to take place. At the same time, the size of total Fund quotas has fallen significantly with respect to the value of global trade or capital flows since 1945.

These outcomes reflect, on the one hand, a reluctance of the major shareholders to increase the size of IMF financial resources on a permanent basis and, on the other hand, a pattern of allocating most of any agreed increase in quotas in the past on an equi-proportionate basis rather than on a selective basis to realign relative quota shares among countries.[8] As a result, certain striking anomalies have resulted; for example, Belgium and the Netherlands have a combined quota (4.5 percent of the total) that is larger than that of China (3.7 percent) and India (1.9 percent), even though each of the latter two economies is much larger than the former two combined, as measured by GDP on a purchasing-power-parity (PPP) basis. More generally, the European countries are overrepresented in the Fund with 32 percent of total quotas, compared with a 17 percent share for the United States, even though the nominal GDP of the two regions is roughly the same size. In addition, European countries are in control of eight of the twenty-four chairs in the Executive Board of the IMF (and a ninth chair on a rotating basis).

In April 2008, a decision was made by the IMF to revise the formula for determining quota shares in the Fund, which would bring about a shift of around 2.7 percent in the relative shares of the advanced and developing countries in the Fund, which were split sixty to forty, respectively. Some improvements were made in the quota formula in that a single formula was established to replace a combination of five formulas that had been in use previously. Changes were also made in the definition of the four variables that have been used in the quota formulas, namely national income, openness, variability, and international reserves. In the case of national income, instead of using nominal GDP in US dollars measured at current exchange rates, this variable is now computed using a weighted average of that measure (60 percent) and GDP in US dollars measured at PPP exchange rates (40 percent). The latter measure tends to increase the size of nominal GDP for developing countries with respect to the former measure because of their lower costs for a standard international consumption basket. In addition, for the measure of variability, its computation was expanded to include net capital inflows along with current receipts.[9]

Notwithstanding these improvements, the revised quota formula has certain defects that continue to bias quota calculation in favor of the advanced countries. One problem is that the computation of openness, which is based on current external receipts and payments (for goods, services, income, and transfers), includes intraunion trade for the European Union (EU), which exaggerates the calculation of quotas for EU countries. Another problem is that the measure of variability, which is based on the standard deviation of current receipts and net capital flows, is highly correlated with openness and national income, and thus also has the effect of biasing the results of the quota formula in favor of the advanced countries. One way of correcting the latter problem would be to use a measure of variability related to the coefficient of variation (i.e., the standard deviation divided by the mean) rather than the standard deviation, or to measure openness and variability with respect to GDP.[10]

The April 2008 decision also adjusted the amount of "basic votes" in the IMF, which are assigned on an equal basis to all its members in addition to their quota-based votes. However, since these shares have not been adjusted upward over time, unlike quota shares, their relative weight in the determination of total voting power has fallen from around 11 percent to around 2 percent. The decision of April 2008 would increase the relative share of basic votes in total voting power to around 5 percent.

At the time of the IMF quota decision in 2008, there was widespread criticism of the result as it only moved a relatively small way in the direction of correcting the imbalance between voting shares of the advanced and developing countries, which should be given more equal weight in the view of many analysts. It was also regrettable that any further review of quotas was to be delayed for a period of five years. Against this background, it is significant that the G20 Leaders agreed at their Summit in September 2009 to reopen the quota issue and to seek a further shift of at least 5 percentage points in the relative shares of advanced and developing countries by early 2011 on the basis of the April 2008 formula. This decision leaves unclear, however, when the defects in that formula and the relative share of basic votes will be reconsidered.

The second aspect of governance reform of the IMF that needs to be addressed is leadership selection. Again, this is an issue that has received much attention since the last reform of the IFA, especially from global civil society groups, which have become an increasingly vocal form of "horizontal accountability" for the Bretton Woods institutions.[11] As noted earlier, leadership selection in the IMF and World Bank has effectively been controlled by the G10 and G7 with the result that the managing director has always been a European, while the president of the World Bank has always been an American. In 2001, the Executive Board of the Fund endorsed certain procedures to allow for a more open process of choosing the managing director, but these have been largely by-passed in the last three appointments. A transparent, merit-based selection process is essential for restoring the credibility and legitimacy of the IMF and World Bank. In this connection, it was symbolically important that at the Annual Meetings of the Fund in October 2008, for the first time, a finance minister from a non-Western country (Egypt) was selected as chair of the IMFC, which had previously been held by representatives of the G7 countries.

New rules for leadership selection should also apply to the three positions of deputy managing director in the IMF. While the position of first deputy managing director has always been assigned to an American, one of the two deputy managing directors has always been from Asia (usually Japan) and the other has been assigned to a representative from Africa or Latin America. In February 2010, Japan's claim on one of the two Deputy Managing Director positions was confirmed, when a former high-ranking official of Japan's Minister of Finance stepped down as deputy managing director, and another one took his place, without any formal selection process involving the nomination and consideration of alternative candidates.

The two communiqués of the G20 issued in November 2008 and April 2009 strongly endorsed an open, merit-based selection process for the appointment of the "heads and senior staff of the international financial institutions," although the qualification "without regard to nationality" that was included in the draft communiqué of April 2009 was dropped in the final version.[12] These declarations hopefully should open the door to the kind of changes in leadership selection noted earlier.

The role of the Executive Board in IMF (and World Bank) operations is the third key area of governance reform. In this regard, there are issues of size, selection process, voting rules, and responsibilities. The creation of an International Monetary and Financial Council or IMF Council, as recommended earlier in this chapter, would require a change in the responsibilities of the Executive Board. Giving more authority and decision-making power to such a council would simply dilute the power of the Executive Board unless it is given a new mandate and greater independence from Fund management. Executive directors now carry a dual function as both senior officers of the IMF and representatives of member governments. These functions do not necessarily coincide, and in practice their role as governmental representatives predominates. Modern practices of corporate governance would suggest a more detached role for the Executive Board, which could be achieved by reducing its role in the day-to-day functioning of the institution and delegating more authority for operational decision making to Fund management. In this context, it would be appropriate to separate the role of the managing director as both chief executive officer of the IMF and chairman of the Executive Board, since there is an inherent conflict of interest in these two responsibilities.[13] It would also make sense for the Board to monitor the management of the Fund in carrying out the strategy set by the IMF Council within a framework of accountability that it would establish. The power to make certain key decisions in regard to IMF operations could be retained by the Board, for example, in the area of budget authorizations and major reforms of IMF policy.

Parallel changes could also be considered in the World Bank, first with the conversion of the ministerial Development Committee to a Development Council. Such a council should be given clear decision-making responsibilities for World Bank activities and could be given a new mandate to oversee all aspects of official development assistance, consistent with its original mandate to oversee the activities of the IFA dealing with the transfer of real resources to developing countries. Accordingly, the roles of the Bank's Executive Board and dual responsibilities of the Bank president as chief executive officer and chairman of the Executive Board should change. The High Level Commission headed by former President of Mexico Ernesto Zedillo in its 2009 report made a strong case for breaking the parallelism in the voting shares of the Bank and Fund, given the different mandates of the two institutions (World Bank 2009). This principle has already been reflected in the voting arrangements for the IDA, which differ from those of the IBRD in that donor and recipient countries have roughly equal shares in its decision making. At the G20 Leaders' Summit in September 2009, it was agreed that a shift of nearly 5 percent in the relative voting shares of advanced and developing countries should be made in the World Bank, which was endorsed by the Development Committee in April 2010, along with the proposal to develop a new formula, distinct from that of the IMF, to support a move toward equity in these shares over time.

As governmental representatives, certain changes are warranted in the selection of executive directors for the Bank and Fund. Under current practice established by the Bretton Woods Agreement, five directors are appointed for indefinite terms by the five largest shareholders (United States, United Kingdom, Japan, Germany, and France), whereas other directors are elected by their constituencies for two-year terms. These arrangements create a substantial disparity in the potential influence of the appointed and elected directors. With a rebalancing of quota shares, as proposed earlier, this distinction has less justification, especially with a change in the responsibility of the Executive Board as discussed in the previous paragraph. In a recent review of the Fund's governance structure, the IMF IEO recommended that all Executive Directors be elected and allowed to form constituencies (IMF IEO 2008). This change could help to reduce the dominance of the European representation in the Board and bring about some consolidation in the number of chairs, which has expanded over time from twelve to twenty-four. Further consolidation could be achieved if the European Union (or the euro-zone countries) agreed to single representation in the Board, consistent with their participation in the WTO, as has been widely recommended. Such a change would also reduce the size of the proposed IMF and Development Councils as their membership follows the arrangement of constituencies established in the Executive Board.

With these changes in the selection of executive directors, it would also make sense to reconsider certain voting rules that now apply to Board procedures. In particular, the 85 percent super majority rule, which applies to the most important decisions under the Fund Agreement, is widely viewed as giving unique power to the United States as the largest shareholder (with 17 percent of quotas). In an effort to restore credibility of the institution and a rebalancing of power-sharing, this rule should be abandoned, with greater reliance on a double majority of voting power and countries, which now only applies to decisions on amendments to the Fund Agreement.

None of the changes in the role of the Executive Board, along the lines proposed here, have been considered formally by the G20. In addition, the Fund, at both the level of the IMFC and the Executive Board, has not reached any consensus on this issue (as of mid-2010), notwithstanding the recommendations of a number of official groups that are pending formal consideration. The Board itself in its preliminary deliberations has been divided on the merits of these proposals, in part because of its attachment to current operating arrangements including its consensual approach to decision making, which has tended to give more weight to the representatives of developing countries. Thus, it is clear that decisions on any changes in the role of the Executive Boards of the Fund and Bank will take some time, not least because they would involve amendments to the Fund and Bank Agreements, which can be a time-consuming process. It is also clear that they cannot be made without high-level political engagement of groups such as the G20, the IMFC, and Development Committee. These bodies should also take up consideration of proposed changes in the operations of the Bank and Fund with developing countries proposed in chapter 6.

The International Adjustment Mechanism

The role of the IMF in the international adjustment process needs to be strengthened to avoid a resurgence of the problem of global imbalances once the recovery from the recent crisis is well entrenched. In this connection, the decision of the G20 leaders at the Pittsburgh Summit in September 2009 to have the IMF play a key role in its peer review or mutual assessment process of macroeconomic policy coordination during 2010 was a positive sign of greater willingness to cooperate with the IMF that was not evident during the multilateral consultation exercise of 2006–7. The willingness of all members to cooperate with the Fund in its surveillance responsibilities could be enhanced with the changes in its governance structure discussed earlier.

However, other changes are needed to improve the IMF's own surveillance exercises, both bilateral and multilateral, on a permanent basis. In regard to bilateral surveillance conducted through the Article IV consultation process, a number of changes have been proposed to strengthen its impact, both substantively and procedurally. Notwithstanding repeated calls to enhance the links between country consultation reports and the analytical and policy framework of the WEO and GFSR exercises, the Fund's latest internal evaluation of the surveillance process continued to identify shortcomings in this regard.[14] In a similar vein, the lessons of the recent crisis make it incumbent on the organization to deepen its understanding of macrofinancial links in country analysis and to integrate more effectively the FSAP exercise with bilateral surveillance.

In terms of process, the Fund's bilateral surveillance mechanism needs to be improved both in terms of its delivery and consequences. The recent crisis has raised again a concern that the policy messages of the IMF in specific country cases were less forceful and direct than they should have been. To a significant extent, this criticism can be attributed to the role of the Executive Board in concluding the Article IV consultation procedure, as noted already in chapter 8. Once the staff team concludes the policy discussions with country authorities for the Article IV consultation, it prepares a report for the Executive Board, which is first approved by Fund management. Following discussion of the report by the Board, a Summing-Up of the Board discussion is issued that signals the conclusion of the procedure and represents the official view of the institution. However, internal reviews by the staff have shown that this process tends to soften the impact of important policy appraisals or critical assessments of a country's policy direction, given the consensual basis on which the Board operates. It is also the case that Board representation for many consultation exercises is often delegated to staff within the director's office below the level of the executive director, thus weakening the peer review aspect of the Board's deliberations. In the Fund's last internal review of surveillance in 2008, a significant share of the staff expressed the view that the Executive Board's involvement in bilateral surveillance provided little value-added to the consultation procedure, which was echoed in the IEO's own survey of Executive Directors.[15]

In this context, the governance reforms discussed in the previous section of this chapter, which would remove the Board from day-to-day responsibility for Fund operations, could lead to an improvement in the consultation procedure. Without the Board's intervention, Fund management could have a freer hand to highlight critical areas of policy, which it and the staff believed a country should address.[16] The managing director of the Fund should also speak out more frequently on the conclusions of selected consultation reports for systemically important countries where significant deficiencies of a country's policy framework are identified. Many have suggested that the IMF managing director should invoke powers it has under Article IV of the Fund Agreement to call for "special or ad hoc consultations" with member countries where cases of severe currency misalignment were present, as a way of bringing pressure of the international community to bear on a country's exchange rate policy. This procedure has only been invoked on two occasions in the last thirty years.[17]

It has also been suggested that bilateral surveillance could be strengthened if a systematic attempt were made by the staff to develop a quantitative rating for each country's macroeconomic policy framework and to evaluate the country's performance in addressing any deficiencies identified.[18] Such an approach could be given more force, for example, if highly satisfactory policy ratings developed in the Article IV consultation procedure were directly linked to access to the Fund's Flexible Credit Line. Other analysts have noted that the Fund's bilateral and multilateral consultation mechanism is better suited for providing information to the financial markets to enable them to act as a disciplining device on member countries' policy choices, as distinct from being a direct influence on policy making, in view of the absence of any real peer review pressure in IMF consultation procedures. This becomes clear when one compares the peer review process of the OECD Economic Policy Committee, for example, in which a policy dialogue takes place between senior policy-making officials of a member government and the rest of the committee based on an assessment of macroeconomic conditions and prospects by the OECD staff.[19] The G20 initiative to involve the IMF directly in its peer review process, outside the formal mechanism of the IMF procedures, is clearly a step in the right direction. A strengthened IMFC perhaps could also play such a role for future multilateral consultation exercises by the Fund.

Whether these changes would be sufficient to strengthen the surveillance process and the international adjustment mechanism remains an open question. Alternatively, should the Fund be given certain enforcement mechanisms to facilitate the adjustment process? This is not a new question, as it was present in the debates at the Bretton Woods Conference and during the first reform of the IFA. During the debates of the Committee of 20 in the early 1970s, it will be recalled, establishing more symmetry in the burden of adjustment for surplus and deficit countries was a central point of dispute between the US and European powers. The use of objective indicators by the Fund was proposed to serve as a benchmark against which financial penalties for excessive reserve build-up, or higher interest charges for larger IMF financing of persistent deficits, would be assessed.

Professor Barry Eichengreen has recently proposed a variant on this idea by suggesting that in the case of a country running persistent external payments surpluses a system could be established that would require it to transfer a portion of its "excess" reserves to the IMF or pay a tax on excess reserve holdings to the IMF (or other agency of the UN) to support development assistance.[20] One appeal of such a proposal is that it would by-pass difficult, technical issues of trying to measure the degree of currency misalignment that may be present in a given country case. However, the experience of the EU in conducting its "excessive deficit" procedure under the Maastricht rules for fiscal policy point to some of the practical and political difficulties of operating a regime of international sanctions, even assuming agreement could be reached on its merits.

To strengthen IMF surveillance in a case of persistent currency misalignment (in particular undervaluation), Arvind Subramanian of the Peterson Institute of International Economics and Aaditya Matoo have suggested that a formal link could be established between the Fund's judgment on currency manipulation and the dispute resolution mechanism of the WTO.[21] The rationale for this link is that the WTO Charter recognizes the role of currency manipulation as a basis for creating an unfair trade advantage and calls on the WTO to seek the views of the IMF in cases of severe currency misalignment. The dispute resolution machinery of the WTO provides a mechanism for enforcing a judgment of the IMF on currency manipulation if countries bring a complaint of trade discrimination. Even if practicable, however, this use of the WTO's dispute resolution authority in IMF surveillance is not a desirable outcome in terms of enhancing the Fund's role in the international adjustment mechanism.

Apart from the proposals discussed earlier for strengthening IMF surveillance within the current system of exchange rate arrangements, others have questioned whether alternative monetary arrangements should be considered as a means of providing a more stable underpinning for the international monetary and financial system. At the official level, this debate was advanced by a proposal of the Governor of the People's Bank of China in March 2009 that consideration should be given to establishing a multilateral reserve system based on a unit such as the SDR rather than single country reserve currencies (People's Bank of China 2009). A similar proposal was made by the Expert Commission of the UN General Assembly on Reform of the International Monetary and Financial System, which was headed by Professor Joseph Stiglitz (United Nations 2009).

Among other things, what these proposals point to is a fundamental asymmetry and certain inequities in the current international monetary system centered on the US dollar as the dominant reserve currency. Since the time of the Bretton Woods Agreement, the dollar has provided the unit of account for most international trade transactions, and it has served as a vehicle currency for most international transactions and a store of value for international reserve accumulation, thus fulfilling all the attributes of an international monetary unit. It is no accident that the US dollar has taken on these functions, given the dominant size of the US economy and the depth and liquidity of its financial markets, which have provided important financial intermediation services and network externalities for the global economy.[22] The advent of the euro has provided an alternative reserve currency for the global system, but the absence of a single fiscal authority to back euro debt instruments and of a single market for euro-based financial assets (only euro-denominated assets in separate national markets) limits its scope to serve as an international reserve money on the scale of the US dollar.

The inequities of the current international monetary arrangement arise from the asymmetry in the burden of adjustment between deficit countries (other than the United States) and surplus countries, which was discussed earlier, and from the requirement on developing countries to transfer real resources to the United States to obtain international reserves. In effect, the asymmetries and inequities of the current system represent a considerable benefit for the United States, as it is one of the few countries that can borrow abroad in its own currency at a relatively risk-free rate of interest, while earning "seignorage" revenue from the wide use of US dollars in private transactions outside its borders.[23]

In principle, these inequities could be eliminated by the adoption of the SDR as the central reserve asset of the international system, as envisaged in the second amendment of the Fund Agreement, if approved by an 85 percent majority of IMF members. Again, this was at the center of the debate on "asset settlement" during the debates of the Committee of 20 at the time of the first reform of the IFA. However, for the SDR to become a truly global reserve currency, a number of changes would have to be made in the SDR mechanism to allow it to be used in private transactions and to facilitate its use as a unit of account for debt instruments. Also, it is unlikely that the United States would willingly agree to such changes to replace the dollar as the principal reserve asset, absent a major loss of confidence in US economic leadership and the role of the US dollar.

Notwithstanding these impediments, consideration could be given to expanding the use of SDRs in the current international monetary arrangements through two mechanisms. One means of doing this would be to continue the policy of SDR allocations on a periodic basis to satisfy the incremental demand for global reserves and to minimize some of the pressure for self-insurance among emerging market economies. Over time, this practice would gradually increase the share of SDRs in total reserves above its current share of around 4 percent. The second mechanism for increasing the use of SDRs in the current system would be to consider the establishment of a Substitution Account in the IMF to absorb and diversify some of the excess reserves held by emerging market economies. This idea was also advanced indirectly by the People's Bank of China in March 2009 and could be seen as a means of providing an orderly diversification of international reserves that would avoid the destabilizing effect on foreign exchange markets of individual country actions to diversify reserves. As in the late 1970s, when this idea was actively debated in the context of concern over a dollar "overhang," some means of covering the potential losses to the IMF inherent in the currency mismatch of dollar assets against SDR liabilities on its balance sheet would need to be found.

The G20 has been silent on any possible reforms to the international monetary system beyond an improvement in the Fund's surveillance procedures. However, the issues related to the role of the SDR as a reserve asset and the establishment of a Substitution Account should be taken up by a strengthened IMF Council.

Improving the International Lender of Last Resort Mechanism

The problem of global imbalances cannot be resolved through improvements in the international adjustment process managed by the IMF, without strengthening the international lender of last resort mechanism of the IFA to minimize the incentives for "self-insurance," The issue of an effective ILOLR mechanism in the IFA, in turn, cannot be divorced from the issue of IMF financial resources.

The international response to the current crisis effectively has established an ILOLR mechanism that is managed by the central banks of the major financial center countries and the IMF. The swap network of the central banks of the United States, the United Kingdom, Japan, Switzerland, and the euro zone, which were put in place during the period from September 2008 to March 2009, together with the creation of the IMF's FCL in March 2009, constitutes the principal elements of this mechanism. Although the FCL was established as a regular new facility of the IMF, the permanent resources of the IMF need to be expanded for it to be potentially available to a wider set of clients beyond the three countries that have been authorized to use it thus far. The swap network, by contrast, was an ad hoc response to the crisis, and it is not clear what criteria were used to select the counterpart countries involved, nor to determine the amounts that could be drawn down under the swap arrangement. The BIS or IMF could take the lead in seeking understandings with the major central banks on putting in place permanent arrangements for a swap network that could be coordinated with the FCL. One could also envisage in the future an arrangement whereby the IMF used existing lines of credit with its NAB creditors to establish separate swap agreements with central banks that have not been included in the existing reciprocal currency arrangements of the major financial center central banks. In addition, the IMF should explore the possibility of cooperative arrangements with existing regional reserve-pooling mechanisms, such as the Latin American Reserve Fund and the Chiang Mai Multilateral Initiative, to enhance its potential as an ILOLR.[24] The decision by the euro zone countries in May 2010 to establish a European Financial Stability Facility, in conjunction with the IMF, is a positive precedent for such a role. It is also the first time since 1978 that the major European countries have recognized a potential role for the IMF in meeting some of their financing requirements.[25]

To mitigate potential moral hazard problems associated with the existence of the Fund's FCL, access should continue to be based on prequalification. However, criteria for access to the FCL should be specified more precisely, and could be linked, as proposed in the previous section of this chapter, to the Fund's Article IV consultation procedure and its overall assessment of a country's macroeconomic policy framework and prospects.

The potential demand for FCL resources could be large, given the limited experience to date. Estimates by Professor Obstfeld and others of the possible range of "precautionary" reserves maintained by emerging market economies suggest an amount of US$1–2 trillion, as an upper bound.[26] Such amounts raise a fundamental question about the size of the financial resources that the Fund should have at its command. Thus far, the G20 has decided to augment Fund resources only on a temporary basis, through an increase in its borrowed resources using the NAB and special bilateral borrowing arrangements with selected member countries.[27] Such an approach was justified by the immediate demands of the crisis and the recognition that an increase in the Fund's permanent resources by means of a quota increase would be a time-consuming process involving parliamentary approval in many member countries.

At the time of the next quota review exercise in January 2011, a significant increase in the overall size of Fund quotas should be considered. To remove the need for political bargaining in determining the size of Fund quotas, consideration should also be given to setting an automatic formula for adjusting the financial resources of the IMF, for example, in relation to the value of total trade and/or foreign capital flows. Restoring the level of Fund quotas in relation to total imports to the ratio that applied when the Fund was established in 1945 would imply an increase in its financial resources to around US$2.2 trillion, compared with around US$335 billion at present.

Another financial concern for the IMF that was only resolved recently by the G20 was a change in its income model. Traditionally, the IMF has relied on earnings associated with its regular lending programs to cover its administrative expenditures. This practice implied that, since the mid-1970s, developing and emerging market countries that borrowed from the Fund were paying for the various technical services it provided, while the advanced countries controlled its lending resources through decisions on quota increases and the size of borrowed resources under the GAB/NAB. After 2003, when there was a pronounced drop in the number of financial arrangements approved by the Fund, the institution began to experience significant operational deficits.

In 2007, an expert group led by Sir Andrew Crockett (the former General Manager of the BIS) recommended a new income model for the Fund that would allow it to sell some of its gold reserves (which were received as part of quota subscriptions from certain countries in past years) and invest these proceeds in interest-earning assets. As a condition for approving this plan, the major shareholders insisted that the IMF undergo a retrenchment exercise to scale down the staffing of the organization to take account of its reduced prospects for lending. Accordingly, a program was established to reduce total staffing for the IMF by around 490 staff during 2008, precisely during the outbreak of the current financial crisis and a renewed demand for IMF financing, which then had to be offset in part by new hiring. In April 2009, the G20 endorsed the changes that would allow the Fund to invest a portion of its gold reserves to create a new source of permanent funding for the IMF.

The Oversight of Global Financial System Stability

The G20 has devoted considerable attention to the issue of global financial system stability, given the nature of the current crisis. The conversion of the FSF to a Financial Stability Board (FSB) with a formal charter, expanded membership, and a permanent secretariat, along with the strengthening of the IMF, reflects this emphasis. The expanded role of the FSB in promoting information exchange and best practices among the major national regulators, coordinating the work of the international standard-setting bodies (such as the BCBS), overseeing the work of supervisory colleges for LCFIs, and developing a framework for cross-border crisis management is appropriate, but these tasks need to be underpinned by a strong system of peer review, which was missing in the work of the FSF. In this connection, the decision of the G20 to link the FSB peer review of each member's regulatory regime with a mandatory FSAP exercise of the IMF and World Bank at least once every five years is a positive development. In addition, consideration should be given to converting the chairmanship of the FSB from a part-time to full-time position (the current chair is governor of the Bank of Italy), and significantly expanding the size of its staff secretariat, in view of its expanded range of responsibilities.

Over time, it is likely that the activities of the FSB will need to take on greater importance, as the requirements for a harmonization of national regulatory practices grow with the expansion of the global financial system. It is also the case that cooperation among the BIS, FSB, and IMF needs to be enhanced, as each of these bodies has been a repository of knowledge on global financial stability issues that operated largely independently in the lead-up to the crisis. A system of staff secondments and the rotation of staff assignments among the three institutions would help to foster closer coordination.

In addition to these institutional considerations, a number of other issues have surfaced in recent debates, which have an important bearing on global financial stability. One is the large information gaps for regulators and global institutions that the crisis has revealed. A second is the role of LCFIs in the international financial system, which the crisis has shown to be "too big to fail." A third issue is the need for new market infrastructure to handle the enormous size of derivative trading in connection with cross-border financial flows. A fourth issue is the possible role of a tax on large financial institutions to deal with the negative externalities they may have on the financial system and on financial transactions in limiting the size of speculative capital flows in international capital markets (a "Tobin" tax). Finally, there is the question of institutional oversight at the international level of capital market integration and capital account restrictions by governments in response to rapid changes in capital flows. Each of these issues is taken up in the paragraphs that follow.

Given that information gaps about the nature of securitized instruments and the interconnections of financial institutions via derivative transactions were central problems in the misperception of risk and the creation of panic in the fall of 2008, it is natural to conclude that a major international effort is needed to improve financial reporting and data collection on financial instruments (in particular, structured financial products), the trading book of banks' balance sheets, and financial transactions of the shadow banking system (off-balance sheet entities, investment banks, hedge funds) both domestic and international. One of the most important gaps was related to OTC derivative positions, in particular for credit default swaps (CDS). Apart from the overall size of the market, which was enormous, very little was known about the counterparties to these transactions before the outbreak of the crisis. As a result, the major financial center countries in the G20 have endorsed the migration of standardized derivative trading to central clearinghouses and organized exchanges, where transactions can be monitored, transfer risk can be minimized, and margin requirements can be set. In addition, in cases where OTC trading in nonstandardized derivative products is still permitted, these transactions should be reported to approved trade repositories to facilitate data collection on counterparty exposures for supervisory purposes.

The work to close information gaps will require much time and effort among all the major institutions of the IFA, including the FSB and its constituent members at the national, regional, and international levels. For this purpose, an Inter-Agency Group on Economic and Financial Statistics was formed at the end of 2008, which is chaired by the IMF, to coordinate a strengthening and expansion of existing international data systems.[28] In this regard, it is important to note that one of the statistical efforts that arose in the context of the second reform of the IFA was the development of indicators on bank soundness on an international basis that only started to be published by the IMF in July 2009, with forty-six economies reporting (including fourteen G20 countries).[29] Unfortunately, these statistics did not serve as useful warning signals for the current crisis because of their focus on microprudential indicators for the traditional banking system, such as capital adequacy, asset quality, and earnings.

The current crisis has engendered a wide-ranging debate about the appropriate size of financial institutions and financial systems, more generally, for the protection of systemic stability. This debate has been particularly strong in the case of the United Kingdom and the United States where the development of a capital market-based financial system (or "shadow" banking system), operating in parallel with the traditional banking system, was most advanced. The considerable increase in financial system profits in relation to GDP, the growing intensity of proprietary trading, and the high concentrations of risk in the capital-market based system have raised questions about the social utility of the financial industry and the dangers of financial institutions that are deemed "too big to fail." The G20 leaders have not taken a view on these questions and, instead, have focused more on the required elements of a systemic financial regulator for the protection of systemic stability, which was either missing or ineffective in the lead-up to the crisis.

The need for a clear identification of responsibility for financial system stability in the national (and international) context is now well established. The institutional arrangements for this reform may vary from country to country, but invariably it will involve an extension in the perimeter of supervision to include any financial institution (bank or nonbank) that is deemed to be systemically important. It will also mean that special regulatory regimes may be put in place for LCFIs, for example, in terms of higher capital requirements, and that new legal regimes will be developed to allow for their orderly resolution in the event of an insolvency. The preparation of contingent "recovery and resolution plans" (or so-called living wills) by LCFIs as an element of cross-border crisis management is actively being pursued. Also, at the international level, colleges of national supervisors have been set up since the end of 2008 with the encouragement of the FSB for some thirty LCFIs (mainly bank holding groups and some insurance companies) to coordinate the international aspects of their supervision.[30]

Beyond these points of agreement, there has been an active debate on both sides of the Atlantic as to whether regulatory authorities should take steps to limit the size of large financial institutions or restrict banks from proprietary trading or investment banking activity (so-called Volcker Rule). In the United States, a somewhat modified version of the Volcker Rule was incorporated in financial reform legislation that was approved by the US Congress in July 2010. The UK authorities have promoted public debate on the idea of prohibiting all trading and lending activity of banks by limiting them to the notion of "narrow" banking. Such a limit would require banks that rely on insured deposits to invest only in highly secure investments such as government securities, thus establishing a distinction between narrow, utility banks to support the basic payments and settlement systems for general commerce, and other financial institutions that would operate in the capital markets.[31]

A strong case can be made for limiting the overall size of banks or bank-holding companies, as economies of scale diminish rapidly once the size of overall assets approaches US$100 billion, while the potential risks of their failure to the broader financial system increase above that amount.[32] The imposition of a tax on the liabilities of large financial institutions could be one way of discouraging undue leverage and risk-taking. As of mid-2010, views within the G20 were sharply divided on these issues: the US government and the European Union have endorsed a special tax or systemic risk levy on banking institutions as a form of "polluter pays" penalty for the risk of financial crisis that they entail, whereas countries such as Australia, Canada, and Japan, as well as some emerging market economies, were opposed to such a tax.[33]

The United Kingdom and other European governments have also popularized the notion of some kind of "tobin" tax or financial transactions tax to limit trading activity of financial institutions. Professor James Tobin proposed the idea of a small tax on foreign exchange transactions in 1978 to limit the scope for highly speculative short-term trading of foreign currencies to reduce exchange rate variability during the post-Bretton Woods era of floating regimes.[34] This idea was raised again during the debates of the second reform of the IFA as a means of limiting capital flow volatility for emerging market economies. A financial transactions tax would be broader in coverage than a "tobin" tax, as it would apply in principle to all financial transactions (domestic and foreign). Given the distortion between the social and private value of much proprietary trading witnessed before the crisis, such a tax could provide one means of aligning these values more closely together and of compensating some of the high social cost of financial crises. However, apart from practical problems in its administration, it would need to be applied uniformly by all countries; otherwise its creation in some countries would simply divert trading activity to other locations.

Where much further work is needed is in developing guidelines for the coordination of resolution authority for LCFIs with large cross-border exposure. The problem now is that there is an inherent conflict between the interests of home and host regulators in dealing with the insolvency of a large financial institution with a presence in different countries, which inevitably leads to the "ring-fencing" of local assets. There can also be a conflict between national regulators that operate under a universal principle of supervision (such as the United States) and those that follow a home country (territorial) approach as in Europe. The development of an effective cross-border resolution mechanism is likely to be a time-consuming process given the reliance on national regimes for the regulation of international financial flows and the need to harmonize and coordinate different legal, regulatory, and fiscal practices involved in national bank insolvency procedures. The creation of a special tax regime to fund such a mechanism also has to be considered, for which there is no consensus within the G20, as noted earlier. Pending the gradual harmonization of resolution regimes and the development of a cross-border resolution framework, it is likely that countries will continue to favor territorial or home country regulatory regimes, in which financial institutions with cross-border activities would be forced to register their foreign branches or subsidiaries as separate local legal entities, which would adhere to host government requirement on capital adequacy and other regulatory norms.[35]

A larger question, which has not been addressed by the G20, is whether jurisdiction for capital market integration and the use of capital controls should be formally vested institutionally within the IFA. Given the growing scope of IMF surveillance over capital account issues and the current emphasis on global financial stability, it would make sense to reconsider the Fund's formal role in relation to capital account transactions of its members. At present, there is no institution within the IFA with formal responsibility or a mandate for monitoring capital account liberalization, in the way the WTO does for trade liberalization and the IMF has done for current account liberalization. This is not a new issue, as will be recalled from the debates on the second reform of the IFA that considered an amendment to the Fund Agreement that would have made capital account liberalization one of the purposes of IMF membership.

Rather than establish capital account liberalization as a purpose of IMF membership in the same manner as current account liberalization, consideration should be given to formally vesting authority in the IMF for monitoring countries' progress in this area, which is consonant with its broader interest in overseeing the integration of capital markets in the global financial system.[36] More specifically, the role of the Fund in the case of countries that now impose capital account restrictions would be to determine with the member the appropriate pace and sequencing of liberalization, when and if the member decided to embark on this process. In this connection, an amendment to the Fund Agreement or policy decision of the IMFC (or IMF Council) to expand the Fund's mandate to cover capital account issues would provide a link between the IMF's interest in monitoring a country's progress in establishing an appropriate regulatory regime for domestic financial institutions under the FSAP program (including possible prudential limits on the cross-border exposure of financial institutions) and its interest in global financial system stability.

On a related matter, some formal reconsideration is needed of the temporary role of capital controls in moderating capital flow volatility for emerging market economies. Formally, this authority of countries is already specified in Article VI of the Fund Agreement, but this provision has generally been viewed as an anachronism in an age of financial globalization. The experience of Malaysia during the Asian financial crisis and that of Chile during its transition to capital account liberalization and recent attempts by Brazil to impose a tax on financial inflows in late 2009 all point to the relevance of this issue. Although the Fund has moderated its antipathy to these kinds of measures during the last ten years, a formal policy on this issue has yet to be adopted. Such a proposal is not meant to suggest that one can return to the early days of the Bretton Woods Agreement and the widespread use of capital controls. However, the continuing problem of capital flow volatility and the severe economic cost of financial crises in emerging market economies would call for some consideration of the possible role for capital controls in dealing with these issues.[37] This point of view is also consistent with the idea that there needs to be some space within the international financial system for different degrees of tolerance for capital mobility, consistent with the stage of a country's development and differences across countries in domestic economic and social goals.

International Financial Regulation

The current crisis has raised calls by some European political leaders and academic experts for the creation of a new global financial regulator to enforce new rules for national supervision and to handle the regulation of LCFIs with large international activity. Professors Ken Rogoff and Carmen Reinhart, echoing the concern of EU leaders such as Gordon Brown and Nicholas Sarkozy, argued in the *Financial Times* (November 18, 2008) that a supranational regulator was necessary to overcome the pressures of domestic lobbies and political interests, which have weakened national supervision and have created regulatory capture by large financial institutions. Such a regulator would also eliminate the problem of regulatory arbitrage and enforce common standards of financial supervision across jurisdictions.

From a global public goods perspective, a global regulatory authority would be an important improvement in the IFA, especially given the rapid advance of financial globalization and the growing need to harmonize regulatory regimes across a number of different national jurisdictions. However, it seems unrealistic to think that the major countries would be prepared at this stage in the development of the IFA to yield a significant degree of sovereignty in the area of regulatory policy to a new supranational organization, especially in view of the gradual, evolutionary development of the architecture to date. Nevertheless, the ongoing reforms within the EU in response to the financial crisis illustrate the need for new supranational institutions to achieve greater coordination of national regulatory regimes to address the challenges of economic and financial integration at the regional level, which may have implications for the future shape of the IFA.[38]

Considerable attention has been given to the problems of international financial regulation within the G20 since the outbreak of the crisis, which was signaled by the expanded scope of the FSB within the IFA. However, rather than a wholesale reform of the current Basel Accord (Basel II), in terms of its three-pillar approach, changes are being made within the existing framework. Given the lengthy process of developing the Basel II framework (eight years), national regulatory authorities have been reluctant to embark on a major, new reform effort. This decision could prove problematic if efforts are not made to reduce reliance on the ratings of credit agencies in determining capital requirements (pillar one) and to strengthen the role of supervision (pillar two), along with the public disclosure by financial firms of their on and off-balance sheet positions (pillar three).

The G20 has generally endorsed a strengthening of capital adequacy standards for banks through an increase in the requirement for Tier I capital above its current level of 4 percent of risk-weighted assets and a change in the quality of such capital by restricting it to common equity and retained earnings. The composition of Tier 2 capital is also likely to be strengthened by the inclusion of certain kinds of convertible securities, which could be converted into common equity shares of a financial institution in times of capital impairment. In this connection, contingent, convertible bonds (or "COCOs") have been proposed. In addition, a consensus exists that capital requirements must be made less procyclical. This change can be achieved by introducing some form of "dynamic provisioning" whereby financial institutions would establish provisions for loan losses on the basis of expected losses through the loan cycle, rather than on the basis of actual or incurred losses as is commonly the practice now. Additional capital buffers can be introduced by supplementing normal capital requirements with a time-varying cyclical component that would be triggered when an increase in bank credit exceeded some normal trend growth during the upswing of a credit cycle, thus putting a break on bank asset expansion. This additional capital buffer could then be drawn down during the downturn of the cycle to cover potential bank losses, without jeopardizing a bank's regular capital position and its ability to maintain normal credit activity.

The G20 has also agreed that capital requirements need to be supplemented by an overall leverage requirement for financial institutions to limit the extent of "regulatory arbitrage" that banks can engage in to take advantage of different risk weightings for assets on their balance sheet. In this connection, a consolidated approach to enforcing regulatory limits needs to be followed that includes both on and off-balance sheet exposures. In addition, the current crisis has shown the need for stricter liquidity requirements for those financial institutions that are active in capital market transactions. The liquidity risk for a mutual fund or pension fund with long-term investments in marketable securities is much less than that of a hedge fund or investment bank that relies on short-term funding and engages in active proprietary trading. The BCBS has proposed a thirty-day liquidity coverage ratio for internationally active banks.[39]

In September 2010, the BCBS announced a revision of its minimum capital standard for banks (so-called Basel III) that would raise the (core) Tier 1 ratio from an effective ratio of 1 percent (as measured by common equity and retained earnings) to 7 percent, including a capital conservation buffer of 2 1/2 percent. The addition of a further countercyclical capital buffer of up to 2 1/2 percent was also recommended, but was left to the discretion of national regulators. In addition, a new leverage requirement of 3 percent for Tier 1 capital in relation to total assets (including off-balance sheet items) was introduced (BCBS Press Release #35/2010; September 12, 2010). While the increase in minimum capital requirements is significant, the new leverage ratio of 33 1/3 seems unduly generous, as does the long phase-in period that runs through the end of 2018.

Microprudential supervision will in the future deal much more critically with issues of executive compensation, and bank supervisors will be empowered to set limits on pay arrangements if these have not been aligned with the long-term value of the financial institution by corporate boards. In April 2009, the FSB issued guidelines on executive compensation of financial institutions that are intended to deal with its procyclical aspects.[40]

The various changes in the tools of microprudential supervision need to be accompanied by a strengthening of the second pillar of the Basel II accord and the discretionary powers of supervisors to ensure that risk management procedures, executive pay, and information disclosure are aligned with the sound operation of financial institutions. However, the role of credit-rating agencies in pillar one of the Basel accord remains a controversial area of debate. Notwithstanding their long-standing use by national regulators in the United States for setting capital risk weights for many kinds of financial instruments and limits on banks' asset allocation, the independence, integrity, and technical reputation of credit rating agencies have been severely damaged by the recent crisis. A strong case exists for removing their role in the regulatory process. At the very least, they need to be regulated by the SEC (in the case of the United States), and the designation of nationally recognized statistical rating organizations (NRSROs) should be open to new entrants. These agencies should also be required to disclose the methodologies they use in the rating of structured finance products, and a "Chinese wall" should be established between their advisory and consulting functions, on the one hand, and rating activities, on the other. Some of these principles have been adopted at the international level in a revision of IOSCO's Code of Conduct Fundamentals for Credit Rating Agencies, which was released in May 2008.

The setting of capital requirements for financial firms is closely related to the accounting rules that are used in determining capital adequacy. The recent crisis has brought to the fore concerns about the role of "fair value" accounting and marked-to-market valuation as an additional pro-cyclical force along with compensation practices and the impact of the Basel Accord. While "fair value" accounting embodied the notions of the efficient market hypothesis, it is not clear that market valuations for certain traded securities during the panic phase of the recent crisis provided an appropriate basis for determining capital requirements against those securities. Under the "mixed attribute" model of accounting practice that has been in place since the mid-1990s (which is embodied in FASB rule #157 in the United States), financial institutions are required to use "fair-value" or marked-to-market accounting for the tradable financial instruments on their trading book and historical cost accounting for assets held to maturity on their loan book.

After the outbreak of the current crisis, there was a divergence between regulators in the EU, which follow International Financial Reporting Standards (IFRS) developed by the IASB and allowed some forbearance in the application of marked-to-market accounting for determining bank capital levels, and regulators in the United States, which follow GAAP (Generally Agreed Accounting Principles) procedures and insisted on the application of "fair value" rules. Reaching a consensus on both sides of the Atlantic on the application of "fair value" accounting during a crisis will require considerable further debate within the IASB and FSB. Similarly, closing the gap between the IFRS, which have been accepted by most countries in the world, and the US accounting system remains a critical challenge for the IFA. The G20 originally set a deadline of June 2011 for achieving a convergence of these two accounting regimes, but this deadline has been extended until the end of 2011 in view of the significant differences that need to be reconciled.

A Sovereign Debt Restructuring Mechanism

Although the recent global crisis did not involve a series of sovereign debt defaults as did the financial crises of the early 1980s and 1990s, the absence of a centralized mechanism to facilitate debt restructuring in situations of unsustainable private debt remains a gap in the IFA. The current problems facing Greece in managing its substantial debt burden, as well as those of other members of the euro zone, point to the need for an international framework to facilitate orderly debt workouts.[41] The G20 has been silent on this aspect of IFA reform. The so-called contractual approach to debt restructuring, which was endorsed during the second reform of the IFA, essentially confirmed the ad hoc procedures that have been in use since the time of the international gold standard. These procedures, as reflected in the experience of Argentina after its default of late 2001, are very costly for debtors and creditors, time-consuming, and inefficient. It was only in June 2010 that the Argentine government reached a preliminary agreement with the majority of the roughly 25 percent of its bondholders who refused to participate in its restructuring offer of 2005.

The widespread use of collective action clauses in sovereign bond contracts under the contractual approach to bond restructuring can be helpful for countries with a relatively simple debt structure that wish to reschedule their bond indebtedness without significant debt reduction. Reliance on collective action clauses can help to resolve problems of creditor coordination and potentially can prevent problems of "free-riding" on the part of recalcitrant creditors who wish to enforce their claims against a sovereign. However, such clauses only apply to the bondholders of a particular sovereign bond issue and do not deal with problems associated with the existing stock of sovereign debt or the treatment of other categories of debt. In this regard, the statutory approach embodied in the idea of a sovereign debt restructuring mechanism is not incompatible with the contractual approach and would only apply in those exceptional cases of a country facing an unsustainable debt burden. The recent history of sovereign bond restructurings suggests that there continues to be a need for a statutory approach within the IFA to deal with cases of unsustainable debt burdens, as voluntary exchanges negotiated under the current ad hoc, contractual approach have not resulted in significant reductions in public debt burdens for the countries involved, while disorderly defaults, such as that of Argentina that do bring about such a result, are highly costly and inefficient.[42]

The appeal of an SDRM-like arrangement associated with the Fund is that it can provide the technical expertise to determine legitimate cases of insolvency and an acceptable range of debt reduction within which a debtor country and its creditors can negotiate a debt restructuring. The IMF can also provide the functional equivalent of "debtor-in-possession" financing, which could be linked to a "stay" on debt service payments and the strict application of its policy of "lending into arrears." Such an arrangement would reduce the need for large "bail outs" of highly indebted countries, while possibly tempering the flow of debt capital to countries in weak fiscal conditions that has been factor in the volatility and procyclicality of capital flows as creditors become more scrutinizing of the credit-worthiness of borrowers.

Summary and Conclusion

The current global crisis has revealed the IFA to be deficient in the provision of a number of public goods that it was intended to provide. To a significant extent, this deficiency reflects a number of problems with its structure and governance, which are beginning to be addressed in the context of high-level discussions within the G20. The shift of responsibility for the oversight of the IFA from the G7 to the G20 is a positive development in that it has recognized the important role that a number of emerging economies need to play in its reform and future management. The next (third) reform of the IFA needs to address issues regarding both its governance and the provision of public goods in five areas: the international adjustment mechanism, the oversight of global financial stability, an international lender of last resort mechanism, the coordination of international financial regulation, and sovereign debt restructuring.

Governance reform is a prerequisite for effective change in all of the five areas just noted. The IFA has become excessively fragmented, with a duplication of functions spread across a number of institutions and bodies and a lack of coordination in certain key areas. The creation of an international council to coordinate the IFA is the first requirement of governance reform. Heretofore, the G7 and now the G20 at the ministerial levels have played this role. However, these bodies are not representative of the majority of nation states and are not based in any formal institutional arrangement. One alternative forum that would meet these criteria is a strengthened IMFC or IMF Council. This body should be given competence to oversee and direct the activities of both the IMF and FSB, which represent the twin peaks of the IFA. One can also envisage a subordinate role for a strengthened Development Council that would oversee and coordinate the activities of development assistance carried out by the IFA.

For the IMFC or IMF Council to be seen as fully legitimate, a number of separate governance reforms are needed in the IMF. These relate to the issues of "voice and vote," leadership selection, and the role of the Executive Board. The main changes that are needed in these aspects of the Fund have been clearly identified, and a number of recommendations have been put forward for debate and decision. The recent crisis has given new momentum to their consideration, but full implementation will require the attention and commitment of the G20 Leaders over the coming years.

In addition to governance reform, decisions are needed on a permanent increase in the financial resources of the IMF if the IFA is to be further strengthened and reformed. The widespread resort to "self-insurance" on the part of developing countries since the end of the last decade has pointed to the need for a larger insurance pool within the IFA and stronger ILOLR function. The IMF is uniquely placed to fulfill this function in coordination with central banks of the advanced countries and regional reserve pooling arrangements. Further allocations of SDRs would also serve to diminish the need for "self-insurance."

Dealing with the problem of self-insurance will help to resolve defects in the international adjustment mechanism, but other changes are needed in the Fund to improve this aspect of the IFA. However, any change in this area will require a commitment of the major systemically important countries to have the IMF play a role in international policy coordination, which it has not been allowed to play heretofore. Expanding the role of SDRs in the international monetary system with a view to its replacement of the US dollar over the long term as the main international reserve asset would also serve to establish a regime with more automaticity to the adjustment mechanism.

The recent global financial crisis and the intensification of financial globalization have revealed significant weaknesses in international financial regulation, as regards both its macroprudential and microprudential dimensions. Before the crisis, the IMF and FSB, which were charged with oversight of global financial stability, mainly addressed the needs of the emerging market and developing countries in adapting to financial globalization and the potential threats that financial instability in these countries posed for the global financial system. The national regulators in the G7 countries were essentially responsible for financial stability in the advanced countries. The recent crisis has shown that this two-tiered system has not been effective. Tighter coordination and harmonization of national regulatory regimes, mandatory participation in FSAP exercises, and a strong peer review process managed by the FSB for all systemically important countries are essential changes if the IFA is to work more effectively.

At the microprudential level, a number of changes are needed in the Basel capital accord. Higher capital requirements for systemically important financial institutions and time-varying capital buffers to deal with the procyclical bias of existing capital requirements, coupled with overall leverage and liquidity requirements, seem to have a broad base of support among the G20. In addition, the perimeter of financial supervision needs to be extended to all systemically important financial institutions and a cross-border resolution framework for LCFIs needs to be established. Changes in the latter area are perhaps the greatest challenge for a system of global financial markets in which regulatory authority is still largely nation-based and will require much further effort to harmonize resolution regimes in the major financial center countries.

A final gap in the IFA is an efficient mechanism to deal with sovereign debt restructuring involving private creditors. Since the mid-1990s, changes in the Paris Club arrangements and the HIPC Initiative have substantially eased problems of debt sustainability for developing countries in respect of official indebtedness. In regard to private debt, however, arrangements for debt restructuring are ad hoc and highly decentralized. Collective action clauses in individual bond contracts can provide a solution for debt servicing problems on a selective basis, but are not effective for countries facing an unsustainable debt burden. The need for an international framework to promote orderly debt restructurings has been given renewed importance by the debt problems that a number of developed countries are facing as a result of the recent financial crisis.

CHAPTER 10

Conclusion

This chapter attempts to bring together the main threads of the previous discussion to understand how the IFA has come to take the shape it has and what needs to be done to make it work better. Since the middle of the last century, there has been a persistent and rapid expansion in global trade and finance, which at first recovered, and then surpassed levels of interdependence observed during the period of the international gold standard. That first era of globalization ultimately broke down because of (a) the growing incompatibility for governments of the international "rules of the game" with the demand for more national policy autonomy, and (b) political conflict among the great powers. By contrast, the current era of globalization has endured for a longer period of time, in part because of the collective governance arrangements that governments have put in place to manage the process of economic and financial globalization. However, the continuing and growing scale of financial crises in the modern era points to important defects in those arrangements, which we call the IFA, that need to be addressed to make the international financial system work more effectively.

The fundamental challenge for the IFA is that, while financial markets have become more integrated across national borders and global in scale, the structures of decision making and political accountability that determine the rules for finance are still mainly nation-based. In the absence of a supranational political structure with the power to establish international rules and regulation, governments need to devise cooperative (collective governance) arrangements that seek to harmonize and coordinate national actions and decisions to support a global financial system that is welfare-enhancing.

The post–World War II arrangements for the IFA, which were centered in the IMF and World Bank under the Bretton Woods system, focused mainly on the recreation of a stable international monetary system through the establishment of fixed, but adjustable, exchange rates and the elimination of restrictions on current account transactions. Apart from the provision of development finance through the World Bank and expectations for a recovery of foreign direct investment, the initial conception of the IFA envisaged a world in which finance would be subject to strict, domestic control and international financial transactions would be limited by nationally administered capital controls. This arrangement was intended to allow for the autonomy of domestic economic policies subject to the constraint imposed by international agreement that current account transactions to support cross-border trade of goods and services would be allowed free of restrictions. The Bretton Woods system, together with the process of trade liberalization under the GATT, provided the foundation for the postwar recovery of global trade and economic activity.

It needs to be recognized that the scope and evolution of the IFA has reflected throughout the period since the end of World War II a shared vision among the major economic powers of the restoration of a liberal economic and financial order. Moreover, given the preeminent status of the US economy within the global system and the principal reserve currency role of the US dollar, the United States has played a vital role in shaping the IFA and in sustaining financial globalization. In view of the size and depth of US financial markets, the onset and spread of financial globalization was seen as beneficial to private financial interests in the United States and consonant with its leading role in the global economy. Without this coincidence of private and public interests, financial globalization in the twentieth century would not have regained and exceeded the level achieved in the nineteenth century.

Since the time of the Bretton Woods system, the IFA has evolved in response to the pace of financial globalization and the need to fill gaps in the coverage and scope of the architecture. Unlike the domain of international trade, financial globalization has proceeded in a largely unchartered fashion, without any systematic oversight at the international level until recent years, mainly in response to market forces. Over time, the IFA has shifted from a stance of strict governance of global finance grounded in the domestic regulation of financial markets and widespread resort to capital controls to one of relatively little, formal governance in more recent times as reflected in a voluntary set of international standards and codes that have sought to harmonize the regulatory and infrastructural aspects of financial markets across countries that would facilitate an expansion in financial globalization. At critical junctures, new problems and challenges posed by financial globalization have led to international agreement on certain responses and adaptation of the IFA to limit the propensity for crisis within an expanding international financial system.

The first such crisis occurred in the early 1970s with the breakdown of the Bretton Woods system of fixed exchange rates, which was largely determined by its inability to control speculative currency attacks by private institutions that found ways to bypass domestic capital controls and fund their international financial transactions in unregulated off-shore (euro-currency) markets. The growth of the eurodollar market was a direct response to the imposition of capital controls by the United States that were intended to limit the expansion of its foreign dollar liabilities. These developments led to the first international effort to monitor the evolution of international capital markets through the G10 central bank governors and their Eurocurrency Standing Committee operating at the BIS, which was followed by the creation of the Basel Committee on Bank Supervision to promote cooperation among the G10 in the regulation of international banks.

More fundamentally, the breakdown of the Bretton Woods system led to the widespread adoption of flexible exchange rates among the advanced countries and the beginning of a phased liberalization of capital controls. The IMF was given a new mandate to exercise surveillance over each member's exchange rate system (according to the arrangements it chose to adopt) to ensure stability of the international monetary system in a manner that would, in the language of Article IV of the Fund Agreement as amended in 1978, "facilitate the exchange of goods, services and capital among members." Direct oversight of capital account transactions and international financial flows, however, was left unspecified within the IFA. The process of capital account liberalization among the advanced countries was guided by the OECD and the European Commission and largely completed by the late 1980s. No effort was made to establish goals in respect of capital account liberalization for the international community as a whole until the late 1990s. The first international agreement to embody certain aspects of cross-border financial liberalization emerged with the WTO and the General Agreement on Trade and Services in 1997, which covered capital flows related to trade in services, and the General Agreement on Trade-related Investment Measures, which proscribed certain restrictions on foreign direct investment.

The first reform of the IFA, which was concluded with the second amendment of the IMF Agreement, represented a sharp move away from a rules-based system administered by the IMF toward a more decentralized structure in which countries were free to choose different exchange rate mechanisms and various cooperative arrangements were pursued to foster global financial stability. The IMF remained the main international institution with responsibility for oversight of the international monetary system, but its surveillance operations competed with a number of separate activities of the advanced countries centered in the BIS, the European Community, the G7, and the OECD, which functioned largely independently of the IMF. Also, membership within the IMF and World Bank became splintered between the advanced, creditor countries and the developing, borrowing countries, as the former group of countries ceased to rely on these institutions for their financing needs. With a growing polarization within the membership between debtor and creditor countries, the power of effective decision making was assumed by the G7 finance ministers, which acted as a de facto steering committee for the IFA.

The next phase in the evolution of the IFA was marked by a series of financial crises in the developing countries during the 1980s and 1990s, which threatened global financial stability. These crises followed a second wave in the development of financial globalization as it began to incorporate the main emerging market economies. The IMF, along with the World Bank acting in a supporting role, was the main institution involved in the management and resolution of these crises, acting under the guidance of the G7. This experience led to the second reform of the IFA, which sought to bring together different elements of crisis management and crisis prevention into a more coherent framework. This reform implicitly assumed that financial globalization was a phenomenon to be encouraged, and that developing countries should take specific steps to address deficiencies in their domestic economic and financial arrangements to accommodate it. The widespread adoption of international standards and codes, together with more transparency and disclosure of economic and financial information by countries and the IMF, was expected to diminish the possibility of future crises and make international financial markets work more effectively. The main institutional innovation in this reform of the IFA was the creation of the Financial Stability Forum, which was intended to bring about closer coordination among the regulatory authorities of the G7 countries, a number of cooperative arrangements that had been established to facilitate international financial transactions, and the main European and Washington-based international institutions. The vast majority of countries were excluded from the activities of the FSF, except indirectly by way of their membership in the IMF and World Bank.

The recent global financial crisis that began in late 2008 has marked the end of a third phase of financial globalization that brought about a further intensification of financial links among the advanced and emerging market economies. This phase was characterized by a significant reduction in the incidence of financial crises in developing countries, growing payments imbalances among systemically important countries, and a major expansion in the use of structured financial instruments and credit derivatives, which were expected to broaden access to international capital markets and minimize the concentration of risk in individual financial institutions. The speed with which problems in an isolated segment of the mortgage finance market of the United States were transformed into a global financial and economic crisis revealed, once again, serious gaps and defects in the IFA that need to be addressed if the global financial system is to function effectively.

The current crisis has revealed problems in the functioning of both the international monetary and financial systems. As a result, a third reform of the IFA is under way, which will need to continue for a number of years, if these problems are to be resolved in a satisfactory way. As a contribution to that debate, the following considerations and recommendations are advanced as essential elements of a successful reform. In the light of the experience summarized earlier, these recommendations are grounded in a certain vision for the IFA that embraces the following assumptions and objectives. First, a stable monetary and financial order is essential for the promotion of global economic prosperity. Second, an effective international adjustment mechanism is essential for stability of the international monetary and financial system. Third, all countries can benefit from a greater degree of participation in the international financial system, but each country needs to determine its own pace and manner of integration. By the same token, countries should have the flexibility to determine the exchange arrangements they consider appropriate for international exchange with other countries, as well as the pace of capital account liberalization, and the temporary use of capital controls to limit speculative capital inflows or outflows, subject to international oversight. Fourth, to facilitate the integration of all countries in the international financial system, facilities for the provision of technical assistance and training in monetary, financial, and regulatory matters need to be available to developing countries. Fifth, for those countries which cannot participate fully in the international financial system and the possibilities of private development finance, a mechanism needs to be in place to facilitate the transfer of real resources to promote their economic growth and convergence with the global economy. Finally, the international system needs to provide mechanisms for the orderly resolution of sovereign debt problems.

In the light of the principles and objectives just mentioned and the impact of the recent crisis, the next reform of the IFA should include, as a minimum, the following specific elements:

1. Political leadership of the IFA should be institutionalized through the creation of an International Monetary and Financial Council or IMF Council comprising finance ministers representing the full membership of the IMF. This council should oversee the activities of both the IMF and the FSB, which are the main centers of activity within the IFA, and act as a forum for policy debate and coordination to deal with systemic threats. This body would essentially replace the G20 at the ministerial/central bank governor level, which is not grounded in any formal institutional organization and lacks legitimacy as it is unrepresentative of most states in the international system. For the IMFC to be seen as fully legitimate, a number of governance reforms need to take place within the IMF regarding "voice and vote," leadership selection, and the role of the executive board, as discussed in chapter 9.

2. An institutional mandate for the oversight of the international financial system needs to be established within the IFA. As noted earlier, this gap within the architecture has existed throughout the period of financial globalization since the time of the Bretton Woods system. The IMF was given a mandate to oversee the international monetary system that covers the exchange arrangements and workings of the international adjustment mechanism that make possible transactions in goods, services, and financial assets without serious disruption. The oversight of global financial system stability has been a shared responsibility of the BIS, the FSF, and the IMF, without a clear delineation of institutional roles and modes of coordination before the recent crisis. This oversight should involve the regular monitoring and analysis of developments in international capital markets and of the actions that individual countries are taking to facilitate or restrain financial globalization. The BIS (together with the CGFS) and the IMF, separately, have been carrying out some of this activity in respect of their reporting on developments in international financial markets. The amendment to the Fund Agreement that was proposed in 1997 to give the IMF formal jurisdiction over capital account transactions of its members would have vested the IMF with more responsibility for the oversight of the international financial system. It is proposed that this amendment be reconsidered and that a formal mandate

for system oversight be given to the IMF. In addition, a clear division of labor among the BIS, FSB, and IMF should be established.

3. The ILOLR mechanism of the IMF should be strengthened by a substantial increase in its quota-based resources to a level of at least US$1 trillion to reduce the incentives for self-insurance by developing countries. The financial resources of the IMF should be adjusted automatically on a periodic basis (e.g., once every five years) on the basis of certain indicators, such as global GDP, total imports or private capital flows. In addition, consideration should be given to establishing a permanent network of swap arrangements among the central banks of the advanced countries. These facilities could be supplemented by an authorization for the IMF to have immediate access to the New Arrangements to Borrow in times of global financial stress to make emergency financing available to countries that do not participate in the swap network. The IMF should also establish cooperative arrangements with existing regional reserve pooling mechanisms to augment the potential resources available to countries participating in those mechanisms.

4. The international adjustment mechanism needs to be improved to avoid the problem of persistent global imbalances that preceded the recent global crisis. This reform will require a strengthening of the Fund's surveillance mechanism through the operation of a peer review procedure within the IMFC or revamped executive board for systemically important countries and more independence for the managing director of the IMF to disseminate the conclusions of its bilateral surveillance exercises without the direct involvement of its executive board in other cases. In cases of significant exchange rate misalignment, the IMF managing director should make strong public announcements of international concern about the country in question and exercise his authority to call for "special consultations" to focus international attention through the IMF on the need for corrective policy action. Active consideration should be given to the possibility of instituting a mechanism of financial penalties for cases of persistent reserve gains or losses.

5. Following the action taken by the IMF in 2009 to make a special allocation of SDRs equivalent to US$250 billion, a procedure should be established to make future allocations on a periodic basis to increase the role of SDRs in the international monetary system. To this end, private holdings and transactions in SDRs should be permitted, and the IMF should encourage the issue of SDR-denominated debt. Active consideration should also be given to the

creation of a Substitution Account in the IMF, which would allow for the diversification of US dollar reserve holdings without destabilizing effects on the international monetary system. Over the long term, these actions would help to prepare the ground for a transition away from single reserve currencies toward an SDR-based international reserve system, which would allow for a more symmetric adjustment mechanism among surplus and deficit countries. Such a system would require, as a long-term goal, the IMF to take on the role of a global central bank in determining the appropriate level of SDR allocations in the international monetary system.

6. The FSB should issue guidelines for financial regulation, which extend the perimeter of financial supervision to all financial institutions that are systemically important (and not just banks) and establish authority for macroprudential supervision at the national level. In addition, the FSB should be given sufficient staff resources and independence to conduct a vigorous peer review examination of the regulatory regimes of its expanded membership linked to mandatory participation in the joint IMF-World Bank Financial Sector Assessment Program. The Basel Accord on capital adequacy requirements should be revised to improve the quantity and quality of Tier I capital and to include differentiated capital requirements for financial institutions depending on their size, reliance on capital market funding, and OTC derivative exposures. The proposed inclusion of a leverage ratio, liquidity requirements, and countercyclical capital buffers will help to deal with some of gaps in regulation that helped to foster the recent global financial crisis. The "second pillar" of supervisory control under the Basel Accord should be strengthened to reduce reliance on internal risk models of large financial institutions and the ratings of credit rating agencies in the determination of risk weights for capital requirements.

7. To deal with the problem of large, complex financial institutions (LCFIs), which are deemed "too big to fail," national regulators should be empowered to enforce a limit on the size of financial institutions. Banks should be limited from engaging in proprietary trading of financial assets. The FSB should develop guidelines for the orderly resolution of LCFIs in cases of insolvency, which would include the preparation of contingent resolution plans ("living wills"), that avoid the disruption and time lapse of normal bankruptcy procedures. A cross-border resolution mechanism also needs to be developed that establishes the respective responsibilities and burden sharing among home and host regulatory authorities for financial institutions with large cross-border

exposures. Pending the establishment of this international framework, the FSB should encourage the development of national resolution regimes on an internationally consistent basis and promote effective coordination among national regulatory authorities through the work of supervisory colleges for large financial institutions.

8. The main financial center countries should establish a special tax (a systemic risk levy) on large financial institutions to offset the systemic risk that they may pose for the financial system. A tax on the noncore liabilities of these institutions (i.e., their total liabilities less insured deposits) would be one appropriate base for such a tax, as such a measure captures the short-term funding instruments (e.g., REPOs and commercial paper) that were the source of their vulnerability during the recent crisis. Such a tax would discourage excessive reliance on these short-term liabilities as leverage for speculative activity, and thus mitigate some of the procyclical behavior of financial institutions that was observed during the recent crisis. It would also provide a revenue source to support national resolution regimes described in the previous paragraph. This tax could be viewed as an alternative to counter-cyclical capital requirements for large financial institutions.

9. Given the explosive growth in credit derivatives and the large counterparty risk they posed for certain financial institutions, the FSB and IOSCO should establish common rules for the transfer of OTC transactions in derivatives to organized exchanges and central clearinghouses. Such a move will bring about more transparency in the nature of these trades, as regards counterparty risk, margin requirements, and reporting. Central clearinghouses need to have strong operational controls, appropriate collateral requirements, and adequate capital, as well as effective regulatory oversight. Non-standardized derivative transactions, which continue to be traded on an OTC basis, should be reported to authorized trade repositories.

10. To eliminate the potentially large, "dead-weight" losses involved in sovereign debt workouts with private creditors, active consideration should be given to supplementing the current ad hoc, contractual approach to debt restructuring for individual bond issues with a sovereign debt restructuring mechanism which would be available to countries facing an unsustainable debt burden. Such a mechanism would also have the benefit of reducing the need for large, official bailouts of severely indebted countries and lowering reliance on debt finance in international capital flows.

The program of reforms to the IFA described earlier is an ambitious agenda, most of which will require considerable time and debate to reach an international consensus on practicable solutions and timetables. But these reforms are essential to support a sound development of the global financial system and minimize the risk of systemic breakdown. The continued attention of the G20 Leaders will be critical for the process of reform to be successful.

The first half of the items listed earlier directly involve the IMF and build on proposals that have been under debate for some time. Governance reform of the IMF is an essential precondition for improving its effectiveness within the IFA, and the target date of early 2011 for a decision on quota realignments provides an opportunity to take up other issues related to its political oversight, mandate, and financial operations. Governance reform and the outcome of the ongoing mutual assessment process of the G20 will help to shape the Fund's role in the international adjustment mechanism. Ultimately, however, for this mechanism to be effective, countries need to recognize the role for strong international oversight in this area and endow the IMF with the authority to bring pressure to bear on countries that are not fulfilling their obligations for exchange rate management under Article IV of the Fund Agreement.

Most of the remaining items on the above list of IFA reforms point to the need for much greater coordination in the area of financial regulation. Again the experience of the recent crisis points clearly to the absence of effective international oversight in this area and weak coordination among national regulators. It appears that certain improvements in the Basel Capital Accord are in prospect, although the proposed timetable for implementing these reforms should be shortened. Much further work is needed in establishing effective resolution regimes for large financial institutions in the main financial center countries that would facilitate over time the development of an international framework. An independent and well-resourced FSB is critical for the success of these regulatory efforts.

The third reform of the IFA will undoubtedly reinforce the need for greater cooperation among nation states in the financial policy and regulatory fields underpinned by a system of peer review that has been a basic hallmark of the architecture since the end of the Bretton Woods system. How long such a governance arrangement can maintain systemic stability as financial globalization proceeds, without a more formal regulatory regime for the international financial system that includes enforcement mechanisms, only time will tell.

APPENDIX

A Brief Guide to the Committees, Groups, and Institutions That Comprise the International Financial Architecture (alphabetical order)

Bank for International Settlements (BIS): www.bis.org

Date established: 1930

Membership as of 2007–8: Fifty-six central banks or monetary authorities of the following countries: Algeria, Argentina, Australia, Austria, Belgium, Bosnia and Herzegovina, Brazil, Bulgaria, Canada, Chile, China, Croatia, the Czech Republic, Denmark, Estonia, Finland, France, Germany, Greece, Hong Kong, Hungary, Iceland, India, Indonesia, Ireland, Israel, Italy, Japan, Korea, Latvia, Lithuania, Macedonia, Malaysia, Mexico, the Netherlands, New Zealand, Norway, Philippines, Poland, Portugal, Romania, Russia, Saudi Arabia, Serbia, Singapore, Slovakia, Slovenia, South Africa, Spain, Sweden, Switzerland, Thailand, Turkey, the United Kingdom, the United States, and European Central Bank.

Where the institution meets: Headquarters of the BIS are in Basel, Switzerland.

Main Function: The BIS was established to act as an agent for the collection and distribution of reparations associated with the Treaty of Versailles after World War I and as trustee for the Dawes and Young international loans, which were issued to finance those reparations. It was also intended to act as a forum for central bank cooperation, which has been its main function up until the present day. Since the end of World War II, it has carried out a variety of trustee and agency functions for its central bank membership, including the investment of foreign reserves. It also hosts the secretariats of the G10, its three committees (BCBS, CGFS, CPSS), the IAIS, and the FSF/FSB, and serves as the Head Office for the International Association of Deposit Insurers (IADI). Its bimonthly Global Economy Meeting, including thirty central bank governors of key industrial and emerging market economies focuses on developments in the global economy and international financial markets, drawing on the Bank's research and statistical activities.

Basel Committee on Banking Supervision (BCBS): www.bis.org/bcbs

Date established: 1974, by the central bank governors of the G10 countries
Membership as of 2007–8: Belgium, Canada, France, Germany, Italy, Japan, Luxembourg, the Netherlands, Spain, Sweden, Switzerland, the United Kingdom and the United States; in March 2009, membership was extended to Australia, Brazil, China, India, Korea, Mexico, and Russia, and in June 2009, membership was extended to Argentina, Hong Kong SAR, Indonesia, Saudi Arabia, Singapore, South Africa, and Turkey.

Where the group meets: At the BIS in Basel, Switzerland (usually four times per year).

Main function: BCBS provides a forum for cooperation on issues related to banking supervision and acts as a standard-setting body on all aspects of banking supervision. It is also a member of the Joint Forum, established in 1996 in coordination with IOSCO and IAIS. The Joint Forum is comprised of an equal number of senior bank, insurance, and securities supervisors and deals with issues common to these three sectors. It has three main subgroups (risk assessment and capital, conglomerate supervision, and customer suitability) and typically meets three times per year.

The BCBS is responsible for one of the twelve core international standards and codes *(Core Principles for Effective Banking Supervision 1997/2006)* that sets out twenty-five basic principles for an effective system of banking supervision, dealing with licensing and structure, prudential regulations and requirements, supervisory methods and powers, and information requirements.

Committee on the Global Financial System (CGFS): www.bis.org/cgfs

Date established: 1971 as the Euro-currency Standing Committee by the
G10 central bank governors; renamed CGFS in 1999 (with revised mandate)
Membership as of 2007–8: Members are deputy governors, other senior officials of central banks, and the Economic Adviser of the BIS; member

institutions include the Reserve Bank of Australia, National Bank of Belgium, Central Bank of Brazil, Bank of Canada, People's Bank of China, European Central Bank, Bank of France, Deutsche Bundesbank, Hong Kong Monetary Authority, Reserve Bank of India, Bank of Italy, Bank of Japan, Bank of Korea, Central Bank of Luxembourg, Bank of Mexico, Netherlands Bank, Monetary Authority of Singapore, Bank of Spain, Sveriges Riksbank, Swiss National Bank, Bank of England, Board of Governors of the Federal Reserve System, and the Federal Reserve Bank of New York.

Where the group meets: Regular Committee meetings are held on the occasion of four of the bimonthly meetings of governors of BIS member central banks in Basel, Switzerland. As of January 2010, the chairman of the CGFS reports to the Global Economy Meeting of the BIS.

Main function: The Euro-currency Standing Committee was initially established with a mandate of monitoring international banking markets, with a focus on monetary policy implications of the rapid growth of offshore Eurodollar markets, and the oversight of BIS collection of international banking and financial statistics. As attention increasingly shifted toward issues of global financial stability and broader questions of structural change in the international financial system, the G10 governors renamed the committee in 1999 and revised its mandate to cover the review of global financial markets with a view to promoting improvements in their functioning and stability.

Committee on Payment and Settlement Systems (CPSS): www.bis.org/cpss

Date established: 1990, by the G10 central bank governors (to replace the Group of Experts on Payment Systems which was established in 1980 and the ad hoc Committee on Interbank Netting Schemes established in 1989)
Membership as of 2007–8: Belgium, Canada, the European Central Bank, France, Germany, Hong Kong, Italy, Japan, the Netherlands, Singapore, Sweden, Switzerland, the United Kingdom, and the United States. In July 2009, membership was extended to Australia, Brazil, China, India, Mexico, Russia, Saudi Arabia, South Africa, and South Korea.

Where the group meets: Until 1999, meetings were held exclusively at the BIS in Basel, Switzerland; since then, the location of meetings has varied. Meetings are now held three times per year—previously two times per year.

Main function: CPSS acts as a forum for central bank cooperation in strengthening financial market infrastructure through the monitoring and analysis of developments in domestic payment, settlement, and clearing systems as well as in cross-border and multicurrency systems. CPSS formulates broad supervisory standards and guidelines and recommends best practices in banking with the expectation that supervisory authorities will take steps to implement them. CPSS undertakes specific studies at its own discretion or at the request of the governors of the Global Economy Meeting. CPSS publishes various reports as well as the Red Book on payment systems, which provides extensive information on the most important systems in the CPSS countries.

CPSS has produced one of the twelve core international standards and codes (*Core Principles for Systemically Important Payment Systems 2001*), which governs the design and operation of payment systems. The principles focus on payment systems (i.e., systems that comprise a set of instruments, procedures and rules for the transfer of funds among system participants), which are intended to apply to systemically important payment systems, whether credit/debit, electronic/manual processing, and electronic/paper-based instruments. A related code *(Recommendations for Securities Settlement Systems 2001)*, which was produced with IOSCO, identifies minimum standards for securities settlement systems.

Development Committee (DC): www.worldbank. org/devcommittee

Date established: 1974, as a joint committee of the Board of Governors of the IMF and World Bank (Joint Committee on the Transfer of Real Resources to Developing Countries)

Membership in 2007/08: Governors of the IMF and World Bank representing the twenty-four constituencies of these institutions; the managing director of the IMF and president of the World Bank serve as *ex officio* members. Official observers include the heads of the UN, UNDP, UNCTAD, FAO, ILO, WHO, WTO, African Development Bank, Arab Bank for Economic Development in Africa, Arab Fund for Economic and Social Development, Arab Monetary Fund, Asian Development Bank, Council of European Development Bank, European Bank for Reconstruction and Development, European Investment Bank, Inter-American Development Bank, International Fund for Agricultural Development, Islamic Development Bank, Nordic Development Fund, Nordic Investment Bank, OPEC Fund for International Development, and West African Development Bank, and the Commissioner for Development and Human Affairs of the EU.

Where the group meets: Development Committee meets twice a year (usually in Washington, DC) on the occasion of the spring (April/May) and Annual (September/October) Meetings of the IMF and World Bank; every third year, the Annual Meetings are convened in one of the member countries on a rotating basis.

Main function: Development Committee provides general oversight of the activities of the IMF and World Bank with developing countries and constitutes a forum for the consideration of global development issues.

European Central Bank (ECB): www.ecb.int

Date established: 1998
Membership as of 2007–8: Governing Council of the ECB comprises six members of its Executive Board as well as the governors of the central banks of the sixteen countries that participate in the common currency of the euro area (including Malta that joined in January 2009).

Where the institution meets: Headquarters of the ECB are in Frankfurt, Germany.

Main function: The ECB is the regional central bank for the sixteen countries of the European Union which participate in the common currency area of the euro area; it fulfills the normal functions of a central bank, in coordination with the central banks of the countries that participate in the euro area.

European Commission (EC): ec.europa.eu

Date established: 1958, with the establishment of the European Economic Community
Membership as of 2007–8: Twenty-seven commissioners appointed by the European Council, subject to the approval of the EU Parliament.

Where the institution meets: Headquarters of the EC are in Brussels, Belgium.

Main function: The EC is the executive body of the European Union, which drafts proposals for EU legislation and acts as the implementing agency for its policies and spending programs.

Financial Action Task Force (FATF): www.fatf.org

Date established: 1989, by the G7
Membership as of 2007–8: Argentina, Australia, Austria, Belgium, Brazil, Canada, China, Denmark, European Commission, Finland,

France, Germany, Greece, Gulf Co-operation Council, Hong Kong, China, Iceland, Ireland, Italy, Japan, Kingdom of the Netherlands (including the Netherlands, the Netherlands Antilles, and Aruba), Luxembourg, Mexico, New Zealand, Norway, Portugal, Republic of Korea, Russian Federation, Singapore, South Africa, Spain, Sweden, Switzerland, Turkey, the United Kingdom, and the United States; there are also twenty-seven international and regional organizations that are Associate Members or Observers of the FATF and participate in its work.

Where the group meets: Each year, the FATF holds three plenary meetings, as well as meetings of various ad hoc groups; most FATF plenary meetings take place in the facilities of the OECD in Paris.

Main function: The Financial Action Task Force (FATF) develops and promotes policies at the national and international level to combat money laundering and terrorist financing. FATF monitors members' progress in implementing measures to counter money laundering through annual self-assessments and more detailed mutual evaluations. FATF also reviews money laundering trends, techniques, and countermeasures and their implications, and promotes the implementation of its recommendations by nonmember countries.

The FATF has produced one of the twelve core international standards and codes *(The 40 Recommendations of Financial Action Task Force 2002)* that sets out principles for the design of countermeasures against money laundering covering the criminal justice system and law enforcement, the financial system and its regulation, and international cooperation. In addition, the *Nine Special Recommendations on Terrorist Financing 2002* provide a set of international standards designed to deny terrorists access to the international financial system and to track down the assets of terrorists. The standards focus on the following issues: ensuring that terrorist financing is listed as a criminal offence in national legislation, the seizure of terrorist assets, the reporting of suspicious financial transactions, international cooperation, and measures to prevent the misuse of remittance systems.

Financial Stability Forum (now Board) (FSF/FSB): www. financialstabilityboard.org

Date established: 1999; in April 2009 it was reconstituted as the Financial Stability Board
Membership as of 2007/08: G7 (with 3 members each representing finance ministry, central bank and regulatory agency), plus the central

banks of Australia, Hong Kong, Singapore, and Switzerland, two representatives each from the BCBS, CGFS, CPSS, IAIS, IMF, and World Bank, and one representative from the BIS, ECB, IASB, Joint Forum, and OECD. In April 2009, membership was extended to all members of the G20, the EC, the Netherlands, and Spain.

Where the group meets: FSF/FSB meets at the headquarters of the BIS in Basel, Switzerland twice a year, prior to the spring and Annual Meetings of the IMF and World Bank,

Main function: The FSF was established by the G7 to foster cooperation among the various national and international regulatory bodies concerned with the promotion of global financial stability. One of its major responsibilities was to oversee the development of twelve core international standards and codes and their implementation.

Group of 7: www.g7.utoronto.ca

Date established: 1975, at the level of finance ministers and central bank governors
Membership as of 2007–8: Canada, France, Germany, Italy, Japan, the United States, the United Kingdom, and Russia.

Where the group meets: In one of the member countries on a rotating basis 3–4 times a year, and in Washington, DC on the occasion of the spring and Annual Meetings of the IMF and World Bank.

Main function: Initially the focus of ministerial level meetings was on issues of macroeconomic policy management and cooperation, but since the late 1980s its agenda has covered a range of economic development and financial stability issues within the purview of the IMF and World Bank affecting developing and emerging market economies.

Group of 10: www.bis.org

Date established: 1961, in connection with General Arrangements to Borrow (GAB) of the IMF
Membership as of 2007–8: Finance Ministers and Central Bank Governors of Belgium, Canada, France, Germany, Italy, Japan, the Netherlands, Sweden, Switzerland, the United Kingdom, and the United States.

Where the group meets: Usually at the BIS on the occasion of its bimonthly meetings of central bank governors, and in Washington, DC on the occasion of the Annual and Spring Meetings of the IMF and World Bank.

Main function: The group was established to administer the GAB, which is a supplementary loan facility for the IMF. It has also served as a consultative forum for the discussion of issues related to the functioning of the international monetary system. It was the locus of early discussions on the adequacy of international reserves under the Bretton Woods system and the development of Special Drawing Rights (SDRs) in the IMF.

Group of 20: www.g20.org

Date established: 1999

Membership as of 2007–8: Finance Ministers and Central Governors of the G7 plus Argentina, Australia, Brazil, China, India, Indonesia, Korea, Mexico, Russia, Saudi Arabia, South Africa, Turkey, the Commissioner of European and Monetary Affairs of the European Union, and President of the European Central Bank; the chairmen of the Joint Development Committee and the International Monetary and Financial Committee, the managing director of the IMF, and president of the World Bank attend as *ex officio* members

Where the group meets: In one of the member countries annually on a rotating basis; since November 2008, the G20 has met 3–4 times years

Main function: The G20 has served as a consultative forum for the discussion of issues related to global economic governance, economic development, and international financial stability that are relevant to the work of the IMF and World Bank

International Association of Insurance Supervisors (IAIS): www.iaisweb.org

Date established: 1994

Membership as of 2007–8: IAIS represents insurance regulators and supervisors from 190 jurisdictions. Since 1999, IAIS has also welcomed insurance professionals as Observers, and there are now more than 120 Observers representing industry associations, professional associations, insurers and reinsurers, consultants, and international financial institutions.

Where the group meets: Annual Conference, Triennial Conferences, and other subgroup meetings take place in a variety of venues. The Executive Committee is located in Basel, Switzerland.

Main function: The IAIS is a forum for cooperation among insurance regulators and supervisors. It is charged with developing international principles and standards for effective insurance regulation and supervision. IAIS is also a member of the Joint Forum, established in 1996 in coordination with the BCBS and IOSCO.

The IAIS has produced one of the twelve core international standards and codes (*Insurance Core Principles 1999/2003*), which define the essential principles for an effective insurance supervisory system, as well as the underlying rationale for each principle and criteria to facilitate comprehensive assessments. The principles apply to the supervision of insurers and reinsurers, whether private or government-controlled.

International Accounting Standards Board (IASB): www.iasb.org

Date established: 2001, by the IASC Foundation, which replaced the International Accounting Standards Committee
Membership as of 2007–8: The IASB is an independent group of fifteen experts in the accounting field appointed by a group of international Trustees. Six of the Trustees must be selected from the Asia/Oceania region, six from Europe, six from North America, one from Africa, one from South America, and two from any region.

Where the group meets: London, UK.

Main function: The IASB is an independent, privately funded, non-profit standard-setting body of the IASC Foundation, committed to developing global accounting standards for general purpose financial statements. IASB cooperates with national accounting standard setters to achieve international accounting standard convergence.

The IASB has produced one of the twelve core international standards and codes (*International Accounting Standards 2002*), which are a set of international financial reporting standards (IFRS) that provide guidance on how transactions and other dealings should be reported in financial statements. Although IASB has no formal authority to enforce compliance, nearly 120 countries (other than the United States that follows its own accounting standard) require the financial statements of publicly traded companies to be prepared in accordance with IFRS. To date, forty international accounting standards have been promulgated by the IASB and by its predecessor group, the International Accounting Standards Committee.

International Federation of Accountants (IFAC): www.ifac.org

Date established: 1977, as the successor to the International Coordination Committee for the Accounting Profession (ICCAP), which was established in 1972.
Membership as of 2007–8: IFAC has 159 members and associates (primarily national professional accountancy bodies) in 124 countries

and jurisdictions. These members and associates represent 2.5 million accountants employed in public practice, industry and commerce, government, and academia.

Where the group meets: The IFAC Secretariat is headquartered in New York.

Main function: IFAC develops international standards on ethics, auditing and assurance, education, and public sector accounting standards through independent standard-setting boards. It also issues guidance to support professional accountants internationally and issues policy positions on topics relevant to the profession.

The International Auditing and Assurance Standards Board of IFAC has produced one of the twelve core international standards and codes *(International Standards on Auditing 2002)* that set out principles for the design, review, and quality control of auditing and related services.

International Monetary and Financial Committee (IMFC): www.imf.org

Date established: 1974, as a committee of the Board of Governors of the IMF which are the Finance Ministers or Central Bank Governors of its member countries

Membership as of 2007–8: Twenty-four Governors of the IMF representing the twenty-four constituencies of its Executive Board; the managing director of the IMF serves as an *ex officio* member. Official observers include the president of the World Bank, the chairman of the Joint Development Committee, the chairman of the Financial Stability Forum (now Board), the general manager of the BIS, the president of the European Central Bank, the heads of the ILO, OECD, UN, UNDP, WTO, and the EU Commissioner for Economic and Monetary Affairs

Where the committee meets: twice a year (usually in Washington, DC) on the occasion of the spring (April or May) and Annual (September or October) Meetings of the IMF and the World Bank; every third year, the Annual Meeting of the committee is held in one of the IMF member countries on a rotating basis.

Main function: IMFC is an advisory body of the IMF Board of Governors that provides general oversight of the activities of the IMF and constitutes a forum for the consideration of international monetary and financial issues.

International Monetary Fund (IMF): www.imf.org

Date established: 1944, at the Bretton Woods Conference and began operations in 1945

Membership as of 2007–8: 185 members (excludes Cuba, North Korea, and Taiwan); Kosovo joined in June 2009 and Tuvalu joined in June 2010

Where the institution meets: Headquarters of the IMF are in Washington, DC.

Main function: IMF is an international financial institution with primary responsibility for oversight of the international monetary system, which it carries out through a variety of bilateral, regional, and multilateral surveillance exercises. It also provides financial assistance to its members in relation to their quota subscriptions for dealing with balance of payments problems, and technical assistance in fiscal, monetary, and statistical functions. Quotas, which currently amount to the equivalent of US$335 billion, are based on a formula that takes account of a member's GDP, its external current receipts and payments, the variability of its external receipts and net capital flows, and its gross foreign reserves.

The IMF has produced three of the twelve core international standards and codes in the areas of data dissemination, fiscal transparency, and monetary and financial policy transparency. The *Special Data Dissemination Standard 1996 (SDDS),* which is intended for countries that are active in the international financial markets, established benchmarks for the coverage, periodicity and timeliness of official statistics, and the basic principles of an independent statistical function. The *General Data Dissemination System 1997 (GDDS)* was established for the guidance of other member countries with somewhat less demanding requirements than the SDDS for the production and dissemination of official statistics.

The *Code on Good Practices in Fiscal Transparency 1998* identifies a set of principles that are intended to guide governments in the public dissemination of information regarding the structure and content of their public finances. The code deals with the clarity of roles and responsibilities of fiscal institutions, open budget processes, public availability of information, and assurances of integrity.

The *Code of Good Practices on Transparency of Monetary and Financial Policies 1999* provides guidance on clarifying the roles, responsibilities and objectives of central banks and other financial agencies, the processes for formulating and reporting their policy decisions, the public availability of information on these decisions, and appropriate standards of accountability and assurances of integrity of these institutions.

International Organization of Securities Commissions (IOSCO): www.iosco.org

Date established: 1983, as an international transformation of its inter-American regional association ancestor
Membership as of 2007–8: 110 ordinary members (country-level financial supervisory bodies); 11 associate members; 72 affiliate members.

Where the group meets: Meets once per year at an Annual Conference, but the venue changes each year; the General Secretariat is located in Madrid, Spain.

Main function: IOSCO was established to facilitate cooperation among national regulators of securities and futures markets. To maintain efficient and stable markets, it develops and promotes standards of securities regulation, drawing on its international membership to establish standards for effective surveillance of international securities markets. IOSCO is also a member of the Joint Forum, established in 1996 in coordination with the BCBS and the IAIS.

IOSCO has produced one of the twelve core international standards and codes (*Objectives and Principles of Securities Regulation 1998*), which sets out thirty principles of securities regulation based on three objectives of securities regulation: investor protection; the promotion of markets that are fair, efficient, and transparent; and reduction of systemic risk.

Organization for Economic Cooperation and Development (OECD): www.oecd.org

Date established: 1961 (succeeded the Organization for European Economic Cooperation which was founded in 1947 to oversee the administration of Marshall Plan aid for Western Europe)
Membership as of 2007–8: Thirty members including Australia, Austria, Belgium, Canada, Czech Republic, Denmark, Finland, France, Germany, Greece, Hungary, Iceland, Ireland, Italy, Japan, Korea, Luxembourg, Mexico, the Netherlands, New Zealand, Norway, Poland, Portugal, Slovak Republic, Spain, Sweden, Switzerland, Turkey, the United Kingdom, and the United States (Chile became a member in May 2010).

Where the institution meets: Headquarters of the OECD is in Paris, France.

Main function: The OECD deals with a broad range of development, economic, environmental, and financial issues relevant to the economic growth and financial stability of its members. A hallmark of OECD operations is its peer review process of member country policies in the areas just noted on a regular basis. Its Development Assistance Committee (DAC) is the major forum for donor coordination among advanced countries and is a primary source of data on overseas development assistance (ODA).

The OECD has produced one of the twelve core international standards and codes (*Principles of Corporate Governance 1999/2004*), which provides guidance on the regulatory, institutional, and legal framework for an effective regime of corporate governance with an emphasis on publicly traded companies. The principles deal specifically with the rights and equitable treatment of shareholders, the role of various stakeholders in corporate governance, guidelines on disclosure and transparency, and the role and responsibility of corporate boards of directors.

Paris Club (www.clubdeparis.org)

Date established: 1956

Membership as of 2007–8: Nineteen members (Australia, Austria, Belgium, Canada, Denmark, Finland, France, Germany, Ireland, Italy, Japan, Netherlands, Norway, Russia, Spain, Sweden, Switzerland, the United Kingdom, and the United States); other countries may be invited to participate on an ad hoc basis in debt negotiations if invited by the concerned debtor country and agreed by the Paris Club membership; observers include the IMF, World Bank, African Development Bank, Asian Development Bank, European Bank for Reconstruction and Development, European Commission, Inter-American Development Bank, and UNCTAD

Where the institution meets: The French Treasury provides meeting space and secretariat support at its offices in Paris, France.

Main function: The Paris Club is an informal arrangement among the major donor countries that handles the negotiation of debt relief agreements with selected debtor countries of official bilateral credits (ODA).

World Bank (www.worldbank.org)

Date established: 1944 at the Bretton Woods Conference and began operations in 1945 as the International Bank for Reconstruction and Development (IBRD)
Membership as of 2007–8: 185 member countries (excludes Cuba, North Korea, and Taiwan); Kosovo became a member in June 2009, and Tuvalu in June 2010

Where the institution meets: Headquarters of the World Bank are in Washington, DC.

Main function: The World Bank provides long-term loans for development purposes, as well as technical assistance in a variety of development policy and structural areas. The Bank raises its financial resources in the international capital markets, with the full faith and guarantee of its members, as well as from bilateral donor contributions. Member country capital subscriptions, until recently, have been based on IMF quotas, but only a relatively small share of these subscriptions has been contributed as paid-in capital.

In addition to the IBRD, the World Bank includes the International Finance Corporation (est. 1956), the International Development Association (1960), the International Center for the Settlement of Investment Disputes (1966), and the Multilateral Investment Guarantee Agency (1988).

The Bank has produced one of the twelve core international standards and codes *(The Principles of Insolvency and Creditor Rights Systems 2001/2005)* that provides specific guidance on the legal framework for creditor rights, risk management, corporate debt workouts, and insolvency, as well as the institutional requirements for their effective implementation.

World Trade Organization (WTO): www.wto.org

Date established: 1995 as the successor agency of the General Agreement on Tariffs and Trade, which operated during 1947–94
Membership as of 2007–8: 153 members, including the EC that represents the twenty-seven member countries of the European Union; there are thirty observer states, most of which are seeking membership, including Russia.

Where the institution meets: Headquarters of the WTO is in Geneva, Switzerland.

Main function: WTO provides a forum for the negotiation of reductions in barriers to international trade in goods and services and oversees the administration and implementation of negotiated agreements. It also maintains a dispute settlement body to handle the adjudication of disputes among its members regarding their compliance with the terms and conditions of negotiated agreements. Two particular features of the WTO, which are relevant to the international financial architecture, are the General Agreement on Trade-related Investment Measures (TRIMs, 1994) and the General Agreement on Trade in Services (GATS, 1997). The former deals with restraints on foreign direct investment that have an impact on foreign trade (such as local content requirements), while the latter calls for the elimination of capital account restrictions related to the liberalization of trade in services (e.g., financial services).

Notes

2 Financial Globalization and the International Financial Architecture

1. Two restrictions in the United States which led to a shift of financial flows to offshore markets were Regulation Q, which placed a ceiling on the yield that banks could offer on retail deposits; and the interest equalization tax of 1963, which increased the cost of funding from overseas sources for domestic firms if it was less than in the United States.

2. This database is described in Lane and Milesi-Ferretti (2007) and can be accessed at the webpage for Professor Lane at Trinity College, Dublin (www.philliplane.org).

3. Data for foreign exchange trading are taken from the Annual Reports of the Bank for International Settlements; the value of global trade is from the statistical yearbooks of the WTO.

4. These relationships among advanced, emerging market and other developing countries are presented in Kose, Prasad, Rogoff, and Wei . (2009).

5. The drivers of financial globalization are explored in an article by Lane and Milesi-Ferretti (2008).

6. This evidence is reviewed and extended in Dell'Ariccia, di Giovanni, Faria, Kose, Mauro, Ostry, Schindler, and Terrones (2008).

7. Economists have also looked at the correlation of national savings and investment ratios across countries to gauge the extent of financial globalization, as divergences between these two ratios imply large current account balances and thus an increase in the accumulation of foreign assets and liabilities. In a famous study by Feldstein and Horioka (1980), the correlation between saving and investment ratios among the advanced countries was found to be very high during the 1970s, but it has declined sharply since then.

8. This evidence and other price-based measures of capital market integration are presented in Obstfeld and Taylor (2004).

9. This index is described in Chinn and Ito (2008), and it is available on the homepage of Professor Chinn (www.ssc.wisc.edu/-mchinn.research.html).

10. The process of capital account liberalization in the industrial countries is described in Mathieson and Rojas-Suarez (1993) and Quirk and Evans (1995).

11. These regional experiments in capital account liberalization are discussed in Abdelal (2007) and Bakker (1996).
12. "Leads" refer to prepayments of obligations before their normal date of payment, and "lags" represent the postponement of such payments beyond their due date. Under the Bretton Woods system, leads and lags were often induced by expectations of exchange rate changes, and thus constituted speculative capital flows.
13. The experience of financial liberalization in selected industrial and emerging market economies after 1973 is reviewed in Williamson and Mahar (1998).
14. The role of AIG, American Express, and Citigroup in pressuring the US government for a relaxation of international barriers to their entry into foreign markets is presented in Raghavan (2009).
15. This evidence is presented in Quirk and Evans (1995).
16. These patterns are based on the indices of capital account liberalization developed by Quinn (1997).
17. For an alternative vision of global financial governance, which shares some common ground with the one presented in this book, see Bryant (2003).
18. The literature on these informal cooperative, or transgovernmental, networks is extensive and includes prominently the writings of Keohane and Nye (2001) and Slaughter (2004).
19. A summary description of each of the committees, groups, and institutions that comprise the IFA is presented in the appendix.

3 The Evolution of the Global Financial Order

1. The trilemma is derived from the policy implications of fixed and flexible exchange rate regimes for the maintenance of internal and external balance, as explained in Obstfeld and Taylor (2004). The discussion in this section follows their presentation.
2. These issues are explored in a recent paper by Aizenman, Chinn, and Ito (2008).
3. The U-pattern of financial globalization is examined fully in Obstfeld and Taylor (2004).
4. This statement is true in terms of net capital flows, and direct investment and bond finance in particular; however, gross capital flows have been far higher in the current era of financial globalization because of the greater diversity of financial instruments being traded.
5. These differences in the two eras of globalization are examined more fully in Bourguinon et al (2002) and Wolf (2004).
6. At the peak of the gold standard in the first decade of the twentieth century, an estimated sixty countries participated in the gold standard in one form or another. This estimate is based on Ahamed (2009).
7. The term "rules of the game" was coined by John Maynard Keynes in 1925 in his writings about the gold standard era (MacKinnon 1993).

8. While in practice, the gold standard adjustment mechanism operated with less automaticity in the short run than implied by the standard textbook model, over time it tended to operate as envisaged. The adjustment mechanism of the gold standard is described in Eichengreen (1996).

9. The role of the gold standard as a "seal of good housekeeping" is discussed in Bordo and Rockoff (1996).

10. This pattern of financing under the gold standard is explored in Bordo and Schwartz (1998).

11. Alan Taylor (2003) has shown that the ratio of foreign investment to GDP for Latin America during the first decade of the twentieth century was 2.7, the highest on record for any developing region, and that foreign investment accounted for around one-third of its capital stock.

12. These defaults are identified in Sturznegger and Zettelmeyer (2006).

13. The work of the British Corporation of Foreign Bondholders is described in Mauro, Sussman, and Yafeh (2006).

14. The terms of debt workouts is examined in Mauro and Yafeh (2003) and Sturznegger and Zettelmeyer (2006).

15. The Venezuelan blockade and other creditor country interventions to force debt repayments are described in Suter and Stamm (1992).

16. The United States declined to join either of these institutions at the time of their creation because of its isolationist sentiment. Instead, three private banking institutions from the US (J.P. Morgan, the First National Bank of Chicago, and the First National Bank of New York) were accepted as original members of the BIS.

17. The work of the League of Nations in the economic and financial spheres as described in this chapter is based on the work of Louis Pauly (1996 and 1997).

18. Beth Simmons (1993) provides an interesting discussion of the events surrounding the establishment of the BIS.

19. The final act of the Bretton Woods Conference in 1944 called for the "liquidation of the BIS at the earliest possible moment" (Mikesell 1994). The debate about the future of the BIS after the Bretton Woods Agreement is discussed in Helleiner (1994).

20. A recent book which describes the rise and fall of cooperation among the central bank governors of France, Germany, the United Kingdom and the United States during the period before the Great Depression is *Lords of Finance* (Ahamed 2009).

21. These rescue operations are described in Bordo and Schwartz (1998).

22. The history of efforts to restore the gold standard after World War I and its role as one of the causes of the Great Depression are examined in Eichengreen (1992).

23. The continued existence of Article VI of the Fund Agreement raises the distinct possibility that provisions of the GATS and TRIMs Agreements of the WTO may be in conflict with the Fund's provision that grants members the discretion to impose restrictions on capital transactions that are

proscribed under the WTO agreements. This issue is examined in a recent paper by Gallagher (2010).

24. This term was never defined in the Articles of Agreement, but could be understood to mean a situation in which the value of a currency was severely misaligned or where the overall balance of payments disequilibrium was unsustainable.

25. It is interesting to note that in the first US (White) Plan for the IMF, members were expected not to default on their external debt obligations without prior consent of the Fund. This requirement was understood as giving the Fund the role of "compulsory arbitration" in cases of debt default (see Horsefield 1969, vol. III). This issue is examined more fully in Helleiner (2008).

26. This term was first used by John Ruggie (1982).

27. The details of the initial quota determination for the IMF are discussed in Horsefield (1969). The preeminent position of the United States was dictated by the fact that the dollar was the only major currency that was convertible for current account transactions, while the US government was in possession of 55 percent of the global supply of gold in June 1945 (as reported in the BIS Annual Report of 1945).

28. This feature of financial transactions in the Fund was borrowed from the practice established for the Exchange Stabilization Fund (ESF) of the US Treasury that was created in 1935 with the profits arising from the devaluation of the US dollar in terms of gold. The ESF made its first loan to Mexico in 1936 and has been used since then to support stabilization loans to countries mainly in Latin America, often in concert with the IMF (see Bordo and Schwartz 2001 and Gold 1988).

29. The primacy of the IMF in the Bretton Woods system was symbolized by the fact that membership in the IMF was set as a requirement for membership in the World Bank.

30. Under Keynes' proposal for an International Clearing Union (ICU), there were limits on debtor and creditor positions that would trigger adjustment actions (Horsefield 1969, vol. III). For two recent discussions of the Keynes' plan for an ICU, see Alessandrini and Fratiani (2009) and Mateos y Lago, Duttagupta, and Goyal (2009). As an alternative to the adjustment rules of the ICU, the Fund Agreement included a "scarce currency" clause under Article VII that would have allowed the Fund to authorize countries to impose exchange restrictions against surplus countries, but this provision has never been invoked.

31. The data for disbursements of Marshall Plan aid and IMF and World Bank lending are taken from Horsefield (1969) and Kapur, Lewis, and Webb (1997).

32. On the relationship between the IMF and the EPU, see Horsefield (1969).

33. Eichengreen (1992) reports that "dynamic instability" was also a concern among analysts during the gold exchange standard of the inter-war period

in relation to potential pressures on the core gold standard countries arising from the accumulation of short-term claims by noncore countries.

4 The Breakdown of the Bretton Woods System and First Reform of the International Financial Architecture

1. These data are taken from MacKinnon (1979).
2. The limitation on the use of GAB funding by only G10 participants was a source of some resentment among IMF members, as it was seen as a departure from the cooperative nature of the IMF and its uniformity of treatment of all members. This issue is discussed in Ainley (1985) and Solomon (1982). The restriction on the use of GAB funding was removed in 1983. The G10 actually includes eleven countries: Belgium, Canada, France, Germany, Italy, Japan, the Netherlands, Sweden, Switzerland, the United Kingdom, and the United States.
3. This line of argument is developed by Gianni (1999).
4. The creation of the SDR is discussed in DeVries (1976) and Solomon (1982).
5. The G10 was also seen as providing the European powers an effective counterweight to the perceived dominance of the United States in the IMF, as recounted in James (1996).
6. These various swap arrangements are discussed in Borio and Toniolo (2006).
7. This arrangement has been described in various books, most recently one by Eichengreen (2007).
8. The problem of "dynamic instability" of the Bretton Woods regime was laid out in Triffin (1960). During the 1960s, there was an active academic debate about the nature of the United States' payments imbalance. One of the measures of this imbalance was the official settlements version, which is calculated as the change in the net short-term foreign liability position of the United States, which was equal to the sum of its current account imbalance plus its long-term investments abroad. This imbalance was said to arise from the role of the United States as the main financial intermediary for the global monetary system, by which it accepted short-term claims from other countries (equivalent to demand deposits of a bank), which it used to invest in longer-term productive assets abroad.
9. This hegemonic approach to international monetary relations was first articulated in Kindleberger (1973).
10. In addition to the IFC and IDA, two other agencies were created within the World Bank Group: the International Center for the Settlement of Investment Disputes in 1966 and the Multilateral Investment Guarantee Agency in 1988.
11. The early history of the research work of the IMF is reviewed in Rhomberg and Heller (1977) and Blejer, Khan, and Masson (1995). Robert Mundell

and J. Marcus Fleming developed the Mundell-Fleming model of monetary and fiscal policies under fixed and flexible exchange rate regimes during the early 1960s while they were both working in the research department of the IMF.

12. The US Federal Reserve did not formally take up its position on the Board of Directors of the BIS until July 1994, even though it had been attending its bimonthly meetings of Central Bank Governors before that date (see 65th Annual Report of the BIS, June 12, 1995).

13. The "Outline of Reform" and other technical documents of the C20 are reproduced in IMF Committee of 20 (1974).

14. Analytical reviews of the C20 debates from participants in the process are provided by Williamson (1977), Solomon (1982) and DeVries (1985).

15. This issue was taken up in the Report of the C20 Technical Group on Disequilibrating Capital Flows, which is available in IMF Committee of 20 (1974) and is further discussed in Abdelal (2007).

16. In 1999, the euro replaced the franc and mark in the valuation of the SDR.

17. From an accounting perspective, when an SDR allocation is distributed to IMF members, the SDRs are classified as an international reserve asset in the balance sheet of the recipient agency, with an offsetting contra-entry in its capital account.

18. Initially, there was a "reconstitution" requirement for SDRs, which required members to maintain an average balance equivalent to at least 30 percent of their allocation, but this was gradually eliminated over time.

19. The debates on establishing a Substitution Account in the IMF are recounted by Solomon (1982) and Boughton (2001). Some of the exchange risk involved in establishing a Substitution Account could have been covered by the income earned by the account from investing in long-term government securities, which would have been larger than the interest paid on short-term SDR liabilities.

20. See, for example, the proposals on the UN Expert Group (Stiglitz Group) on reform of the international monetary system (United Nations 2009).

21. The ideas and proposals for a NIEO were formally presented in a "Declaration and Program of Action on the Establishment of a New International Economic Order" that was adopted by the UN General Assembly in May 1974.

22. This aspect of the NIEO debates is taken up in Little (1982).

23. The G77 specifically envisaged the creation of an International Debt Commission to deal with problems of official debt restructuring (Rogoff and Zettelmeyer 2002). The Paris Club evolved out of a process of ad hoc informal meetings of certain European creditors with developing country debtors in the mid-1950s to make arrangements for the settlement of their arrears on official debt service. These meetings were usually organized and hosted by the French Treasury in Paris. Over time, the IMF came to

play an important supporting role for the Paris Club, as its agreements on debt relief were almost always conditioned on the prior negotiation by the debtor country of a financial arrangement with the Fund.

24. The evolution of the Paris Club and debates on official debt restructuring are described in detail in Rieffel (2003).

25. This feature of the revolving, short-term nature of IMF financing based on quota contributions of its members has often been characterized as similar to that of a credit union.

26. Technically, under Article V (section 4) and Article IX (section 2) of the Fund Agreement, the Fund can accept collateral as a guarantee for its financial assistance. In 1962, the Fund accepted gold collateral for two purchases by Egypt (UAR) (Horsefield 1969 vol. I), but this procedure has not been used since that time.

27. These figures are taken from DeVries (1985).

28. This interpretation can be found in the writings of Joseph Gold, who served as General Counsel of the IMF at the time of the second amendment (Gold 1980).

29. "Surveillance over Exchange Rate Policies," IMF Decision No. 5392-(77/62), April 29, 1977

30. These figures are taken from DeVries (1985). In the case of the United States, the amounts approved under stand-by arrangements included only purchases of the gold or reserve tranche which was not subject to IMF conditionality.

31. These stabilization mechanisms are described in Ungerer (1990).

32. Because of the requirement of uniformity of treatment in Fund operations, the second amendment of the Fund Agreement included an amendment of Article V, section 12, which specified that "balance of payments assistance may be made available on special terms to developing countries in difficult circumstances, and for this purpose the Fund shall take into account the level of per capita income."

33. In addition to the Euro-currency Standing Committee, which was established in 1971, the Basel Committee on Bank Supervision was created in 1974, and the Group of Experts on Payments Systems (which became the Committee on Payments Systems and Settlements) was formed in 1980.

34. The history of discussions surrounding the possible creation of a Financial Support Fund in the OECD is discussed in Cohen (1997).

35. This point is brought out in DeVries (1985).

36. The emergence and evolution of the G7 process has been extensively covered in Baker (2006) and Hajnal (2007).

37. The so-called Plaza Accord of 1985 was probably the high-water mark of coordinated exchange rate action among the G7 in an effort to sustain the reversal of a period of sharp dollar appreciation during the first half of the decade.

38. For a good overview of the evolution of the G7 process of policy coordination, see Sobel and Stedman (2008).

39. The Fund's role in the G7 surveillance process is fully described in Henning and Bergsten (1996) and Boughton (2001).
40. This point of view is put forward by Henning and Bergsten (1996).
41. These results are presented in Von Furstenberg and Daniels (1992).
42. Many of these proposals have been associated with the Peterson Institute for International Economics; see, for example, Henning and Bergsten (1996). For a similar view by a Canadian participant at the deputies' level, see Dobson (1991). A more recent critique of G7 multilateral surveillance can be found in Kenen, Shafer, Wicks, and Wyplosz (2004).

5 Emerging Market Financial Crises and the Second Reform of the International Financial Architecture

1. Data for the IMF are taken from DeVries (1985) and for commercial bank lending from the World Bank's World Development Indicators database.
2. Since oil export receipts of the OPEC countries were deposited with large international banks operating in the eurodollar market centered in London, the pricing of deposits and loans was based on the six-month LIBOR (London interbank offer rate). Medium-term credits to oil-importing counties carried a variable interest rate, which was set at a margin or spread above LIBOR and adjusted on a six-monthly basis.
3. This information is taken from Rieffel (2003), which describes in detail the bank rescheduling process that operated under the so-called London Club approach during the debt crisis of the 1980s.
4. This figure is cited by William Cline in Kenen (1994).
5. The role of the IMF in handling the debt crisis during the 1980s is fully explored in Boughton (2001).
6. In 1983, the major international banks established the Institute of International Finance in Washington, DC to develop their own economic intelligence service on the major debtor countries to bring a second opinion on country conditions and prospects to the London Club process.
7. This approach to economic reform was first identified as the "Washington Consensus" in a much-cited paper by John Williamson (1990).
8. This point is made, among others, by Boughton (2001) in his retrospective on the Fund's role in the debt crisis. There have been many attempts to assess the impact of IMF and World Bank structural adjustment lending, which are summarized in Easterly (2006).
9. Under the Brady Plan, countries negotiated with the banks from a menu of different options for the cancellation of their bank debt, including the direct purchase of their debt in the secondary market at a discounted value (cash buybacks), the issue of par bonds for the face value of their debt at a below market interest rate, the issue of discount bonds paying a market rate of interest for an amount below the face value of the debt, and

debt-equity swaps. Further details are provided in Boughton (2001), Cline (1995), and Rieffel (2003).

10. These data are provided in Rieffel (2003).

11. In an important departure from normal Fund procedure, many of these loans took the form of "lending into arrears," which meant that the IMF would not require that the borrowing country be current in its debt service obligations, as normally required for its financial assistance. This policy, which shifted the Fund's influence in favor of the debtor country, was conditioned on evidence that the borrower was making a "good faith" effort to finalize its negotiation of a debt agreement with the banks.

12. The 1988 Basel Accord established five risk weights (0, 10, 20, 50, and 100 percent) to determine the capital charge applicable to different types of assets and loans on a bank's balance sheet. For example, debt securities issued by the US and other OECD governments carried a risk weight of zero, which implied that no capital charge was required, whereas consumer loans carried a risk weight of 100 percent, which implied a full capital charge of 8 percent.

13. The policy challenges of managing large private capital inflows have continued to be a matter of concern for many countries up until the present time. For a discussion of policy options, see chapter 3 of the IMF World Economic Outlook for October 2007 (IMF 2007).

14. This study was prepared by Mathieson and Rojas-Suarez (1993).

15. In 1995, in the wake of the first financial crisis of the 1990s in Mexico, the Executive Board revised its Surveillance Decision of 1977 to include an additional indicator to be used in determining whether member countries were pursuing appropriate exchange rate policies, which related to "unsustainable flows of private capital" (Decision No. 5392-[77/63], April 29, 1977, as amended). Also in 1995, the communiqué of the G7 leaders meeting in Halifax for the first time included a recommendation that "the IMF consider extending its obligations on convertibility of current account transactions to a staged liberalization of capital account transactions," which is available at www. G7.utoronto.ca.

16. A recent study by Chwieroth (2010) provides insight, on the basis of access to internal Fund documents, into the evolution of IMF staff thinking on approaches to capital account liberalization.

17. Analyses of the crisis cases can be found in Beim and Calomiris (2001) and Mishkin (2006).

18. The phenomenon of "twin crises" has been extensively studied in the economic literature and was first identified by Kaminsky and Reinhart (1999).

19. Paul Krugman was one of the first economists to present a theoretical framework for understanding balance of payments crises (Krugman 1995). Reinhart and Rogoff (2009) provide a comprehensive empirical study on the causes and consequences of financial crises.

20. The term "original sin" was first introduced in the writing of Barry Eichengreen and Ricardo Hausmann (1999).

21. The term "sudden stops" was first introduced in the writing of Guillermo Calvo (1998). Since the real exchange rate is defined as the nominal exchange rate (in foreign currency terms) times the ratio of foreign prices to domestic prices and foreign prices are fixed, a drop in domestic expenditure would lead to a decline in domestic prices that implies an increase (depreciation) in the real exchange rate.

22. The first G7 Summit to take up issues related to the reform of the international financial architecture was in Halifax (1995). For an overview and summary of these summits and the work of the G7 finance minister and central bank governors, see Baker (2006) and Hajnal (2007).

23. The G20 emerged out of informal meetings that had taken place under the aegis of the G22 and G33 beginning in April 1998. From 1999 until September 2008, the G20 met annually. The managing director of the IMF, the president of the World Bank, and the chairs of the IMFC and Development Committee have attended these meetings as ex officio members (G20 2008).

24. There is a growing academic literature on the role of political forces in IMF lending decisions, which is evaluated in Vreeland (2007) and Steinwand and Stone (2008).

25. The procedures and conceptual framework involved in IMF financial arrangements are discussed in Fischer (1997) and Mussa and Savastano (1999).

26. Two widely commented articles at the time were Feldstein (1998) and Goldstein (2000).

27. This evidence is provided by Robert M. Stern in a background paper for an IEO evaluation of the Fund's role in Trade Policy (Stern 2009); see also the discussion on Korea in IMF IEO (2003).

28. An evaluation of structural conditionality in IMF programs conducted by the IMF Independent Evaluation Office in 2007 concluded that the average number of structural conditions in Fund-supported programs had not declined, but that there had been a shift in the composition of these conditions toward core areas of IMF expertise (i.e., tax policy, public expenditure management, and financial sector issues) (IMF-Independent Evaluation Office 2007). The use of structural conditions as performance criteria in IMF financial arrangements was eliminated in April 2009 (IMF Public Information Notice 09/40; April 3, 2009).

29. Professor Joseph Stiglitz (2003) has been a particularly vocal critic of the Fund in this context.

30. The IMF's response to Malaysia's use of capital controls is discussed in IMF IEO (2005).

31. Malaysia's experience with capital controls and some of the associated literature is reviewed in Johnson et al (2006).

32. Article VI of the Fund Agreement, Section 1, says that "A member may not use the Fund's general resources to meet a large or sustained outflow of capital . . . and the Fund may request a member to exercise controls to prevent such use of the general resources of the Fund." Furthermore, Section 3 declares that "Members may exercise such controls as are necessary to regulate international capital movements."

33. A summary of the IMF Board's discussion of this policy is provided in Public Information Notice (PIN) no. 03/37 of March 21, 2003, which is available at www.imf.org.

34. The IMF's involvement in Argentina has been examined in Mussa (2002) and the IMF IEO (2004).

35. In September 2009, the Argentine government made a first attempt to reach an accommodation with private bondholders whose claims were still in default, which was accepted by a large share of these creditors in late June 2010.

36. The IMF proposal for the establishment of an SDRM was presented in Krueger (2002). Hagan (2005) provides an analysis of the debates surrounding its establishment.

37. For a recent report supporting the application of these principles, see IIF (2008).

38. The lack of representation of major emerging market economies in many of the standard-setting bodies has led to complaints by these countries that their interests have not adequately been taken into account. This issue is examined in Walter (2008).

39. Barry Eichengreen was an early proponent of the two-corner solution for exchange rate policy (2002); see also Fischer (2001 and 2007).

40. The phenomenon of "fear of floating" was first identified by Calvo and Reinhart (2002).

41. The debate on the capital account amendment to the IMF Agreement is discussed in Abdelal (2007) and Chwieroth (2010).

42. Magud and Reinhart (2006) provide an evaluation of the experience of developing countries in the use of capital controls.

6   The Challenge for Developing Countries in a World of Financial Globalization

1. Throughout this discussion, the term "development finance" refers broadly to the availability of external finance to developing countries from both private and official sources. Official development finance refers to both concessional loans and grants from multilateral financial institutions such as the IMF and World Bank, and official development assistance (ODA) from bilateral agencies.

2. These trends are discussed in the World Bank's Global Development Finance report of 2002.

3. The role of remittances as a form of development finance is explored in Kapur (2004) and chapter 2 of the April 2005 IMF World Economic Outlook. While remittances represent, on average, around 3–4 percent of GDP for developing countries, in some countries, such as Guyana, Haiti, Honduras, and Lebanon, they represent 20 percent of GDP or more.

4. This literature is reviewed in Henry (2007).

5. These effects are summarized in Prasad and Rajan (2008).

6. This evidence is presented in Prasad (2007).

7. There is a rich literature on the links between financial development and economic growth, which are examined and summarized in Levine (2008).

8. The problems of information and control that afflict developing financial markets are explored in Beim and Calomiris (2001).

9. The first ten years of the FSAP are reviewed in IMF and World Bank (2009).

10. The Asian Bond Initiative and other official efforts to support local bond markets in the Asian region are discussed in Elson (2006).

11. These developments are reviewed in Committee on the Global Financial System (2009).

12. This literature is reviewed in Roodman (2007).

13. This evidence is presented in Prasad, Rajan, and Subramanian (2007).

14. The terms "planners" and "searchers" are taken from Easterly (2006). Professor Sachs's views on the need for a "Big Push" in development assistance can be found in Sachs (2005) and (2009).

15. A good example of a "needs-based" assessment of the financial requirements to overcome a "poverty trap" and achieve the MDGs for a trio of African countries is provided in Sachs, McArthur, Schmidt-Traub, Kruk, Bahadur, Faye, and McCord (2004).

16. The work of the Central Asia Institute is explained in Mortenson and Relin (2007).

17. The Harrod-Domar model, which linked growth, savings, and the incremental capital-output ratio, was the basis for "capital fundamentalism" and has had a continuing influence on development planning since its formulation in the late 1930s.

18. The role of the "deep determinants" of growth (i.e., institutions, geography, and trade) is discussed in many recent studies, for example, Rodrik, Subramanian, and Trebbi (2004).

19. Meier (2005) provides a detailed discussion of the evolution of thinking about economic development in the post–World War II era.

20. Birdsall, de la Torre, and Caicedo (2010) provide an interesting assessment of the influence of the Washington Consensus on economic policy making in Latin America since the debt crises of the early 1980s.

21. This concept is associated with the writings of Anne Krueger; see, for example, Krueger (1990).

22. The report and background studies of the World Bank Commission on Growth and Development (so-called Spence Commission) can be found

at www.growthcommission.org and in World Bank Growth Commission (2008).

23. Professor Duflo was the recipient of the John Bates Clark Medal in 2010 for the best academic economist under the age of forty and was profiled in an article in the New Yorker magazine (Parker 2010).
24. These recommendations are similar to those of the High Level Panel on UN System-wide Coherence (UN 2006).
25. A number of options in this area are examined in Perry (2009).
26. Information for the World Bank's trust fund activities is reported in its annual Trust Fund reports which are available at www.worldbank.org.
27. The Center for Global Development has been a leading advocate for an independent external evaluation of World Bank programs; see, for example, Center for Global Development (2006).
28. These conclusions are presented in an evaluation conducted by an outside group of academic experts led by Professor Angus Deaton (World Bank 2006).
29. These concerns were raised in World Bank IEG (2008a and 2008b).
30. The withdrawal of the Fund from long-term concessional lending to low-income countries was recommended in the Report of the External Review Committee on Bank-Fund Collaboration (World Bank 2007).
31. In July 2009, the Executive Board of the IMF approved a number of changes in its lending facilities for low-income countries: the Poverty Reduction and Growth Facility was converted into an Extended Credit Facility; the Exogenous Shocks Facility was converted to the Rapid Credit Facility; and a new Short-term Credit Facility was created for concessional financing of short-term balance of payments assistance (IMF Press Release 09/268, July 29, 2009, which is available at www.imf.org).

7 Financial Globalization and the Onset of the Global Financial Crisis of 2008–9

1. These data are taken from McKinsey Global Institute (2008).
2. These data are presented in a speech by Andrew Haldane of the Bank of England (Haldane 2010).
3. These data are derived from the database available in Laeven and Valencia (2008).
4. The possible explanations for the Great Moderation are examined in Davis and Kahn (2008).
5. These issues are explored in Ferguson, Hartmann, Panetta and Portes (2007).
6. Gross foreign reserves are defined as gross official reserves minus gold, as reported in IMF International Financial Statistics.
7. The recent growth of sovereign wealth funds is explored more fully in Elson (2008).

8. For a discussion of the recent impact of international banks in developing countries, see World Bank (2008), chapter 3.

9. A number of studies have been written to explain the causes of the financial crisis in the United States during 2007–8; see, for example, Bailey, Litan, and Johnson (2008) and Brunnermeier (2009).

10. In the case of the US Federal Reserve, this thesis is based on the application of the so-called Taylor Rule, which has proved to be a reliable predictor of, and explanation of, central bank policy actions over the medium-term. For its application to the recent crisis, see Taylor (2009).

11. In a recent study (Greenspan 2010), the then chairman of the US Federal Reserve defended the low interest rate policy of the US central bank on the grounds that such a policy was needed to prevent the problem of deflation that Japan experienced in the 1990s after the bursting of a bubble phenomenon in that country.

12. From the late 1990s, the rise in housing prices in the United States was exceeded in a number of countries of the European Union and in Central and Eastern Europe.

13. The estimate for the relative share of "shadow" banking system assets is cited in Sheng (2009) and IMF (2009a).

14. The data on the growth of credit default swaps are taken from Bailey, Litan, and Johnson (2008).

15. These data are provided in Acharya and Richardson (2009), ch. 1

16. The mechanics of structured finance products is explained in Bailey, Litan and Johnson (2008) and Coval, Jurek, and Stafford (2009).

17. These figures on the relative share of AAA-rated structured finance products are taken from Coval et al (2009).

18. The purchase and sale of credit default swaps (CDS) in the OTC market, instead of through organized exchanges or central clearinghouses, avoided certain reporting, monitoring, and margin requirements.

19. Much of the moral hazard in GSE lending must be attributed to the fact that these institutions were strongly encouraged by the US Congress to expand their acquisition of mortgage-backed securities to support low-income housing as a policy goal, with minimal or inadequate supervision.

20. Research studies have shown that large universal banks with an asset value equal to or exceeding US$100 and market capitalization equal to or exceeding US$20 billion received a premia in stock valuation with respect to smaller banks as a benefit for their perceived access to the federal safety net (Brewer and Jagtiani 2009). Studies have also demonstrated that large banks face lower funding costs than smaller banks, which represents an annual subsidy of around US$35 billion for the 18 largest US banks (Haldane 2010).

21. It has been estimated that the share of investment bank assets supported by overnight repos rose from 12.5 per cent in 2001 to 25 per cent in 2007 (Bailey, Litan, and Johnson 2008).

22. These data are cited in Adrian and Shin (2009).
23. The mechanics of the repo market are explained in Adrian, Burke, and McAndrews (2009).
24. There have been many critiques of the unrealistic assumptions underlying mainstream macroeconomic and financial paradigms that led economists and policy makers to ignore the risks that were building prior to the recent crisis; see, for example, Colander et al (2009).
25. One academic who has long argued against the fallacy of applying standard (Gaussian) probability theory to the analysis of financial markets is Benoit Mandelbrot (Mandelbrot and Hudson 2004). A more recent critique of the methods of modern quantitative finance can be found in Taleb (2007).
26. One behavioral economic theorist who has received much recognition in the wake of the current crisis is Daniel Kahneman, the Nobel laureate in economics for 2002; see Clift (2009).
27. This estimate is cited in Caballero, Farhi, and Gourinchas (2008).
28. See the testimony of former Federal Reserve Board Chairman Greenspan before the House Committee on Oversight and Government Reform (Hearings on the Role of Federal Regulators in the Financial Crisis, October 23, 2008).
29. The pattern of dollar funding across international financial markets that gave rise to a shortage of US dollar liquidity and "safe haven" investments in US treasury securities is analyzed in McGuire and von Peter (2009).
30. Data on global financial flows and stocks are taken from McKinsey Global Institute (2009).

8   The Role of the International Financial Architecture in Crisis Prevention and Crisis Management

1. The term "exorbitant privilege" was first used in relation to the US dollar by the French Finance Minister, Valery Giscard d'Estaing, during the 1960s.
2. See, for example, Chapter 3 of the April 2005 WEO and Chapter 1 of the September 2005 GFSR for clear warnings about the risks involved in global imbalances.
3. For the views of Alan Greenspan, see Greenspan (2007), and for those of Professor Cooper, see Cooper (2008).
4. Professors Obstfeld and Rogoff have written extensively on the problem of global imbalances; see, for example, Obstfeld and Rogoff (2004) and (2009). Wolf (2008) provides an extensive evaluation of these contrasting views about global imbalances.
5. The conclusions of the Fund's multilateral consultation procedure can be found in IMF Press Release 07/72 (April 14, 2007), which is available at www.imf.org.

6. In its communiqué of April 2007, the IMFC took note of the concluding statement of the multilateral consultation, which indicated that the multilateral consultation discussions "have contributed to an improved understanding of the issues (related to global imbalances) and each other's positions . . . We agreed to meet again when developments warrant" (IMF Press Release 07/72; April 14, 2007).

7. For a highly critical assessment of the Fund's bilateral surveillance of China's exchange rate policy, see Mussa (2008).

8. From July 2008 through late June 2010, the PBC reverted to its previous pattern of pegging the value of the renminbi to the US dollar.

9. These conclusions can be found in IMF-IEO (2007).

10. A recent manifestation of this same attitude was revealed in an evaluation of the IMF Independent Evaluation Office on "IMF Interactions with Member Countries," which was completed in November 2009. This report included the results of a survey conducted with policy authorities in the advanced countries, in which less than half of the respondents indicated that they wanted the Fund to play a role in international policy coordination and in the analysis of spillover effects from their policies (see Companion Paper One on IMF Interaction with Advanced Countries in IMF-IEO 2009).

11. Schinasi (2006) provides a good overview of the scope and requirements for assessing financial system stability.

12. The origins of the "macro-prudential" approach in BIS work are discussed in Clement (2010).

13. See Committee on the Global Financial System (2005), which is cited in Coval, Jurek, and Stafford (2009).

14. The role of the FSF Chairman in the meetings of the IMFC is noted in Peretz (2006). Mr. Peretz was a UK representative in the IMF Executive Board for a number of years.

15. This view and others regarding the work of the FSF are presented in Davies and Green (2008). Mr. Davies was the first Chairman of the UK Financial Services Authority, which was an institutional member of the FSF.

16. In its report to the IMFC of October 2007, the FSF reported that "members noted that macroeconomic conditions generally remain strong, underlying credit problems have been limited to a small proportion of credit instruments, and the capital of regulated institutions has remained at sound levels" (Statement of FSF Chair to the IMFC in October 2007—FSB Press Releases, which are available at www.fsb.org). The last part of this sentence suggests an unawareness among regulators in the advanced countries of the extent of off-balance sheet risks that large banks had been assuming in the prelude to the recent crisis.

17. The GFSR has been issued since 2001 and replaced earlier reports of the Fund's Research Department on International Capital Markets: Developments and Prospects.

18. In this connection, it is interesting to note that the Fund concluded in one of its early reviews of its role in the period leading up to the crisis that surveillance tended to downplay "tail risk" in the advanced countries, and that the IMF's formal vulnerability exercises involved only the emerging markets (IMF 2009b).

19. This example from Chapter II, p. 1 of the IMF Global Financial Stability Report (April 2006) was cited in the Turner Review of March 2009 (p. 85) of the UK Financial Services Authority (Financial Services Authority 2009).

20. The conclusions of the Fund's internal review of its surveillance exercises with selected advanced countries (Germany, Switzerland, the United Kingdom, and the United States) are presented in IMF (2008).

21. Financial Services Authority (2009), p. 86.

22. This view is conveyed in IMF IEO (2009), Companion Paper Two—IMF Interactions with Emerging Economies.

23. For an authoritative analysis of this problem, see Danielson et al (2001).

24. The role of "fair value" or mark-to-market accounting in the financial crisis has been the subject of much debate and controversy, which is summarized and evaluated in Laux and Leux (2010).

25. These issues are discussed in Acharya and Schnabl (2009), Bailey, Litan, and Johnson (2008) and Brunnermeier (2009).

26. The development of the Basel I and II Accords is examined in detail in Tarullo (2008).

27. This interpretation of the Basel II Accord is consistent with that presented in Claessens, Underhill, and Zhang (2008).

28. The role of the IIF in the design of the Basel II Accord is discussed in Claessens et al 2008, Tarullo (2008), and Lall 2009.

29. The Chiang Mai Initiative and the development of a regional financial architecture in East Asia are discussed in Elson (2006).

30. These figures are cited in Claessens, dell'Aricia, Igan, and Laeven (2010).

31. The demise of Lehman Brothers has been discussed in a number of recent books, including that of former US Treasury Secretary Paulson (2010), which provides a day-by-day accounting of the events surrounding its failure and the immediate aftermath.

32. This case, along with others, is discussed in BCBS (2010).

33. Government actions to support the financial sector are discussed in Claessens et al (2010).

34. The need for this policy action was highlighted in the IMF's World Economic Outlook exercise of April 2008.

35. These data are reported in IMF Fiscal Affairs Department (2009).

36. The swap lines of the US Federal Reserve and other central banks are discussed in McGuire and von Peter (2009) and Goldberg, Kennedy, and Mu (2010).

37. In May 2010, the Federal Reserve reopened five of these bilateral swap lines with the central banks of Canada, the euro zone, Japan, Switzerland,

and the United Kingdom for a period of eight months in the wake of market turmoil arising from the sovereign debt crisis in Greece.

38. Shortly after the decision on the FCL, the Fund announced a doubling in its normal, annual/cumulative access limits to 200/600 per cent of a member's quota, as well as the terms of a new High Access Precautionary Arrangement for countries that could not qualify for the FCL (IMF Public Information Notice 09/140, April 3, 2009, which is available at www.imf.org).

39. These arrangements are reviewed and discussed in IMF (2009f).

40. The New Arrangements to Borrow were established in 1997 to provide supplementary financing to the IMF from the G10 and sixteen other advanced and emerging market economies. In April 2009, its potential membership was extended to thirty-nine member countries.

9 The Third Reform of the International Financial Architecture

1. The creation of such a council is a key recommendation of the UN Commission of Exports (chaired by Professor Joseph Stiglitz) on Reform of the International Monetary and Financial System (United Nations 2009).

2. The sixteen countries are Bangladesh, Brazil, Canada, China, France, Germany, India, Indonesia, Italy, Japan, Nigeria, Pakistan, Russia, Spain, the United Kingdom, and the United States (Rueda-Sabater, Ramachandran, and Kraft 2009).

3. This recommendation was also advanced in the report of the De Larosiere Committee (European Commission 2009).

4. While the membership of the FSB was expanded, it should be noted that it still excludes representatives of two bodies (FATF and IFAC) that play important roles in the international standards and codes program overseen by the FSB.

5. The Charter for the FSB can be found on its website (www.financialstabilityboard.org). The FSB has established a Steering Committee and Standing Committees for Vulnerabilities Assessment, Supervisory and Regulatory Cooperation (including for supervisory colleges and cross-border crisis management), and the Implementation of Standards and Codes (FSB Press Release #14/2009; April 2, 2009).

6. Similar concerns have been raised by Kawai and Pomerleano (2009) and the Group of 30 (2009).

7. A convenient summary of various proposals for the reform of IMF governance can be found in IMF (2009e). Truman (2008) provides an authoritative, nonofficial view on many aspects of IMF reform.

8. As specified in the Fund Agreement, quotas in the Fund are reviewed once every five years and adjusted upward if agreed to by 85 percent of the membership. Since 1945, there have been eight increases in Fund quotas, the last in 1998.

9. While this reform of the quota calculation was approved by the Executive Board and Governors of the Fund, it has yet to be approved by 85 percent of total voting shares, as required under the Fund Agreement.

10. A careful analysis of the revised quota formula, along with suggestions for further improvement, is provided in Bryant (2008).

11. Horizontal accountability is to be distinguished from the vertical accountability of the formal governance arrangements of the Bretton Woods institutions that are mediated through the Executive Board, the IMFC, and Development Committee, and the Boards of Governors, which are responsible to member governments and national parliaments, and ultimately the citizens of each country. Since the 1990s, global civil society groups have complained about the weakness of these governance chains in the IMF and World Bank, and more broadly within the IFA, and the presence of a "democratic deficit" in the deliberations and decision-making of its constituent bodies. These groups, which are disproportionately present in the advanced countries, have been effective in demanding more transparency and disclosure of IMF and World Bank operations, which has increased their horizontal accountability. For an early discussion of the role of these groups in global governance, see Woods (2001).

12. The draft communique of the G20 was printed in the *Financial Times* on March 31, 2009.

13. These issues and proposals were examined in detail in an evaluation of the IMF Independent Evaluation Office on IMF Governance (IMF IEO 2008), as well as in the recommendations on governance reform of the Civil Society (Fourth Pillar) consultations with the IMF (New Rules for Global Finance Coalition 2009).

14. See, for example, IMF (2009a and 2009b).

15. See discussion in IMF (2008) and IMF IEO (2008).

16. This approach was endorsed in a study of the Council of Foreign Relations (Dunaway 2009). A similar recommendation was made by the Manuel Committee, although it would retain the prerogative of the Executive Board to discuss Article IV consultation reports in selected cases (IMF 2009d).

17. The utilization of the authority to call for "ad hoc consultations" was highlighted in the 2007 revision of the Fund's surveillance decision.

18. Such an approach was proposed in Ostry and Zettelmeyer (2005).

19. This perspective is brought out in a study by Lombardi and Woods (2008).

20. This and other reform proposals were discussed in Eichengreen (2009).

21. This proposal was presented in Matoo and Subramanian (2008).

22. The dominant role of the US dollar in the operations of the international monetary system is discussed in Goldberg, Kennedy, and Mu (2010).

23. The value of seignorage revenue accruing to the United States from the international use of the dollar is currently estimated to be around US$30 billion a year (Goldberg 2010). The ability of the United States to borrow

in its own currency, while investing abroad in foreign currencies, also implies that it benefits from valuation gains whenever the US dollar depreciates in value.

24. In June 2009, the ASEAN plus 3 countries (China, Japan, and Korea) agreed to multilateralize the Chiang Mai Initiative, which was accomplished in June 2010 with a reserve pool of US$120 billion.

25. Since 1978, the only countries in the Euro zone that have made purchases from the Fund (prior to that of Greece in May 2010) were Cyprus (1979–80), Portugal (1983–84), and Slovakia (1993–94).

26. This range of financing was noted in Obstfeld, Shambaugh, and Taylor (2009).

27. Through March 2010, the IMF had negotiated bilateral lines of credit for an aggregate amount of US$250 billion with sixteen member countries. In addition, commitments had been received from thirty-nine member countries for an increase in the resources under the New Arrangements to Borrow (NAB) from around US$50 billion to around US$550 billion.

28. This work was described in a joint FSB-IMF report on Information Gaps for the G20, dated October 29, 2009 (FSB and IMF 2009).

29. This information is reported in Johnston, Psalida, de Imus, Gobat, Moswami, Mulder, and Vazquez (2009).

30. The list of these institutions was reported in the Financial Times of November 30, 2009.

31. See, for example, a speech by Bank of England Governor Mervyn King of October 20, 2009, and chapter 3 of its Financial Stability Report of December 2009, which are available at www.bankofengland.co.uk.

32. The literature on economies of scale in banking is reviewed in Haldane (2010).

33. At the request of the G20, the IMF considered various options for taxing the financial sector, and recommended the imposition of a tax (or "financial stability contribution") on certain balance sheet items of financial institutions and a "financial activities tax" on the sum of a financial institution's profits and employee remuneration (IMF 2010). Professor Shin of Princeton University has proposed a tax on noncore liabilities of large financial institutions as a macro-prudential regulatory tool (Shin 2010).

34. The "tobin tax" was first proposed in Tobin (1978).

35. These issues are explored in the report of the Warwick Commission (2009). The report of the BCBS Cross-Border Bank Resolution Group examines the complexities of developing a cross-border resolution framework and the interim steps that are necessary (BCBS 2010).

36. The report of the Manuel Commission (IMF 2009e) also addressed this issue and recommended an amendment to the Fund Agreement to establish capital account liberalization as a purpose of IMF membership.

37. For a recent example of rethinking in the IMF on this issue, see Ostry, Ghosh, Habermeier, Chanon, Qureshi, and Reinhart (2010).

38. The Report of the De Larosiere Group laid out a number of recommendations for strengthening the European system of financial regulation and supervision, which have been largely endorsed by the EU (European Commission 2009).

39. The proposed changes in the Basel II regime have been laid out in a consultative document of the Basel Committee on Banking Supervision (BCBS 2009). While the membership of the BCBS was expanded in 2009 to include all of the G20 members and the process of revising the Basel Accord has been more open than in the past, it is still the case that most developing countries are excluded from the Committee's deliberations.

40. These guidelines are set out in the document of the FSB entitled "Principles for Executive Compensation" (April 2, 2009), which is available at www.financialstabilityboard.org

41. The creation of a regional debt restructuring mechanism within the EU has been recommended by economic experts at the Bruegel think-tank in Brussels (Pisani-Ferry and Sapir 2010) and the Centre for Economic Policy Studies (Gros and Mayer 2010).

42. This case experience is reviewed in Finger and Mecagni (2007) and Panizza, Sturznegger, and Zettelmeyer (2009).

Bibliography

Abdelal, Rawi (2007), *Capital Rules: The Construction of Global Finance* (Cambridge, MA: Harvard University Press)

Acharya, Viral and Matthew Richardson (2009), *Restoring Financial Stability: How to Repair a Failed System* (New York: John Wiley)

Acharya, Viral and Philipp Schnabl (2009), "Do Global Banks Spread Global Imbalances? The Case of Asset-Backed Commercial Paper during the Financial Crisis 2007–09" (paper presented at the 10th Annual Research Conference of the IMF, November 5–6, 2009, available at www. imf.org)

Adrian, Tobias and Hyun Song Shin (2009), "Money, Liquidity and Monetary Policy" *American Economic Review*, vol. 99(2): 600–605 (May)

Adrian, Tobias, Christopher Burke, and James McAndrews (2009), "The Federal Reserve's Primary Dealer Credit Facility" *Current Issues in Economics and Finance*, vol. 15(4), August (Federal Reserve Bank of New York).

Ahamed, Liaquat (2009), *Lords of Finance: The Bankers Who Broke the World* (New York: Penguin Press)

Ainley, Michael (1985), "Supplementing the Fund's Lending Capacity" *Finance and Development*, vol. 22(2): 41–45 (June)

Aizenman, Joshua, Menzio Chinn, and Hiro Ito (2008), "Assessing the Emerging Global Financial Architecture: The Trilemma's Configurations over Time" NBER Working Paper #14533, December

Alessandrini, Pietro and Michele Fratianni (2009), "Resurrecting Keynes to Stabilize the International Monetary System," *Open Economic Review*, vol. 20: 339–358

Alexander, Kern, Rahul Dhumale, and John Eatwell (2006), *Global Governance of Financial Systems: The International Regulation of Risk* (New York: Oxford University Press)

Bailey, Martin Neil, Robert Litan, and Matthew Johnson (2008), "The Origins of the Financial Crisis," Fixing Finance Series Paper #3 (Brookings Institution), November, available at www.brookings.edu

Baker, Andrew (2006), *The Group of Seven: Finance Ministries, Central Banks and Global Financial Governance* (London and New York: Routledge)

Bakker, Age F. P. (1996), *The Liberalization of Capital Movements in Europe: The Monetary Committee and Financial Integration 1958–1994* (Dordrecht, Boston and London: Kluwer Academic Press)

BIS, *Annual Reports* (Basel: Bank for International Settlements) various issues

Basel Committee on Bank Supervision (2009), "Consultative Document on Strengthening the Resilience of the Banking Sector" (December), available at www.bis.org/bcbs

Basel Committee on Banking Supervision (2010), "Report and Recommendations of the Cross-Border Bank Resolution Group" (March), available at www.bis.org/bcbs

Beim, David and Charles Calomiris (2001), *Emerging Financial Markets* (New York: McGraw Hill)

Birdsall, Nancy, Augusto de la Torre, and Felipe Valencia Caicedo (2010), "The Washington Consensus: Assessing a Damaged Brand," Center for Global Development Working Paper #213 (May), available at www.cgdev.org

Blejer, Mario, Mohsin Khan, and Paul Masson (1995), "Early Contributions of *Staff Papers* to International Economics," *IMF Staff Papers*, vol. 42: 707–733

Bradford, Colin and Johannes Linn (editors) (2007), *Global Governance Reform: Breaking the Stalemate* (Washington, DC: Brookings Institution)

Brewer, Elijah and Julapa Jagtiani (2009), "How Much Did Banks Pay to Become Too Big To Fail and to Become Systemically Important?" Federal Reserve Bank of Philadelphia Working Paper 09–34 (December)

Bordo, Michael and Anna Schwartz (1998), "Under What Circumstances, Past and Present, Have International Rescues of Countries in Financial Distress Been Mounted?" NBER Working Paper #6824 (December)

——— (2001), "From ESF to IMF" NBER Working Paper #8100 (January)

Bordo, Michael and Barry Eichengreen (eds.) (1993), *A Retrospective on the Bretton Woods System* (Chicago and London: University of Chicago Press)

——— (2002), "Crises Now and Then: What Lessons from the Last Era of Financial Globalization?" NBER Working Paper #8176 (January)

Bordo, Michael and Hugh Rockoff (1996), "The Gold Standard as a 'Good Housekeeping Seal of Approval,'" *Journal of Economic History*, vol. 56(3): 389–426

Borio, Claudio and Gianni Toniolo (2006), "!30 Years of Central Bank Cooperation: A BIS Perspective" Bank for International Settlements Working Paper #197 (February)

Borio, Claudio, and I. Shim (2007), "What Can Macro-Prudential Policy Do to Support Monetary Policy?" Bank for International Settlements Working Paper #242 (December)

Boughton, James (2001), *The International Monetary Fund 1979–1988: The Silent Revolution* (Washington, DC: International Monetary Fund)

Bourguinon et al (2002), "Making Sense of Globalization" CEPR Policy Paper #8 (July), Center for Economic Policy Research

Brunnermeier, Markus (2009), "Deciphering the Liquidity and Credit Crunch 2007–08" *Journal of Economic Perspectives*, vol.23(1): 77–100 (Winter)

Brunnermeier, Markus, Andrew Crockett, Charles Goodhart, Avinash Persaud, and Hyun Song Shin (2009), *The Fundamental Principles of Financial Regulation* (Geneva Reports on the World Economy #11) January

Bryant, Ralph (2003), *Turbulent Waters: Cross-Border Finance and International Governance* (Washington, DC: Brookings Institution)

—— (2008), "Reform of IMF Quota Shares and Voting Shares: A Missed Opportunity" Policy Paper (April 8) (Washington, DC: Brookings Institution)

Caballero, Ricardo, Emmanuel Farhi, and Pierre-Olivier Gourinchas (2008), "Financial Crash, Commodity Prices and Global Imbalances," *Brookings Papers on Economic Activity* (Fall): 1–68

Calvo, Guillermo (1998), "Capital Flows and Capital Market Crises: The Simple Economics of Sudden Stops," *Journal of Applied Economics*, vol. 119(3): 1131–75

Calvo, Guillermo and Carmen Reinhart (2002), "Fear of Floating," *Quarterly Journal of Economics*, vol. 107(2): 379–408

Center for Global Development (2006), "Rescuing the World Bank: A CGD Working Report and Selected Essays" (Washington, DC: Center for Global Development)

Chinn, Menzie and Hiro Ito (2008) "A New Measure of Financial Openness" *Journal of Comparative Policy Analysis*, vol. 10(3): 307–320 (September)

Chwieroth, Jeffrey M. (2010), *Capital Ideas: The IMF and the Rise of Financial Liberalization* (Princeton, NJ and Oxford: Princeton University Press)

Claessens, Stijn, Geoffrey Underhill, and Xioke Zhang (2008), "The Political Economy of Basel II: The Costs for Poor Countries," *World Economy*: 313–344

Claessens, Stijn, Giovanni dell'Aricia, Deniz Igan, and Luc Laeven (2010), "Lessons and Policy Implications from the Global Financial Crisis," IMF Working Paper #10/44 (February)

Clement, Piet (2010), "The Term 'Macro-prudential': Origins and Evolution," Bank for International Settlements *Quarterly Review* (March): 59–67

Clift, Jeremy (2009), "Questioning a Chastened Priesthood" *Finance and Development*, vol. 46(3): 4–7

Cline, William (1995), *International Debt Reexamined* (Washington, DC: Peterson Institute for International Economics)

Cohen, Benjamin (1997), "The Financial Support Fund of the OECD: A Failed Initiative" Princeton Essays in International Finance No. 204 (International Finance Section, Department of Economics, Princeton University)

Cohen, Jessica and William Easterly, Editors (2009), *What Works in Development? Thinking Big and Thinking Small* (Washington, DC: Brookings Institution)

Colander, David, Michael Goldberg, Armin Haas, Katarina Juselius, Alan Kirman, Thomas Lux, and Brigitte Sloth (2009), "The Financial Crisis and Systemic Failure of the Economics Profession," *Critical Review*, vol. 21(2–3): 249–268

Committee on the Global Financial System (2005), "The Role of Ratings in Structured Finance: Issues and Implications" Publication #23 (January), available at www.bis.org/cgfs

Committee on the Global Financial System (2006), "Housing Finance in the Global Financial Market," CGFS Paper 26 (January)

———— (2009), "Capital Flows and Emerging Market Economies" Working Paper #33 (January)

Cooper, Richard (2008), "Global Imbalances: Globalization, Demography and Sustainability," *Journal of Economic Perspectives*, vol. 22(3): 93–112

Coval, Joshua, Jakub Jurek, and Erik Stafford (2009), "The Economics of Structured Finance," *Journal of Economic Perspectives*, vol. 23(1): 3–26

Danielson, Jon, Paul Ermbrechts, Charles Goodhart, Con Keating, Felix Muenich, Olivier Renault, and Hyun Song Shin (2001), "An Academic Response to Basel II" LSE Financial Markets Group Special Report #130 (May)

Davies, Howard and David Green (2008), *Global Financial Regulation: The Essential Guide* (London: Cambridge Polity Press)

Davis, Steven and James Kahn (2008), "Interpreting the Great Moderation: Changes in the Volatility of Economic Activity at the Macro and Micro Levels," *Journal of Economic Perspectives*, vol. 22(4): 155–180

Dell'Ariccia, Giovanni, Julian di Giovanni, Andre Faria, Ahyan Kose, Paulo Mauro, Jonathan Ostry, Martin Schindler, and Marco Terrones (2008), "Reaping the Benefits of Financial Blobalization" IMF Occasional Paper #264

DeVries, Margaret Garritsen (1976), *The International Monetary Fund 1966–1971: The System Under Stress*, vol. I: Narrative (Washington, DC: IMF)

———— (1985), *The International Monetary Fund 1972–1978: Cooperation on Trial*, Vol. I: Narrative and Analysis (Washington, DC: IMF)

Dobson, Wendy (1991), *Economic Policy Coordination: Requiem or Prologue?* (Washington, DC: Peterson Institute for International Economics)

Dunaway, Steve (2009), "Global Imbalances and the Financial Crisis" CFR Special Report #49 (New York: Council on Foreign Relations), March

Easterly, William (2006), *The White Man's Burden: Why the West's Efforts to Aid the Rest Have Done So Much Ill and So Little Good* (New York: Penguin Press)

Eichengreen, Barry (1992), *Golden Fetters: The Gold Standard and the Great Depression 1919–1939* (Oxford: Oxford University Press)

———— (1996), *Globalizing Capital: A History of the International Monetary System* (Princeton, NJ: Princeton University Press)

————. (2002), *Financial Crises and What to Do About Them* (New York: Oxford University Press)

———— (2007), *Global Imbalances and the Lessons of Bretton Woods* (Cambridge: MIT Press)

———— (2009), "Out of the Box Thoughts About the International Financial Architecture" IMF Working Paper #09/116 (May), available at www.imf.org

Eichengreen, Barry and Michael Mussa (1998), Capital Account Liberalization: Theoretical and Practical Aspects" Occasional Paper 107 (Washington, DC: IMF)

Eichengreen, Barry and Ricardo Hausmann (1999), "Exchange rates and Financial Fragility" NBER Working Paper #7418 (November)

Elson, Anthony (2006), "The Emergence of a Regional Financial Architecture in Asia: Recent Developments and Prospects," *World Economics*, vol. 7(3): 167–184 (October/December)

——— (2008), "Sovereign Wealth Funds and the International Monetary System," *Whitehead Journal of Diplomacy and International Affairs*, vol. 9(2): 71–82 (Summer/Fall)

European Commission (2009), *The De Larosiere Report on Cross-Border Financial Supervision* (Brussels) February

Feldstein, Martin (1998), "Refocusing the IMF," *Foreign Affairs* (March/April): 20–33

Feldstein, Martin and Charles Horioka (1980), "Domestic Saving and International Capital Flows," *Economic Journal*, vol. 90(358): 314–329

Ferguson, Roger, Jr., Philipp Hartmann, Fabio Panetta, and Richard Portes (2007), *International Financial Stability* (Geneva Reports on the World Economy #9) November

Financial Services Authority (2009), "The Turner Review: A Regulatory Response to the Global Banking Crisis" (March), available at www.fsa.gov.uk

Financial Stability Forum (2008a), *Report on Enhancing Market and Institutional Resilience* (Basel: Bank for International Settlements), April

——— (2008b), *Report on Enhancing Market and Institutional Resilience: A Follow-Up on Recommendations* (Basel: Bank for International Settlements), October

Financial Stability Board and IMF (2009), "The Financial Crisis and Information Gaps: A Report to the G20 Finance Ministers and Central Bank Governors" (October 29), available at www.imf.org

Finger, Harold and Mauro Mecagni (2007), "Sovereign Debt Restructuring and Debt Sustainability: An Analysis of Recent Cross-Country Experience" IMF Occasional Paper #255

Fischer, Stanley (1997), "Applied Economics in Action: IMF Programs," *American Economic Review*, vol. 87(2): 23–27

——— (2001), "Exchange Rate Regimes: Is the Bipolar View Correct?," *Journal of Economic Perspectives*, vol. 15(2): 3–24

——— (2007), "Exchange Rate Systems, Surveillance and Advice," a paper presented at the 8th Jacques Polak Annual Research Conference of the IMF, November 15–16, available at www.imf.org

Gianni, Curzio (1999), "'Enemy of None But a Common Friend of All?' An International Perspective on the Lender of Last Resort Function" Princeton Essays in International Finance #214 (June) (International Finance Section, Department of Economics, Princeton University)

Gallagher, Kevin (2010), "Policy Space to Prevent and Mitigate Financial Crises in Trade and Investment Agreements," G24 Policy Discussion Paper #58 (May)

Gold, Joseph (1980), "The Rule of Law in the International Monetary Fund" IMF Pamphlet Series No. 32 (Washington, DC: International Monetary Fund)

——— (1988), "Mexico and the Development of Practice of the IMF," *World Development*, vol. 16(10): 1127–1142 (October)

Goldberg, Linda, Craig Kennedy, and Jason Mu (2010), "Central Bank Swap Lines and Overseas Dollar Funding Costs," Staff Report #429, Federal Reserve Bank of New York (January)

Goldstein, Morris (2000), "IMF Structural Programs," a paper prepared for an NBER Conference on Economic and Financial Crises in Emerging Market Economies in Woodstock VT (October 19–21), available at www.iie.com

Greenspan, Alan (2007), "Balance of Payments Imbalances" The Per Jacobsson Lecture, October 1, 2007 (Washington, DC: Per Jacobsson Foundation)

———— (2010), "The Crisis" paper presented at the Brookings Panel on Economic Activity in March, available at www.brookings.edu

Gros, Daniel and Thomas Mayer (2010), "How to Deal with Sovereign Default in Europe," Centre for Economic Policy Studies Policy Brief #202 (May 17)

Group of Lecce (2009), "Reforming Global Economic Governance: A Proposal to the Members of the G-20" (February) available at www.isufi.unile. it/?GruppoDiLecce

Group of Twenty (2008), "The Group of 20—A History" available at www.g20. org

———— (2009a), "Enhancing Sound Regulation and Strengthening Transparency" Working Group #1 Final Report (March)

———— (2009b), "Reinforcing International Cooperation and Promoting Integrity in Financial Markets" Working Group #2 Final Report (March)

Group of Thirty (2009), *Financial Reform: A Framework for Financial Stability* (New York) January

Hagan, Sean (2005), "Designing a Legal Framework to Restructure Sovereign Debt," *Georgetown Journal of International Law*, vol. 36(2): 299–402

Hajnal, Peter (1999), *The G7/G8 System: Evolution, Role and Documentation* (London: Aldershot Publishers)

————. (2007), *The G8 System and the G20: Evolution, Role and Documentation* (Burlington: Ashgate Publishing)

Haldane, Andrew (2009a), "Why Banks Failed the Stress Test," Bank of England Speech (Bank of England, London) February 13, available at www.bankofengland.co.uk

————. (2009b), "Rethinking the Financial Network," Bank of England Speech (Bank of England, London) April

————. (2010), "The $100 Question" Bank of England Speech (Bank of England, London) March

Helleiner, Eric (1994), *States and the Reemergence of Global Finance: From Bretton Woods to the 1990s* (Ithaca, NY: Cornell University Press)

————. (2008), "The Mystery of the Missing Sovereign Debt Restructuring Mechanism," *Contributions to Political Economy*, vol. 27: 91–113

Henning, C. Randall and Fred Bergsten (1996), *Global Economic Leadership and the G7* (Washington, DC: Peterson Institute for International Economics)

Henry, Peter Blair (2007), "Capital Account Liberalization: Theory, Evidence and Speculation," *Journal of Economic Literature*, vol. 45(4): 887–935

Horsefield, Keith (1969), *The International Monetary Fund: Twenty Years of International Monetary Cooperation,* Vol. I Chronicle and Vol. III Documents (Washington, DC: International Monetary Fund)

Institute of International Finance (2008), "Principles for Stable Capital Flows and Fair Debt Restructuring in Emerging Markets: Report on Implementation of the Principles Consultative Group" (October), available at www.iif.com

IMF, *Global Financial Stability Report* (Washington, DC: International Monetary Fund), various issues

IMF *World Economic Outlook* (Washington, DC: International Monetary Fund), various issues

IMF (2008), Triennial Surveillance Review: Background Information and Statistical Appendix (September), available at www.imf.org

———— (2009a), "Initial Lessons of the Crisis" (February), available at www.imf.org

———— (2009b), "Initial Lessons of the Crisis for the Global Financial Architecture and the IMF" (February), available at www.imf.org

———— (2009c), "Lessons of the Financial Crisis for Future Regulation of Financial Institutions and Markets and for Liquidity Management" (February), available at www.imf.org

———— (2009d), "Report of the Expert Group on Governance Reform" (Manuel Report) available at www.imf.org. (March)

———— (2009e), "Review of Recent Crisis Programs" (September), available at www.imf.org

———— (2010), "A Fair and Substantial Contribution by the Financial Sector: Final Report for the G20" (June), available at www.imf.org

IMF Committee of 20 (1974), *International Monetary Reform: Documents of the Committee of 20* (Washington, DC: International Monetary Fund)

IMF Fiscal Affairs Department (2009), "The State of Public Finances Cross Country Fiscal Monitor: November 2009," IMF Staff Position Note #09/225, available at www.imf.org (November)

IMF Independent Evaluation Office (2003), *The IMF and Recent Capital Account Crises: Indonesia, Korea and Brazil* (Washington, DC: International Monetary Fund)

IMF Independent Evaluation Office (2004), *The IMF and Argentina, 1991–2001* (Washington, DC: International Monetary Fund)

———— (2005), *The IMF's Approach to Capital Account Liberalization* (Washington, DC: International Monetary Fund)

———— (2007), *The Fund's Exchange Rate Advice* (Washington, DC: International Monetary Fund)

———— (2007), *Structural Conditionality in IMF-Supported Programs* (Washington, DC: International Monetary Fund)

———— (2008), *Governance of the IMF: An Evaluation* (Washington, DC: International Monetary Fund)

IMF Independent Evaluation Office (2009), *IMF Interactions with Member Countries* (Washington, DC: International Monetary Fund)

IMF and World Bank (2009), "The Financial Sector Assessment Program after Ten Years: Experience and Reforms for the Next 10 Years" (August), available at www.imf.org

James, Harold (1996), *International Monetary Cooperation since Bretton Woods* (New York and Washington, DC: Oxford University Press and IMF)

Johnson, Simon, Kalpana Kochhar, Todd Mitton, and Natalia Tamirisa (2006), "Malaysian Capital Controls: Macroeconomics and Institutions," IMF Working Paper #06/51 (February)

Johnston, R. Barry, Effie Psalida, Phil de Imus, Jeanne Gobat, Mangal Moswami, Christian Mulder, and Francisco Vazquez (2009), "Addressing Information Gaps," IMF Staff Position Note #09/06 (March)

Kaminsky, Graciela and Carmen Reinhart (1999), "The Twin Crises: The Causes of Banking and Balance of Payments Problems," *American Economic Review*, vol. 89(4): 473–500 (June)

Kapur, Devesh (2004), "Remiitances: The New Development Mantra?" G24 Discussion Paper #29, available at www. G24.org

Kapur, Devesh, John Lewis, and Richard Webb (1997), *The World Bank: Its First Half Century* (Washington, DC: Brookings Institution), Vol. I: History

Kawai, Masahiro and Michael Pomerleano (2009), "International Stability Architecture for the 21st Century," a commentary on www.voxeu.org (July 31)

Kenen, Peter (ed.) (1994), *Managing the World Economy* (Washington, DC: Peterson Institute for International Economics)

Kenen, Peter, Jeffrey Shafer, Nigel Wicks, and Charles Wyplosz (2004), "International Economic and Financial Cooperation: New Actors, New Players, New Responses" Geneva Reports on World Economy (London: Center for Economic Policy Research)

Keohane, Robert and Nye, Joseph P. Jr. (2001), *Power and Interdependence: World Politics in Transition* (Boston: Little Brown, 3rd Edition)

Kose, Ayhan, Eswar Prasad, Ken Rogoff, and Shang-Jin Wei (2009), "Financial Globalization: A Re-appraisal," *IMF Staff Papers*, vol. 56(1): 8–62

Kindleberger, Charles (1973), *The World in Depression, 1929–1939* (Berkeley: University of California Press)

Krueger, Anne (1990), "Market Failures and Government Failures," *Journal of Economic Perspectives*, vol. 4(3): 25–41

——— (2002), "A New Approach to Debt Restructuring" (Washington, DC: International Monetary Fund), April

Krugman, Paul (1995), *Currencies and Crises* (Cambridge: MIT Press)

Laeven, Luc and Fabian Valencia (2008), "Systemic Banking Crises: A New Database," IMF Working Paper #08/224 (November)

Lall, Ranjit (2009), "Why Basel II Failed and Why Any Basel III Is Doomed" Global Economic Governance Working Paper #2009/52 (October), Center for Global Economic Governance, Oxford University

Lane, Phillip and Gian Maria Milesi-Ferretti (2007), "The External Wealth of Nations," *Journal of International Economics*, vol. 73(2): 223–250 (November)

───── (2008), "The Drivers of Financial Globalization," *American Economic Review*, vol. 98(2): 327–332 (May)

Laux, Christian and Christian Leux (2010), "Did Fair Value Accounting Contribute to the Financial Crisis?," *Journal of Economic Perspectives*, vol. 24(1): 93–118 (Winter)

Levine, Ross (2008), "Finance, Financial Sector Policies and Long-Run Growth" (with Asli Demirguc-Kunt), Working Paper #11 for the Commission on Growth and Development (Washington, DC: World Bank)

Little, I. M. D. (1982), *Economic Development: Theory, Policy and International Relations* (New York: Basic Books)

Lombardi, Domenico and Ngaire Woods (2008), "The Politics of Influence: An Analysis of IMF Surveillance," *Review of International Political Economy*, vol. 15(5): 711–39

MacKinnon, Ronald (1979), *Money in International Finance: The Convertible Currency System* (New York: Oxford University Press)

───── (1993), "The Rules of the Game: International Money in Historical Perspective," *American Economic Review*, vol. 31(1): 1–44

Magud, Nicolas and Carmen Reinhart (2006), "Capital Controls: An Evaluation" NBER Working Paper #11973 (January)

Mandelbrot, Benoit and Richard Hudson (2004), *The (Mis)behavior of Markets: A Fractal View of Risk, Ruin and Reward* (New York: Basic Books)

Mateos y Lago, Isabelle, Rupa Duttagupta and Rishi Goyal (2009), "The Debate on the International Monetary System," IMF Staff Position Note #09/26 (November)

Matoo. Aaditya and Arvind Subramanian (2008), "Currency Undervaluation and Sovereign Wealth Funds: A New Role for the World Trade Organization" Working Paper 08-2 of the Peterson Institute for International Economics (January), available at www.iie.com

Mathieson, Donald J. and Liliana Rojas-Suarez (1993), "Liberalization of the Capital Account: Experiences and Issues" IMF Occasional Paper #103 (March)

Mauro, Paolo, Nathan Sussman, and Yishay Yafeh (2006), *Emerging Markets and Financial Globalization: Sovereign Bond Spreads in 1870–1913 and Today* (Oxford and New York: Oxford University Press)

Mauro, Paolo and Yafeh, Yishay (2003), "The Corporation of Foreign Bondholders" IMF Working Paper #03/107 (May)

McGuire, Peter and Goetz von Peter (2009), "The US Dollar Shortage in Global Banking and the International Policy Response," Bank for International Settlements Working Paper #291 (October)

McKinsey Global Institute (2008), "Mapping Global Capital Markets: Fifth Annual Report" (October), available at www.mckinsey.com/mgi

───── (2009), "Global Capital Markets: Entering a New Era" (September), available at www.mckinsey.com/mgi

Meier, Gerald (2005), *Biography of a Subject: An Evolution of Development Economics* (New York and Oxford: Oxford University Press)

Mikesell, Raymond (1994), "The Bretton Woods Debates: A Memoir" Princeton Essays in International Finance No. 192 (International Finance Section, Department of Economics, Princeton University) March

Mishkin, Frederic (2006), *The Next Great Globalization: How Disadvantaged Nations Can Harness Their Financial Systems to Get Rich* (Princeton, NJ and Oxford: Princeton University Press)

Morris, S. and H. Shin (2008), "Financial Regulation in a System Context," *Brookings Papers on Economic Activity*, Fall, pp. 229–274

Mortenson, Greg and David Oliver Relin (2007), *Three Cups of Tea* (New York: Penguin Group)

Moyo, Dambisa (2009), *Dead Aid* (New York: Farrar, Straus and Giroux)

Mussa, Michael (2002), "Argentina and the IMF: From Triumph to Tragedy," Policy Analyses in International Economics #67 (Peterson Institute for International Economics)

——— (2008), "IMF Surveillance over China's Exchange Rate Policies" in Morris Goldstein and Nicholas Lardy (eds.), *Debating China's Exchange Rate Policies* (Washington, DC: Peterson Institute for International Economics)

Mussa, Micahel and Miguel Savastano (1999), "The IMF Approach to Economic Stabilization," *NBER Macroeconomics Annual* : 79–118

New Rules for Global Finance Coalition (2009), Report on the Civil Society (Fourth Pillar) Consultations with the International Monetary Fund on Reform of IMF Governance (September), available at www.new-rules.org

Nier, Erlend (2009), "Financial Stability Frameworks and the Role of Central Banks: Lessons from the Crisis," IMF Working Paper #09/70 (April)

Obstfeld, Maurice and Ken Rogoff (2004), "The Unsustainable US Current Account Position Revisited," NBER Working Paper #10689 (November)

——— (2009), "Global Imbalances and the Financial Crisis: Products of Common Causes," Paper presented at a Conference of the Federal Reserve Bank of San Francisco on Asian Economic Policy, October 18–20

Obstfeld, Maurice and Alan M. Taylor (2004), *Global Capital Markets: Integration, Crisis and Growth* (New York: Cambridge University Press)

Obstfeld, Maurice, Jay Shambaugh, and Alan Taylor (2008), "Financial Stability, the Trilemma, and International Reserves" NBER Working Paper #14217 (August)

Ostry, Jonathan and Jeromin Zettelmeyer (2005), "Strengthening IMF Crisis Prevention," IMF Working Paper #05/206 (November)

Ostry, Jonathan, Atish Ghosh, Karl Habermeier, Marcos Chanon, Mahvash Qureshi, and Dennis Reinhart (2010), "Capital Inflows: The Role of Controls," IMF Staff Position Note #10/04 (February)

Panizza, Ugo, Federico Sturznegger, and Jeromin Zettelmeyer (2009), "The Economics and Law of Sovereign Debt and Default," *Journal of Economic Literature*, vol. 47(3): 651–698 (September)

Parker, Ian (2010), "The Poverty Lab: Transforming Development Economics, One Experiment at a Time," *New Yorker Magazine* (May 17): 79–89

Paulson, Henry (2010, *On the Brink* (New York: Hachette Book Group)

Pauly, Louis (1996), "The League of Nations and the Foreshadowing of the IMF" Princeton Essays in International Finance No. 201 (International Finance Section, Department of Economics, Princeton University) December

———— (1997), *Who Elected the Bankers? Surveillance and Control in the World Economy* (Ithaca, NY: Cornell University Press)

People's Bank of China (2009), "Reform the IMF," Speech by Governor Zhou Xiachuan (March 23), available at www.pbc.cn/english

Peretz, David (2006), "Global Financial Stability," Expert Paper #3 in the Report of the International Task Force on Global Public Goods, sponsored by the Yale University Center for the Study of Globalization

Perry, Guillermo (2009), *Beyond Lending: How Multilateral Banks Can Help Developing Countries Manage Volatility* (Washington, DC: Center for Global Development)

Pisani-Ferry, Jean and Andre Sapir (2010), "Europe Needs a Framework for Debt Crises," *Financial Times* (April 29)

Prasad, Eswar (2007), "India's Approach to Capital Account Liberalization" Institute for the Study of Labor Discussion Paper #3927, January

Prasad, Eswar, and Raghuram Rajan (2008), "A Pragmatic Approach to Capital Account Liberalization," *Journal of Economic Perspectives*, vol. 22(3): 149–172

Prasad, Eswar, Raghuram Rajan, and Arvind Subramanian (2007), "Foreign Capital and Economic Growth," *Brookings Papers on Economic Activity*, Spring, 153–230

Quinn, Dennis (1997), "The Correlates of Change in International Financial Regulation," *American Political Science Review*, vol. 91(3): 531–551

Quirk, Peter and Owen Evans (1995), "Capital Account Convertibility: Review of Experience and Implications for IMF Policies" IMF Occasional Paper #131 (October)

Raghavan, Chrakravarthi (2009), "Financial Services, The WTO and Initiatives for Global Financial Reform," G24 Discussion Paper, available at www.G24. org

Rajan, Raghuram and Arvind Subramanian (2008), "Aid and Growth: What Does the Cross-Country Evidence Really Show?" *Review of Economics and Statistics*, vol. 90(4): 643–655 (November)

Reinhart, Carmen and Ken Rogoff (2009), *This Times Is Different: Eight Centuries of Financial Folly* (Princeton, NJ: Princeton University Press)

Rhomberg, Rudolph and Robert Heller (eds.) (1977), *The Monetary Approach to the Balance of Payments* (Washington, DC: International Monetary Fund)

Rieffel, Lex (2003), *Restructuring Sovereign Debt: The Case for Ad Hoc Machinery* (Washington, DC: Brookings Institution)

Rodrik, Dani, Arvind Subramanian, and Franciso Trebbi (2004), "Institutions Rule: The Primacy of Institutions over Integration and Geography in

Economic Development," *Journal of Economic Growth*, vol. 9(2): 131–165 (June)

Rogoff, Ken and Jeromyn Zettelmeyer (2002), "Bankruptcy Procedures for Sovereigns: A History of Ideas, 1976–2001," IMF Working Paper #02/133 (August)

Roodman, David (2007), "MacroAid Effectiveness Research: A Guide to the Perplexed" Working Paper #137, Center for Global Development (Washington, DC), available at www.cgdev.org, December

Roubini, Nouriel and Brad Setser (2004), *Bailouts or Bail-Ins? Responding to Financial Crises in Emerging Economies* (Washington, DC: Peterson Institute for International Economics)

Rueda-Sabater, Enrique, Vijaya Ramachandran, and Robin Kraft (2009), "A Fresh Look at Global Governance: Exploring Objective Criteria for Representation" Center for Global Development Working Paper #160 (February) available at www.cgdev.org

Ruggie, John (1982), "International Regimes, Transactions and Change: Embedded Liberalism in the Postwar Economic Order," *International Organization*, vol. 36(2): 379–415

Sachs, Jeffrey, John McArthur, Guido Schmidt-Traub, Margaret Kruk, Chandrika Bahadur, Michael Faye, and Gordon McCord (2004), "Ending Africa's Poverty Trap" *Brookings Papers on Economic Activity*, Spring: 117–240

Sachs, Jeffrey (2005), *The End of Poverty: Economic Possibilities for Our Time* (New York: Penguin Press)

———— (2009), *Common Wealth: Economics for a Crowded Planet* (New York: Penguin Press)

Schinasi, Gary (2006), *Safeguarding Financial Stability: Theory and Practice* (Washington, DC: IMF)

Sheng, Andrew (2009), *From Asian to Global Financial Crisis: An Asian Regulator's View of Unfettered Finance in the 19990s and 2000s* (New York: Cambridge University Press)

Shin, Hyun Song (2010), "Non-Core Liabilities Tax as a Tool for Prudential Regulation," A Policy Memo (February 19), available on Professor Shin's personal website (hyunsongshin.org)

Simmons, Beth (1993), "Why Innovate? Founding the Bank for International Settlements," *World Politics*, vol. 45(3): 361–405 (April)

Slaughter, Anne-Marie (2004), *A New World Order* (Princeton, NJ: Princeton University Press)

Sobel, Mark and Louellen Stedman (2008), "The Evolution of the G7 and International Policy Coordination," U.S. Treasury Department Occasional Paper #3 (July)

Solomon, Robert (1982), *The International Monetary System, 1945–1981* (New York: Harper and Row)

Steil, Ben (2009) "Lessons of the Financial Crisis" CFR Special Report #49 (Council on Foreign Relations, New York), March

Steinwand, Martin and Randall Stone (2008), "The International Monetary Fund: A Review of Recent Evidence," *Review of International Organizations*, vol. 3(2): 123–149

Stern, Nicholas, Jean-Jacques Dethier, and F. Halsey Rogers (2005), *Growth and Empowerment: Making Development Happen* (Cambridge and London: MIT Press)

Stern, Robert M. (2009), "Trade in Financial Services—Has the IMF Been Involved Constructively?" Background Paper (BP/09/05) for the IMF IEO Evaluation of "IMF Involvement in Trade Policy Issues," available at www.imf.org/ieo

Stiglitz, Joseph (2003), *Globalization and Its Discontents* (New York: Norton)

Sturznegger, Federico and Jeromyn Zettelmeyer (2006), *Debt Defaults and Lessons from a Decade of Crises* (Cambridge: MIT Press)

Suter, Christian and Hanspeter Stamm (1992), "Coping with Global Debt Crises, Debt Settlements, 1820–1986," *Comparative Studies in Society and History*, vol. 34(4): 645–678

Taleb, Nassim (2007), *The Black Swan: The Impact of the Highly Improbable* (New York: Random House)

Tarullo, Dan (2008), *Banking On Basel: The Future of International Financial Regulation* (Washington, DC: Peterson Institute for International Economics)

Taylor, Alan (2003), "Foreign Capital in Latin America in the 19th and 20th Centuries" NBER Working Paper #9580 (March)

Taylor, John (2009), "The Financial Crisis and the Policy Responses: An Empirical Analysis of What Went Wrong" NBER Working Paper #14631 (January)

Tobin, James (1978), "A Proposal for Monetary Reform," *Eastern Economic Journal*, vol. 4(3–4): 153–159

Triffin, Robert (1960), *Gold and the Dollar Crisis* (New Haven, CT: Yale University Press

Truman, Edwin editor (2008), "Reforming the IMF for the 21st Century," Special Report #19 of the Peterson Institute for International Economics (April)

Ungerer, Horst (1990), "The European Monetary System: Recent Developments" IMF Occasional Paper #73

United Nations (2006), *Report of the High Level Panel on UN System-wide Conference* (New York: United Nations), November

——— (2009), *Report of the Commission of Experts of the President of the United Nations General Assembly on Reforms of the International Monetary and Financial Systems (Stiglitz Group)* (New York: United Nations)

Von Furstenberg, George and Joseph Daniels (1992), "Economic Summit Declarations, 1975–1989: Examining the Written Record of International Cooperation" Princeton Essays in International Finance No. 72 (International Finance Section, Department of Economics, Princeton University)

Vreeland, James (2007), *The International Monetary Fund: Politics of Conditional Lending* (New York: Routledge)

Walter, Andrew (2008), *Governing Finance: East Asia's Adoption of International Standards* (Ithaca, NY and London: Cornell University Press)

Williamson, John (1977), *The Failure of World Monetary Reform, 1971–1974* (New York: New York University Press)

———— (1990), "What Washington Means by Policy Reform" chapter 2 in Williamson, J. (ed.), *Latin American Adjustment: How Much Has Happened?* (Washington, DC: Peterson Institute for International Economics)

Williamson, John and Molly Mahar (1998) "A Survey of Financial Liberalization" Princeton Essays in International Finance No. 211 (International Finance Section, Department of Economics, Princeton University) November

Wolf, Martin (2004), *Why Globalization Works* (New Haven, CT: Yale University Press)

———— (2008), *Fixing Global Finance* (Baltimore: Johns Hopkins University Press)

Woods, Ngaire (2001), "Making the IMF and World Bank More Accountable," *International Affairs*, vol. 77(1): pp. 83–100 (January)

World Bank (2002), *Global Development Finance* (Washington, DC: World Bank)

———— (2005), *Economic Growth in the 1990s: Learning from a Decade of Reform* (Washington, DC: World Bank)

———— (2006), "An Evaluation of World Bank Research, 1998–2005" (a report by an academic team led by Professor Angus Deaton), available at www.worldbank. org

———— (2007), Report of the External Review Committee on Bank-Fund Collaboration (Washington, DC: World Bank), available at www.worldbank. org

———— (2009), Repowering the World Bank for the 21st Century: Report of the High-Level Commission on Modernization of World Bank Group Governance (Zedillo Commission), available at www.worldbank.org

World Bank Growth Commission (2008), Final Report and Background Studies (Washington, DC: World Bank)

World Bank Independent Evaluation Group (2008a), "Using Training to Build Capacity for Development: An Evaluation of the World Bank's Project-based and World Bank Institute Training," available at www.worldbank.org/ieg

———— (2008b), "Using Knowledge to Improve Development Effectiveness: An Evaluation of World Bank Economic and Sector Work and Technical Assistance 2000–06" (September), available at www.worldbank.org/ieg

Index

Note: A page number followed by "n" indicates a reference in the Notes section of the book.

CPSIA information can be obtained at www.ICGtesting.com
Printed in the USA
LVOW072122090412

276895LV00005B/28/P